A CUP OF CAPPUCCINO
FOR THE ENTREPRENEUR'S SPIRIT™

A CUP OF CAPPUCCINO

FOR THE ENTREPRENEUR'S SPIRIT™

find your passion and live the dream™

Women Entrepreneurs' Edition I

ENTREPRENEURS' STORIES TO INSPIRE AND ENERGIZE YOUR
ENTREPRENEURIAL SPIRIT

JERETTA HORN NORD
LOU C. KERR

Foreword by Amilya Antonetti

Cover design by Karen Lemley

To order additional copies of this book, contact:

Jeretta Horn Nord
Entrepreneur Enterprises LLC
405-747-0320
jeretta@acupofcappuccino.com
www.acupofcappuccino.com

CONTENTS

To all women who have found their passion and are living the dream and to all who aspire to *live the entrepreneurial dream.*

FOREWORD

Enjoying a cappuccino and talking about entrepreneurship are two of my favorite things. A cappuccino is often mistaken for "a cup of coffee," which it is not. If you have ever experienced that perfect cappuccino where each element from the froth, flavor, temperature and texture all come together creating that perfect cup, you absolutely know the difference and how hard it is to find. Similarly, an entrepreneur is often mistaken for a "business person" when he or she is actually a unique blend of instinct, risk taking, opportunism and intelligence. Just like making a perfect cappuccino takes practice, patience, and a good machine, entrepreneurship requires a high level of commitment, a whole lot of patience and a good team.

My journey into entrepreneurship started as early as my first memories. Even though "being an entrepreneur" was not understood by me or my family, the qualities and instincts of a budding entrepreneur were alive and well in my DNA. Marching to a different tune, seeing what others could not see in everyday situations, and the comfort I felt in going the opposite way of others were the first signs that my journey was going to be on the road less traveled.

Years later, when my infant son became ill, I would draw on every aspect of my entrepreneurial DNA in order to fight for his survival. These instincts were not the norm, but were critical in finding a solution to my son's health issues. This solution resulted in launching Soapworks, Inc. and becoming an integral part of pioneering the "Green" movement that is readily accepted today. This is far from the thinking of the 1990s when I was being escorted out of meetings for the "insanity" of a movement that the experts believed would never be acknowledged in mainstream consumer markets.

As unique as entrepreneurs are in the business arena, our skills and interests vary greatly. Some entrepreneurs are "mad inventors," while others create a job for themselves or are interested in launching a product. I thrive on my ability to see the world with my instincts rather than depending on just what I know and my talent for bringing groups of diverse people together for a common goal and motivating them to make changes. This is what led me to a life of entrepreneurship. I believe when instinct takes advantage of an opportunity that is aligned with purpose and passion, you have an entrepreneur. This is, I believe, the art of entrepreneurship.

It was a pleasure to meet Jeretta at the United States Association for Small Business and Entrepreneurship Conference where I was the keynote speaker for the Entrepreneurship and Inspiration section. I admire her efforts to capture inspiring stories that highlight how individuals can take the entrepreneurial path for different reasons, yet share the entrepreneurial mentality. Each entrepreneur has had twists and turns, triumphs and setbacks, exhilaration and heartache, but every step has led them—like me—to a greater understanding of his or her purpose and self; one that is uniquely their own. It's a journey that forces self-discovery, tests what we believe are our limits, and most importantly changes us and our families, communities and the world. With each story you will see the entrepreneur's journey to find her passion, purpose, inspiration and hope. You will also see that we have created a "life by design" that we are blessed to live each day.

Amilya Antonetti
www.Amilya.com

INTRODUCTION

The *Cappuccino* book series features collections of true short stories written to inspire, energize and teach the reader. The stories include adversities, challenges, triumphs, and successes experienced by the entrepreneur to help *you* discover passion and basic principles so that you too can live the entrepreneurial dream.

According to the Kauffman Foundation, most American voters view entrepreneurship as key to solving the current U.S. economic crisis. Three out of four Americans aspire to be entrepreneurs. So what is entrepreneurship and what does it take to be a successful entrepreneur? There are numerous definitions for entrepreneurship. The one I use is simple: *Rearranging resources to create value.* Entrepreneurs have a mindset that typically exemplifies the following: passion, perseverance, work ethic, integrity, risk taking, determination, taking action, relationships, focus and, many would say, faith. With the proliferation of technology, entrepreneurs must utilize the Internet and other technology to be competitive, including e-marketing, social networking, online collaboration techniques and accessing unlimited resources that are available online.

Women are starting ventures faster than any other segment of business owners. Most of the women featured in this book have started their own companies; however, a few are entrepreneurs in a nontraditional sense, often referred to as intrapreneurs, within a business or corporation. The Women Entrepreneurs' Edition features stories from sixty extraordinary women entrepreneurs from five countries and eighteen states, each telling a story that will touch your heart and your head. A diverse group of entrepreneurs are included, ranging from an artist who has a home-based business and markets her work on the Internet to 'Rocket Girl', a rocket scientist who focuses on engineering innovative business strategies offering advice on being an expert where there is none.

Stories are powerful! The featured women entrepreneurs in this book have shared their stories so that other women can be successful. Women are looking for inspiration, encouragement and education. They need role models, mentors, and the motivation that comes from knowing other women before them overcame obstacles to enjoy success and self-confidence. The following by Joyce Johnson Rouse titled *Standing on the Shoulders* personifies what the women featured in this book are all about—*Women Helping Women*:

*I am standing on the shoulders of the ones
who came before me*

I am stronger for their courage, I am wiser for their words

I am lifted by their longing for a fair and brighter future

I am grateful for their vision, for their toiling on this Earth

*We are standing on the shoulders of the ones
who came before us*

*They are saints and they are humans, they are angels,
they are friends*

*We can see beyond the struggles and the troubles
and the challenge*

*When we know that by our efforts things will be better
in the end*

They lift me higher than I could ever fly

Carrying my burdens away

I imagine our world if they hadn't tried

We wouldn't be here celebrating today

*I am standing on the shoulders of the ones
who came before me*

I am honored by their passion for our liberty

I will stand a little taller, I will work a little longer

*And my shoulders will be there to hold the ones
who follow me*

They lift me higher than I could ever fly

Carrying my burdens away

I imagine our world if they hadn't tried

We wouldn't be so very blessed today

*I am standing on the shoulders of the ones
who came before me*

I am honored by their passion for our liberty

I will stand a little taller, I will work a little longer

*And my shoulders will be there to hold the ones
who follow me*

We've come a long way, but we must embrace the idea of *women helping women,* so that our lives and the lives of future generations continue to improve. My goal is to empower women with *A Cup of Cappuccino for the Entrepreneur's Spirit* as the vehicle. Through the stories, events, and our philanthropy program, women will be inspired, motivated and gain knowledge. The following are some examples:

- Providing scholarships to assist first generation women entrepreneurs with start-up funds based on business plan proposals.
- Providing micro financing for women entrepreneurs in underdeveloped countries through Kiva.org.
- Giving inspirational presentations to entrepreneurs and aspiring entrepreneurs.

- Facilitating events featuring panels of women entrepreneurs who tell their stories and provide advice to entrepreneurs or those who aspire to be entrepreneurs.

- Providing a collection of inspiring and educational stories in *A Cup of Cappuccino for the Entrepreneur's Spirit* to make a difference in the lives of those who read them.

- Distributing one- and two-story booklets including stories from the *Cappuccino* book series with the intent of promoting the featured entrepreneur, the book and motivating others.

Each woman featured in this book has presented her story from an entrepreneur's point of view with passion and enthusiasm. When reading these stories, you will learn that your positive thoughts and actions can bring you success. You will find out how to overcome obstacles specific to women that many of the featured entrepreneurs overcame. Whatever you want in life is yours, if you (1) know what you want, (2) have the passion to go after it and (3) apply the lessons you will learn in the following entrepreneurs' stories.

To secure the future of our nation, we must ensure that entrepreneurs have the skills, knowledge and inspiration they need for success. Read, enjoy, and *find your passion and live the dream.*

ACKNOWLEDGMENTS

Jeretta Horn Nord

I would like to extend my most sincere appreciation to the following individuals:

Entrepreneurs and aspiring entrepreneurs for their interest and enthusiasm, both as contributors and readers, in *A Cup of Cappuccino for the Entrepreneur's Spirit* book series. Entrepreneurs hold the key to economic recovery and now more than ever entrepreneurs and aspiring entrepreneurs need inspiration and education.

Lou C. Kerr for sharing my dream of empowering women entrepreneurs worldwide through stories of adversities, challenges, triumphs and successes. Many extraordinary women are featured in this book because of their respect and admiration for Lou and what she has done to help women be the best they can be through education and mentoring.

Amy Wells for her assistance in interviewing, writing and editing stories for this edition. Her brilliance and passion have helped bring each of these stories of women entrepreneurs to life and truly made a difference in the quality of the Women Entrepreneurs' Edition of *A Cup of Cappuccino for the Entrepreneur's Spirit.*

Cindy Patterson Thompson for writing Volume II and the upcoming Momtrepreneurs' Edition of *A Cup of Cappuccino for the Entrepreneur's Spirit.* Her enthusiasm, creativity and unique ideas have helped take the *Cappuccino* book series to a whole new level.

My husband, Daryl, for believing in my vision and for his love and support. And to our son, Nicholas, for his never-ending optimism and enthusiasm.

Lou C. Kerr

To my family and friends and the staff and trustees of The Kerr Foundation who believed in my idea that if one "reaches for the moon they might just touch a star," I appreciate you. To all the young ones who have yet to spread their wings and hit the wind, or fight a storm, or feel the warmth of successful sunlight on their faces, I wish you greatness.

To the women in organizations like the International Women's Forum and the Women Presidents' Organization and special visionaries like Julie Weathers, Vickie Karnes, and others at Oklahoma State University, I thank you for your continued support, encouragement and stories.

To the true entrepreneur, Jeretta Horn Nord, who captured the stories and life experiences of such a vast group of extraordinary people, it has been a pleasure to work with you. You are truly gifted and talented.

SUBMIT YOUR STORY

Are you an entrepreneur with a story to share? Join us in our quest to encourage others by describing your unique journey to becoming an entrepreneur! The series of books, *A Cup of Cappuccino for the Entrepreneur's Spirit,* captures entrepreneurs' true stories, which are written to inspire, energize and teach the reader. The stories include adversities, challenges, triumphs, and successes experienced by the entrepreneur to help readers discover passion and basic principles they can use to live the entrepreneurial dream.

The *Cappuccino* series of books includes Volumes I, II and the Women Entrepreneurs' Edition I of *A Cup of Cappuccino for the Entrepreneur's Spirit.* Future editions will include Momtrepreneurs, Native Entrepreneurs, Extraordinary Entrepreneurs, Women Entrepreneurs II, Young Entrepreneurs, Ecopreneurs, Internet Entrepreneurs, Global Entrepreneurs, Social Entrepreneurs, Disabled Entrepreneurs, African American Entrepreneurs, Australian Entrepreneurs, New Zealand Entrepreneurs and others.

If you are interested in sharing your story to inspire others, the format and guidelines are located on the website at www.acupofcappuccino.com. Just click on Submit Story.

Enjoy, get inspired, and learn from the best as you read the following stories.

CHAPTER 1

EXTRAORDINARY, EXCELLENT AND EMPOWERED

*We all have the extraordinary coded within us,
waiting to be released.*

—Jean Houston

The most beautiful things in the world are not seen nor touched. They are felt with the heart.

—Helen Keller

THE EXTRAORDINARY ENTREPRENEUR

Lou C. Kerr—"I want to do and be everything," was my response when adults asked me what I wanted to be when I grew up. That little girl's wide-eyed dreams have evolved into a lifetime spent trying to make a difference. I have spent much of my life committed to creating additional opportunities for women in an effort to aid in their advancement in business and leadership. My goal is to help women be the best they can be through education and mentoring.

I grew up as one of ten children and learned to be innovative so I could earn my own money. At seven years of age, I picked up golf balls that were left behind, cleaned them with bleach, and resold them to golfers. Later, I worked as a floral designer, waitress, and bookkeeper. In high school, I loved economics because we conducted experiments in the stock market. After graduating from high school, I worked in a photography shop before accepting a job as a receptionist for KWTV.

In 1969, I began my first real entrepreneurial venture after convincing a banker to loan me $25,000 so I could open an exclusive dress shop, The Jade Boutique. In 1972, I made a decision to sell the shop. During this same year, I married my husband, Robert S. Kerr, Jr., and stayed a busy housewife while taking up golf and tennis. I also traveled a lot and helped with political campaigns.

In 1982, I became involved at The Kerr Foundation, Inc., a philanthropic organization that provides funding to charitable causes both locally and nationally. In 1986, four new Kerr Foundations were formed and my husband, Robert, and I became the President and Secretary of the current Kerr Foundation. Today, I serve as President and Chair of this foundation, which has given more than $25 million to charities and projects including arts and media, medical, agriculture, and historic preservation.

I have always been extremely involved in organizations, activities, boards, and philanthropic endeavors. In 1992, I formed a partnership between the Oklahoma Chapter of the International Women's Forum (IWF) and Oklahoma State University to host the annual Women's Business Leadership Conference. Women leaders from across the nation who have experienced personal and professional success speak each year to an ever increasing number of women. The IWF is an organization of pre-eminent women of significant and diverse achievements who help prepare future generations of women leaders. The Oklahoma IWF accomplishes similar goals with a strong local network. I also work to further enhance the status of women as an appointee to the Oklahoma Commission on the Status of Women and as a member of the Women's Leadership Board at the Kennedy School of Government at Harvard University and the advisory board of the Women Presidents' Organization.

To promote the rich traditions of American Indian arts and culture, I founded Red Earth, Inc. in 1983. The museum hosts a respected collection of more than fourteen hundred items of Native American fine art, pottery, basketry, textiles, and beadwork. Both traveling and permanent exhibits are featured.

My philosophy is that entrepreneurs must commit to giving back to the community from the time they first start their business. Money is not the only way to give back. You can join an advisory board, become a mentor, or volunteer your time. You can never give too much. As long as you are involved, whatever you are able to give—your time, expertise, or financial commitment—you are helping others and will be intrinsically rewarded.

I continue to look to new opportunities and issues that will enable me to expand my knowledge base and personal experience while continuing to give back unselfishly to what I believe in most: people and the community. Find *your* passion. Ordinary women can be extraordinary entrepreneurs through education and commitment!

Lou C. Kerr

KEY SUCCESS FACTORS: Passion, Education, Mentoring, Integrity, Giving Back, Relationships

WEBSITES: www.thekerrfoundation.org, www.iwforum.org

SOCIAL MEDIA: Facebook, Twitter

EDITOR'S NOTES: Lou C. Kerr serves as President and Chair of The Kerr Foundation, Inc. and is founder and Chair of the Oklahoma International Women's Forum. She has committed her time, expertise, and funds to numerous organizations. Lou currently sits on the board of directors for multiple organizations including the International Women's Forum, Lyric Theatre, Committee for a Responsible Budget, the Women's Leadership Board of the John F. Kennedy School of Government at Harvard University, Women Presidents' Organization (co-founder) and others.

Kerr chaired the Oklahoma Centennial Commission, the State Capitol Preservation Commission for almost two decades, and continues to serve on the Oklahoma Status of Women Commission. Lou was appointed by President Clinton to the 1995 President's Oklahoma City Scholarship Fund Advisory Board, which funded scholarships for children who lost parents or were severely disabled as a result of the Oklahoma City bombing.

Among numerous awards from the International Women's Forum, Lou Kerr has won the "Women Who Make a Difference" and the "Leading Lights" awards. Lou received the Inaugural "Woman of Valor" Award from *travelgirl* magazine.

Kerr was a NAPA Honorary Fellow and was inducted into the Philanthropy World Hall of Fame. She is listed in the Oklahoma Women's Almanac, and was named one of eighteen of Oklahoma's Most Influential Women in 2001 by *Oklahoma Family* magazine. Oklahoma Governor Henry issued a proclamation naming March 2, 2005 as "Lou C. Kerr Day."

Lou enjoys tennis and traveling and is one of the most admired and respected individuals I know. Lou C. Kerr is truly an extraordinary entrepreneur!

*The important thing is to take the first step. Get going!
If you find you are pursuing the wrong objective …
change it. Just get going and don't stop.*

—Lucy Jarvis

BRINGING THE WORLD
TO AMERICA

Lucy Jarvis—If I could have chosen to live any time during the whole history of civilization, I would have chosen the very years I've lived. I've seen all the changes—radio, TV, computers. It's a very exciting world. At ninety-two, I'm often asked what keeps me young. I say, "Rage! R-A-G-E!" I get excited about something that should be done, I fight for it and that passion runs through my veins and keeps me young.

My mother made me believe there wasn't anything I couldn't do. When I was young, she made me go to dancing school, take piano and elocution lessons, and even attend a class that taught me all the social graces—how to walk into a room, sit in a chair and set a table. I couldn't believe she was making me take all these boring classes when I could have been out with my friends.

She said, "You'll have plenty of time to hang out. I'm giving you the tools now so that when you walk into a room, no matter where in the world you are, you will be able to feel comfortable, at home and happy in your own skin. Whether you're with kings or beggars, you will never walk into a room and feel out of place." Because of my mother, I knew I could accomplish anything and everything.

My career in television actually began while I was a food editor at *McCall's* magazine. I wrote a story about a doctor from Johns Hopkins who was doing experimental work on a Vitamin B complex that could forestall the graying of hair.

I followed him for about a year and then wrote my article. It was the most bombastic thing we'd ever printed. The circulation doubled, and I was invited on everybody's television programs to talk about it. I thought to myself, the most elaborate issue on a printed magazine will get you a million, maybe two million readers. The simplest show ... the dumbest television show ... will get you at least ten million viewers. I was in the wrong business!

I stopped working at *McCall's* when I was married and had two babies, Barbara and Peter, one right after another. At that time, I really wanted to spend my time with my children. I did a lot of what could have been construed as production work because I became chairman of many fundraising causes and political organizations. When my children were in school full time, I practiced what I call a bit of healthy neglect and I got back into the industry.

In 1956, I joined a woman named Martha Rountree, the creator and originator of *Meet the Press*, when she developed a new program called *Capitol Close Up*. Our first guest was then President Dwight D. Eisenhower. Our second guest was then Vice President Richard Nixon. Our third guest was a man who had never before been on television, J. Edgar Hoover. We had a very auspicious beginning.

After my work on *Capitol Close Up*, I was asked by a very famous executive producer to go with him to NBC, and in 1958, I became the producer of a weekly show called *The Nation's Future*. The show featured a debate on both sides of an issue that impacted Americans.

I learned early on that to be successful, I had to be resourceful, persistent and full of moxie. I understood the power of the words, "I'm an executive producer at NBC, and I want to talk to you about a project we're doing." That's precisely how I got astronaut John Glenn and cosmonaut Herman Titov in the same room at the same time discussing what it was like to be in outer space.

Neither the Russians, the Americans nor anybody else had any way of bringing those two gentlemen together, because the U.S. and Soviet Union were very competitive in those days. I knew I needed to start at the top, so I went to the White House. I asked President Kennedy if I could get these two men together in the same room at the same time in front of a camera, could I have exclusivity on John Glenn?

The President replied, "It will never happen, so why not?"

Next I called the Russians. I asked them if I could get John Glenn and Herman Titov in the same room at the same time in front of a camera, could I have Herman Titov exclusively? The Russians wanted to know where the interview would be done.

I said, "Washington."

The Russians wanted to know, "How will we know if we apply for a visa for Titov, he will get a visa?" The State Department had recently denied another cosmonaut's visa request.

I said, "I'll call you back."

I went to see the Secretary of State, Dean Rusk, and said, "I want to get these two guys in the same room at the same time in front of the cameras. I have an exclusive on Glenn from the President. I can get Herman Titov here, but the Russians won't apply for a visa unless they know you're going to approve it. Will you give him a visa?"

The Secretary of State said, "How can I give him a visa if he hasn't applied?"

I said, "Let me see if I understand this. You'll give him a visa if he asks for a visa, but he won't ask for a visa unless he knows you'll give him a visa?"

He finally said, "If he asks, we'll give him a visa."

And that's how I got Herman Titov invited to the United States and on a program with John Glenn, exclusively for NBC. The other networks had to come as guests and were not allowed to interview him. How's that for moxie?

During my twenty-two years at NBC, I had great experiences and did many things. I was filming at the Kremlin during the Cuban missile crisis … only I didn't know it was the Cuban missile crisis at the time. In Vienna, President Kennedy introduced me to Nikita Khrushchev by saying, "This lady would like to do a film on the Kremlin, and I think we should allow her to do it. It would be good for both of us."

Two months later I got a call asking me to come to Moscow to do the film. The Kremlin had never been filmed before and has never been filmed since. I filmed the entire Kremlin … every inch of it … using sixty thousand feet of film.

While I was filming, I noticed something was going on, but didn't know what it was. I complained to the American ambassador that it looked like Khrushchev was going to back out on appearing on film.

The ambassador asked, "No one's thrown you out of there?"

I said, "No, no, no."

He asked me how much time I had left to film. I had three to four days. He suggested I finish and pack up everything and go home. "And don't stir up anything," he said.

When I asked him why he was saying that, he replied, "Kennedy and Khrushchev are having an argument."

On the way out three days later, I sent a cable to Pierre Salinger, the White House press secretary: "I hear Kennedy is having an argument with Khrushchev. Couldn't he have waited until I finished? He's lousing up my film."

Later President Kennedy said to me, "I told Khrushchev that if he got the missiles out of Cuba, I would get Lucy Jarvis out of the Kremlin." He had a great sense of humor even under stress.

My film on the Kremlin was the first film for television that was shot and broadcast in color. At that time it seemed like such an innovation. It was the beginning of technology and changes in the industry. The moment we went into television was the big change. But when we went from black and white to color, there was no stopping what we could do.

My next project was filming the Louvre in Paris, France. That film was also shot in color. I made the museum curators understand that if they let us in, the world would see the Louvre, not just a handful of people. I received the French government's prestigious Chevalière de l'Ordre des Arts et des Lettres award for that film. I was the only woman to win that for many years. At that time there were only five foreigners who had ever received the award—four American men and me.

I was also the first person allowed into China with cameras to film the Forbidden City. It was the first time the People's Republic of China entered U.S. living rooms. Other films for NBC included one on Scotland Yard, another on Buckingham Palace, and one at the White House on the Medal of Honor winners with President Kennedy, who was my greatest booster and hero. I also filmed a story on the invention of the shunt that made dialysis possible, sparking a debate about accessibility of that lifesaving treatment. While doing a story on the diamond trade in South Africa, I was also given the opportunity to film the very first human heart transplant by Dr. Christiaan Barnard.

While I was at NBC, I organized all the other women, many of whom had advanced degrees in various subjects. No matter how educated or experienced they were, however, women were not allowed in the unions affiliated with the television or entertainment worlds. I was the only female producer at NBC at the time and felt it was important to organize the women who were with me then. Even though I was the "token" executive, I put them all together with a lawyer and they filed a class action suit, which they won.

I made the decision to leave NBC when Barbara Walters convinced me I should go with her to ABC. I was very anxious for her to make her presence felt. There were no women on prime time news broadcasts, and NBC was not willing to give her that spot. ABC was. They also offered Barbara the opportunity to do four special interviews a year. So I went with her to produce the interviews while she was doing the prime time news. In those days, having a female co-anchor the news was earth-shattering.

By then I decided it was time to start my own business, and in 1980 I became the first woman in the industry to start my own production company, Creative Projects. We produced television, film and theatrical projects. I started off by producing Barbara Walters' interview with Barbra Streisand. I also produced a feature film with Bette Davis called *Family Reunion*. I brought *Sophisticated Lady,* the Duke Ellington musical, to Russia and we performed it in Russia, Georgia and Leningrad. I also presented the first Russian musical to the United States and we performed on Broadway. It was an extraordinary time, and I was a very busy lady.

In starting my own company, I had to rely on courage, belief and passion in what I was doing. I could no longer just sign a chit and throw it in the outbox for someone else to pay. If I had to sign a check, I had to make sure there was money in the bank.

I also found it was important to understand the value of your product. You can't just fly blindly. Whether it's underwritten by a sponsor or network, or if you've financed it yourself, the project has be attractive, desirable and sellable. You have to know your own value and the value of the product you're making and you must know your market. That's true whether it's a dress or shoes or cereal or a television show.

But I believed I could do it, and the people who worked with me believed in me too. We had a great time. I put together a really incredible staff. Some are still with me. It's been over twenty years, and we've been enjoying the work ever since. We've had some successes and some failures, but plenty of fun. We are now called Jarvis Productions LLC.

In picking my subjects, I was really interested in doing programs that took me outside the United States so that I could show Americans what the rest of the world looked like and how people lived. Doing films on the Kremlin or the Louvre was not just about filming a building or artwork. It was about the people who lived in those countries: their traditions, their culture, their histories, their hopes and dreams. And it gave viewers a sense of what the rest of the world was like. We live in a shrinking world and need to understand each other and learn to live with each other. We're still a long way away from this, but at least I feel that I helped, to some extent, to shrink the gap and make peace a possibility in the world. Lyndon Johnson once said to me, "Most Americans never go more than one hundred miles from where they were born. With your programs, you bring the world into everybody's homes."

For people who think they've done everything and want to retire, I tell them I don't believe in retirement. I believe you have to re-tire. Take the old tire and put new treads on it and keep going. Don't sit back on your haunches and say I'm retiring. No way.

For young people, I advise that you have to have the courage to follow your dreams. A lot of young people don't know what they're going to do after they graduate. Should they go to graduate school, law school, medical school or perhaps go to Wall Street? I told my granddaughter, Serena, "You're twenty-two years old. You have seventy or so years ahead of you to do the most wonderful things. Change your mind. Have four or five careers. The important thing is to take the first step. Get going! If you find you are pursuing the wrong objective ... change it. You've got all those years ahead of you to make mistakes and make them better. Just get going and don't stop."

I didn't get to film the Kremlin by knocking at the door and waiting for someone to open up. I didn't get to China by waiting for someone to invite me in. If you believe strongly enough and are passionate enough in what you believe, you will make it happen. I did.

Lucy Jarvis

KEY SUCCESS FACTORS: Resourcefulness, Taking Advantage of Opportunities

EDITOR'S NOTES: Lucy Jarvis was recently elected a Giant in American Broadcasting by the Library of American Broadcasting. Two years ago, the Paley Center (formerly Museum of Radio and Television) elected her into its elite group "She Made It."

Lucy Jarvis and her films have received many awards, including: six Emmys, three Christophers and two Peabodys. In addition, she was the first female recipient of the Chevalière de l'Ordre des Arts et des Lettres.

You get in life what you have the courage to ask for.

—*Oprah Winfrey*

ENTREPRENEUR
EXTRAORDINAIRE!

Lynne Hardin—"I cannot wait for my next adventure!" As I think about my life and past experiences, examining where I have been, what I have done, and who I am today, I see several threads running through my life that wove the entrepreneurial fabric I donned as a child and still wear today. I didn't consciously decide at an early age to become an entrepreneur. I didn't even know the word! Rather, the "guiding threads" I chose to follow led me there naturally, as they will anyone who selects them as part of the weave of their own tapestry: responsibility, relationships, service, action, intention, expectation and trust. Here's how they worked for me.

I was born in California, the second child in a family of seven children. Birth order and a compromising spirit made it only natural that I become the organizer and facilitator of my younger siblings. I learned very early that if we worked together, each with certain responsibilities, we could achieve our goals. As in most large families, we were without a great deal of financial resources and our goals generally involved a need for spending money. It was in this spirit that we bonded together on several adventures that included collecting soda bottles for resale, setting up lemonade stands, mowing lawns, plus dozens of other things that provided funding for our needs and wishes, all of which gave us a sense of accomplishment. We learned that working together, assuming responsibility for the things we wanted, taking action to get them and trusting we would have them were our pathway to freedom.

Following high school graduation, I moved to Florida to attend college. Having a need and a desire is always the mother of invention and I needed to pay for school. Relying on internal initiative and past strengths, I funded my education by teaching swimming and scuba diving at Skipper's Dive Shop.

I then moved to Dallas, Texas, and began a job as an airline hostess with Braniff International Airlines. Their tag line, "If You've Got It, Flaunt It," matched perfectly the Emilio Pucci designed uniform consisting of go-go boots, miniskirts and false eyelashes.

Life was interesting, but somewhat shallow, and I yearned for more. I seized an opportunity to work with Braniff out of Travis Air Force Base in California, flying troops into Vietnam under military contract. I moved to Tiburon, in Marin County and began traveling the world, flying to Hawaii, Japan, the Philippines, Vietnam and Thailand. It was an extraordinary time in the history of our country, and I was a "walking question mark" during that period.

While flying, I would be with somber, young troops, transporting them into a war zone. In my other world, I returned to the "Love-In," "California Dreamin'" culture where sit-ins and concerts promoting peace and love were daily fare. The juxtaposition of those two worlds makes me pause even now. Although I was working for others at that particular time, doing so brought me a depth of experience intellectually, emotionally and philosophically, that I could not have duplicated on my own at that tender age. And the young, naïve me blossomed from the experiences of being able to dwell in both worlds.

In the 1970s, I was inspired by a televised special about the Cayman Islands, and I considered starting a business there. Although ready to make the move, I consulted with Joe Kingery, the owner of Skipper's Dive Shop where I had worked during my college days. He suggested that Key West, Florida, would have the same island feel, with a better business environment; and because of the trust I developed in him through our prior working relationship, I listened. Key West became the destination. It made perfect sense, given my background in aquatics and athletics.

They say timing is everything, and I agree. But it has been my experience that the timing so crucial to success as an entrepreneur is not necessarily the timing of being in the right place at the right time, as most people suggest. Rather, it is the timing of one's recognition of the many opportunities that surround us daily, and one's willingness to take action in response to those opportunities. Life has shown me that there are endless possibilities that I may choose to follow in work and in play, but if I don't discern them to begin with, or I don't act when they appear, then even the perfect opportunity may go unnoticed and one day may simply blend into another. Timing is not luck. Rather, it is a matter of remaining aware and open to the magic that surrounds us and having the will to take action.

As the universe would have it, my arrival in Key West coincided with the island's annual Holiday Tennis Tournament. I entered it and won, providing me with wonderful connections to the island's tennis crowd and an instant reputation as being good at the game. I discovered that California's "sport de jour" and land of athletic plenty was remarkably different from the Key West reality. There was only one hotel in Key West that had tennis courts. This hotel also had a very large swimming pool. Tennis and swimming … I could see another business opportunity beginning to take shape. It was perfect! I negotiated a win-win relationship with the hotel owner, offering to teach tennis lessons, swimming lessons, scuba diving and water exercise classes (both to the hotel's guests as well as the locals). This provided the owner with a wonderful benefit for his guests that no other hotel could offer, bringing goodwill and inclusiveness to the locals, too. He, in turn, provided me with a venue to make a living.

My first client was a guest at the hotel; he wanted to take tennis lessons but he did not have a proper pair of shoes. My simple desire to serve the customer resulted in my offer to take him to the store to buy tennis shoes, which planted the seed for my new business. More negotiations with the hotel owner allowed me to convert two cabanas into retail shops. We sold dive equipment as well as tennis clothes and equipment. Thus, the Key West Tennis and Scuba Center and the Key West Tennis Club were born.

After saving $600, I went to market in Miami, bought a few pairs of Adidas tennis shoes and some tennis wear on consignment, making my initial investment minimal. I continued to grow the retail product lines, which allowed me to introduce Key West to the tennis attire considered customary in California. The point is, my client's need for shoes was "timing," but it could have begun and ended with a trip to the store. Entrepreneurs' "timing" is recognizing a need when it occurs, then taking action while the opportunity is ripe. That's timing, when opportunity meets ingenuity!

From these early experiences, I also learned that networking connections, as well as business and personal relationships, enriched my life immeasurably and opened doors that may have otherwise remained closed. Such relationships have linked me to many new and interesting opportunities throughout my life. For example, as a result of my experience with the hotel owner in Key West, I was hired as a consultant for a resort tennis facility in need of financial restructuring in Ft. Lauderdale, Florida. This, in turn, led to a contract with a developer in St. Petersburg, Florida, who was considering the purchase of a tennis club as part of a two-hundred-acre residential development. That association culminated in my marriage to the CEO of the financial institution involved in financing the development.

Life at that point was as good as it gets. We had each other, a very large home on fifteen acres of waterfront property for which the monthly mortgage payment was equivalent to my annual earnings at certain times in my earlier careers. We had it all: a healthy child, and all the physical comforts of which many only dream: boats, planes and pilots for my husband and a stable of horses for me. I began competitively show-ing Jumpers, as an amateur/owner on the Grand Prix Horse Show Circuit and became a member of Two Rivers Hounds.

Of course, the only thing that is constant in life is change, and the highs that we were enjoying were soon confronted by the financial crisis of the mid 1980s. Banks and savings and loans began to fail all across the country, and my husband's was among them. As the bank succumbed, so did the marriage. Everything was gone. The stock that I personally purchased in the bank was worthless. All my personal investments with the bank and related companies were gone, as well as all of our marital assets. The bank allowed me to remain in the house for a period of time, and I was awarded $200 per month for child support. Alimony was not an option.

Did I mention earlier that I believe a successful entrepreneur takes action and then takes more action? When things didn't go at all the way I had planned, I called upon those guiding principles to get me through. My heart was breaking, but my entrepreneurial spirit was still functioning. I was determined to survive, as I now had a young son to take care of, as well as myself.

I moved to Palm Beach, Florida. I was familiar with the Polo Club there as it was a stop on the horse show circuit. I thought I might be able to sell my horses and keep my head above water. Instead, a realtor showed me a parcel of property located at the Palm Beach Polo Club, which I was able to secure with a meager deposit. Within a short period of time, this same realtor approached me with an offer to sell the prop-erty for a profit.

Again, timing was the major factor. Yes, the fact that the prop-erty was for sale was "being there at the right time," but I also could have determined that I had no business buying any-thing in my particular dilemma and moved along to the horse stables. Instead, I recognized an opportunity and took action where others may have created reasons not to move. The experience was a gift to me, and I accepted it. Trusting in myself, in my intuition and in my ability to change lemons into lemonade, just as in my youth, was the pathway to freedom.

My next adventure began in the fall of 1991, when I was visiting my sister in Oklahoma City. A new school, the Oklahoma School of Science and Mathematics (OSSM) was hiring a Development Officer to raise funds, and I made an inquiry. I was hired, and my son and I moved to Oklahoma. I began working in January of 1992 to help the school meet its funding goals and become a leader in its field.

It was not long after my move to Oklahoma, however, that a truly life-changing event took place. While driving to work, a truck hit me hard, spinning my car three hundred and sixty degrees and leaving me trapped and unconscious inside my little Mazda Miata. An ER doctor was in the vehicle in front of me and immediately came to my aid. He saw that I was not breathing and readied himself to perform an emergency tracheotomy. Suddenly I gasped for air, defying all the odds. But as the Jaws of Life began to extract me from my crumpled car, a seizure followed. I slipped into a coma, which lasted for three days.

According to the medical team, the chances for my survival were questionable and prospects of my recovery very low. Perhaps this is where sheer will, determination and my own spiritual philosophy took over. After regaining consciousness, my main concern was getting back to work. Deadlines were racing to a close, and OSSM needed the capital campaign to move forward or risk losing the matching funds that had been offered. Three weeks, and some serious internal fortitude later, I returned to work.

Due to the severity of my head injury, however, I had lost my short-term memory and was now dependent on others to give me the proper directions as I drove my son to school or myself to work. My brain was not connecting the dots. Managing to stay the course, funding for OSSM was secured. I am delighted and proud of the school's success, having been part of that in a small way.

Looking back on that experience, I see the threads weaving tightly together to help raise me out of that life-threatening situation. I was not willing to accept my prognosis. Instead, I trusted in my ability to heal completely and that became the only option. I assumed responsibility for my health and for the commitment I had undertaken with OSSM. There were times in my confusion that it would have been easier to step back and be "sick." But moving forward was all I could do, and moving forward was all I intended to do. The combination of all of those threads brought success in recovery and in my work, and they continue to run through the fabric of my being today.

During that time of trying to remember and recover, a friend asked, "Why did you come back?" She was asking why I chose to return to this life from the throes of death, when I was clearly on the brink of leaving … twice. I was jolted by the question, and it led to yet another adventure. I began to ask "why"? And as the initial answer would come, I asked "why" again, going deeper and deeper into what life meant to me. This journey, which was my response to my friend's question, resulted in my authoring *The Magic of Why for Re-membering Your Soul©*. *The Magic of Why®* is a process, including a book, DVD and CDs, which takes the reader out of the governing dynamic of fear, competition and lack, and into another reality of love, cooperation and abundance.

Writing *The Magic of Why®* was important; but practicing the process on a daily basis has been life-changing. Within every situation, I am now looking for ways to cooperate rather than compete. Because this is an expanding universe, there is more than enough for everyone. Competition is not necessary to get ahead, when in fact a win-win approach to life is far easier to do and can be an extremely lucrative means to an end. *The Magic of Why®* process is rooted in the covenant that we must "love" ourselves and others; we must "trust" ourselves and others;

we must "care" about ourselves and others; and we must be willing to "share" our gifts with others. Then, we must "allow" everyone to do the same … in their own way. By passing this along from one person to another, one generation to another, we can manifest this new governing dynamic. It is a choice.

I am eternally grateful for the gifts, as well as the challenges in my life. My life has been perfectly orchestrated by the God of my understanding. Without the love and support of my son, family, friends and God's hand gently guiding me, none of this would be possible. It is not how many times we fall that matters; what does matter is that we get back up and try again.

To all of the women out there, I say this: You are without limits. Consider your inner potential and desires, and use your power to create your dreams. If you know your "Why" you will create your future.

Everything in the universe is delicately connected and there are no accidents. Be receptive to the abundance that is yours.

My life is extraordinary because I expect nothing less.

Lynne Hardin

KEY SUCCESS FACTORS: Timing, Trust, Responsibility, Service, Relationships, Action, Intention, Expectation.

RECOMMENDED BOOKS: *The Magic of Why* by Lynne Hardin, *Outliers: The Story of Success* by Malcolm Gladwell, *The Field: The Quest for the Secret Force of the Universe* by Lynne McTaggart, *The Women's Millionaire Club* by Maureen G. Mulvaney, *Atlas Shrugged* by Ayn Rand.

WEBSITE: www.magicofwhy.com

EDITOR'S NOTES: Lynne Hardin is President and CEO of Integrated Solutions, Inc. She is a Certified Professional Facilitator (CPF) and much of her work has been in the areas of health, education, and public policy. Ms. Hardin has initiated legislation, creating a landmark breast cancer bill, which funds under-served women in Oklahoma. Ms. Hardin has experience in international trade, real estate development and funding. She is the author of the book and process called *The Magic of Why®* and has received multiple awards and honors from both U.S. and internationally based organizations. She continues to work with many philanthropic foundations.

KEY SUCCESSES AS AN ENTREPRENEUR

- Consulted on fundraising and marketing with a candidate running for President of the United States of America
- Invited as a delegate to "The Global Peace Initiative of Women Religious and Spiritual Leaders" sponsored by the United Nations and held in Geneva, Switzerland
- Produced the original Oklahoma productions of *The Vagina Monologues*, starring Eve Ensler
- Consulted with medical doctors to consider prevention and cure, rather than disease management as a business
- Founded the International Water for Life Foundation
- Authored and developed *The Magic of Why®*
- Initiated and coordinated the passage of the Oklahoma breast cancer bill
- *The Journal Record* Woman of the Year *Fifty Making a Difference*
- Member of the International Women's Forum
- Chapter Chair, Women Presidents' Organization-OKC Chapter
- Initial Board "Ft. Lauderdale to Key West" Yacht Race
- Business consulting with clients in Canada, Japan and Saudi Arabia
- Coordinated individual defense to enjoin stockholder suit: *Jennings vs. Park Bank*, creating a precedent-setting award to stockholders over the FDIC

Independence is happiness.

—Susan B. Anthony

THE ART OF
ENTREPRENEURSHIP

Sheri Orlowitz—Taking risks is what all good actors do. There's no path, no safety net, no step-by-step instructions. Studying the craft, promoting oneself in the face of daunting odds (the younger, the prettier, the better-connected), and most of all, starting again after rejection … that's all a part of the life of an actor. I was an actor in New York City for ten years, and nothing could have prepared me better for the life of an entrepreneur.

I come from a long line of entrepreneurs: my father, my grandfather, and my great grandfather all worked for themselves. I'm sure most children spend time with their fathers tossing a ball, gardening, going to a movie. From the time I was eleven, I did my father's books. When I wasn't reconciling his accounts, I was being quizzed. Intellectual pursuits were of the utmost importance in my house, and my father spent much of his time attempting to develop my mental prowess. My upbringing was indeed one of rarified privilege. Once I reached the other side of college, however, I was expected to make my own way.

My passion was acting, and I pursued it with enthusiasm. After earning my MFA in theater, I headed to New York City to study with the greats: Stella Adler and Uta Hagan. I dedicated myself to learning and practicing "the Method," a process by which an actor fully immerses herself in the world of the character she's portraying. I loved creating a character and expressing that life on stage. The work was sporadic but rewarding.

When I became ill at twenty-seven, I could no longer escape into a world of my own making. The reality of my situation sunk in: I was aging in an industry that rewards youth, gainful employment was never going to be guaranteed, and a steady paycheck would most likely remain elusive. The idea that I might not be a success by the ripe old age of twenty-nine compelled me to make a change. Once again, I did what a lot of good actors do: I went to law school.

As a successful debater in college, I felt law school was something that would suit my personality type and interests. I was right. I excelled at my studies and even started the school's first law journal. I had my choice of jobs when I graduated, and chose a position with the Justice Department. I found government work to be a great fit. My years of preparing for acting roles taught me how to prepare for cases, and my preparation paid off. I never lost a case or a motion while I was at the Justice Department.

A brutal commute led me into private practice—that's really the only excuse I have. Private practice was the path to success and money (and a shorter commute), but it wasn't me. I'm a firm believer that when life is too comfortable, there's no need to create anything new. Let's just say, I was uncomfortable in private practice, so I started looking for other opportunities.

As luck would have it, I found two simultaneously: a twenty-unit condo development in Washington, D.C., and the opportunity to partner in a leveraged buyout. I hadn't intended to jump into two projects, but I felt both opportunities were right and decided to pursue them even though I found myself over-stretched. When I was trying to pull the money together for the projects, I felt like I was holding a dustpan and trying to sweep up whatever scraps I could.

The leveraged buyout came to me through the ex-owner of Piper Aircraft. I knew it was a great opportunity, but I didn't have a clue how to raise money. Entrepreneurs just dive in and figure things out and that's what I did. I spoke to probably five hundred people and was able to unearth opportunities from the most unexpected places to finance that crazy leveraged buyout. As compensation, I was given the title CFO. Now I had absolutely no experience as a CFO—I had only taken one semester of accounting. And here I was with a thirty- to forty-million dollar company and none of it was cash—it was all debt and debt instruments. With my feet to the fire, I learned about finance and how to be a CFO. It was not pretty in the beginning, but I learned by simply doing it. I believe that's the best way to learn and gives birth to the most creative ideas.

That experience prepared me for my next venture: buying two manufacturing companies that became part of Shan Industries. When I was trying to raise money for that project, I was turned down by over one hundred and fifty people. My ego was tested. My mettle was tested. I had absolutely no experience in manufacturing, but I surrounded myself with smart individuals who focused on their areas of expertise and taught me about the industry in the process.

As I made the purchases, I did my due diligence. Unfortunately, the parent company of one of the businesses did not disclose issues prior to the purchase. Litigation ensued. Luckily one of my partners was a lawyer. Entrepreneurs can get bogged down in every kind of issue: legal, environmental, financial. That's why it is imperative to have competent people around you. If I had focused on the legal battle, I could have gone crazy and bankrupted the company. I had faith that our general counsel was handling the situation, and I was able to focus on the bigger picture of running the business. Having competent partners makes all the difference—you can't grow if you're micromanaging.

As I built my business, I found it important to rely on my wit and gut. The fun part of being an entrepreneur is trying out new things. You have a blank canvas and can draw on it any way you like. You are basically creating something and living by what you do, which can often be a bit of a rollercoaster ride. Everyone enjoys the ride up, but I don't know many entrepreneurs who aren't losing their stomachs a bit on the ride down. It's imperative to be able to weather that plunge down and hang on until you head back up again.

One such plunge occurred when I faced a very serious health crisis. I had spent the previous seven years grooming my CFO to take my place, so I hoped for a seamless transition that would enable me to work as I was able and focus on getting well. As validating as it is to *be* the company as its leader, any one person's indispensableness isn't necessarily healthy for a company. No matter the preparation, it is impossible to know if someone is going to be able to perform until curtain time. It became readily apparent that my CFO would not be able to fill my shoes as Shan Industries' resident entrepreneur. It is indeed an empty stage when your company lacks an entrepreneur. My board had been used to me being the Energizer bunny of our company—the cheerleader, the boss, the heart of the business. It was a humbling period to realize my company might not survive without me at its helm.

Part of the challenge of entrepreneurship is that it requires a skill set that is not easily defined. It's not a CEO, it's not a CFO. It's an art, not something quantifiable. Creating opportunity out of disaster is the art of entrepreneurship ... that's the single most important quality. It's easy to be an entrepreneur when everything is going great. It's hard to be an entrepreneur when things are going sour.

Entrepreneurs must also be the safety net for people in their organizations who can't perform. It's a delicate situation to avoid bruising egos of those without an entrepreneurial bent; it's important to motivate them in other ways. Being an entrepreneur requires a certain risk profile, personality type and an ability to rely on your instincts. When you have created and built a company, how do you replace yourself? Through my illness, I discovered that no one could do exactly what I do. I couldn't simply turn the company over to someone else and rest. After ten years, it was clear that I needed to sell my companies and move on to something else.

As a Jewish woman in a male-dominated industry, I've had my fair share of obstacles over the years, but I believe obstacles can become opportunities. I don't care who you are, there are going to be obstacles. Being a woman can be a positive or a negative depending on how you play it and view it. I think it's hard not to let challenges that present themselves due to your gender color any experience. The fact that I'm a woman has played a part in my success because it has pushed me on to the next thing and the next thing and the next thing. You don't like me because I'm a woman? Fine. I'll go do something else. I've learned not to be afraid to give voice to such discrimination and move on to something better.

After this most recent economic downturn, a whole host of entrepreneurs are coming out of the woodwork because they have no choice. They say that necessity is the mother of invention, innovation, and creation. People have been put through the mill and because of that they will create great stuff. When you're knocked out of your comfort zone, that's when you create.

That's where I am now ... outside of my comfort zone. I sold my companies and have no idea what I'm going to do next. I've spent the last five months being vetted for a presidential appointment—Assistant Secretary of Manufacturing. It's a position where I feel I could make a big difference and provide great value to the administration. I've fully immersed myself in the manufacturing industry for twenty years and have seen first-hand the entrepreneurial nature of government work. If given the opportunity to serve, I would fully dedicate myself to that venture. If someone else is selected, well, I'm sure there's a property out there just ripe for development, a business to buy, or another role to play.

Sheri Orlowitz

KEY SUCCESS FACTORS: Passion, Enthusiasm, Taking Risk

EDITOR'S NOTES: Sheri Orlowitz has achieved success in a variety of fields. After acting on the stages of New York for ten years after college graduation, Sheri pursued a law degree and worked in the legal field for a large law firm and the Federal government. When private industry caught her interest, Sheri provided executive leadership to companies in manufacturing and real estate development. Along the way she gave her time to various charitable and civic organizations.

Sheri began her career in manufacturing working with senior management at Magnetic Data Technologies/DBI, Inc. to develop a leveraged buyout plan to raise capital for acquisitions. This experience led to Chief Operating and Chief Financial Officer positions with the company. At the same time, Sheri founded Orlovon LLC, a real estate development company that developed and sold upscale condominiums in the historic Adams Morgan neighborhood of Washington, D.C.

Three years later Sheri returned to manufacturing as founder, Chief Executive Officer, and Chairman of the Board of Shan Industries. She grew this company to revenue of $18 million in the competitive plastics and metal stamping industry. Among her successes at Shan industries, she recruited, hired and directed senior executives, initiated penetration of government markets, led a major acquisition and overcame potentially crippling environmental issues of this company created by the previous owner.

Outside the business world, Sheri has given her time and expertise to various charitable and civic organizations. She served as a delegate for the Department of State's Business Women's Summit and the Department of Commerce's First Domestic Trade Mission to the Gulf Coast. She also served on the President's National Women's Business Council and the Women's Leadership Forum. Sheri is dedicated to helping children, since they have the least amount of power and the quietest voices. She's worked on stopping human trafficking, sexual abuse, promoting early education and the health, safety and welfare of children. Sheri founded the Orlowitz-Lee Children's Advocacy Center in 2000 and has worked as an ambassador to the Global Coalition to End Human Trafficking NOW since 2005.

We go, sometimes, to art for safety, for a haven of order,
serenity; for recognizable even traditional beauty,
for anticipation with certainty that the art form
will take us past our mundane selves into
a deepness where we also reside.

We go, sometimes, to art for danger; to be riveted
by experiencing the strange, by understanding suddenly
how uncanny the familiar really is. We go to be urged,
shaken into reassessing thoughts we have taken
for granted, to learn other ways of seeing, hearing.
To be excited. Stirred. Disturbed.

—*Toni Morrison*

WHY ART?

Mary Frates—I go to art for life. It is what I live. But I cannot call myself an artist. To me, that label is reserved for truly creative people. I have only been a participant. I have danced, sung, made films, installed exhibitions, produced programs, directed an arts organization and did whatever was necessary to make art programs flourish. In the process I learned to raise money, to lead an organization, to navigate the world of politics and non-profits, and to stay the course. And most importantly, I learned from artists who taught me to see the world through their eyes.

Women mentors have shaped my life. My mother, Marcella Craver Young, was my first mentor. She loved the arts and took me to every community concert in our small Oklahoma community. She insisted that I study piano and dance. And she saw the educational value of travel. She was fun and demanding and is very much alive for me today although she has been dead for many years.

My second mentor was Kathryn Bloom, Director of the Arts and Education program of the John D. Rockefeller III (JDR 3rd) Fund in New York. Kathryn hired me to direct a project in Oklahoma and her stern discipline and generous support forged my professional development in the arts.

The third mentor is my daughter, Dr. L. Lloys Frates. Dr. Frates has worked in a township in Soweto, taught Women's Studies at UCLA and is currently an executive at Renewable Resources, a company in Los Angeles. From childhood on, she has been my lodestar. Her humor, keen intelligence, and love for humanity and the earth have been a source of inspiration to me.

And what about the other women who have made such a difference in my life? I call them mini mentors and maxi friends who share the same vision. Mary Gordon Taft, a colleague who worked side by side with me for twenty-five years is such a person as is Molly Shi Boren who chaired my board and led with courage and commitment. Betty Price, Director of the State Arts Council, held my hand and parted waves for me at the state capitol. In the modest story that I have to tell, all these women are part of my tale.

When I was a youngster growing up in Ponca City, Oklahoma, I was terribly shy. My mother dreamed that I would become a ballet dancer, even though her genetic pool had passed on shallow hip sockets that would eventually give out and need to be replaced. The idea of being on stage terrified me, but in the process of enduring this terror, I was exposed to the world of dance and classical music. I will never forget the day I saw Maria Tallchief dance for the first time. Years later, she would be the first artist I would hire to teach at the Oklahoma Arts Institute, a program that would become my life's work.

I attended a small Catholic college for women in Washington D.C., my mother's idea of a proper education. There, I found myself in another world, far from Ponca City. I was one of two students west of the Mississippi and one of the few students who had graduated from a public high school. I found myself in a mix of young women who were daughters of leaders from foreign countries. I felt very alone, and even more so when my only pal and roommate flunked out due to her failure to meet the rigid academic requirements. Dating was difficult because of strict curfews. However, I found the key to escape the gray stone walls of the college. Students were encouraged to participate in art and political activities and hours were generously extended for these outings. So, I went to every symphony at Constitution Hall, every theater production (Greek tragedy became a favorite), and any dance concert or poetry reading that I could find.

Another escape route was politics. I joined the Young Republicans and the Young Democrats. I went to receptions where I met Fidel Castro, Nikita Khrushchev, Richard Nixon and whoever else would shake my hand or talk to me. I marched at the White House protesting the Russians and their siege on democracy in Eastern Europe. This activity did not find favor with my college president, not because she did not support my position but because a picture of me waving a sign that read, "Mikoyan is a Rat!" made the front page of the *Washington Post*. She explained that the language was not becoming to me or to our school. I asked her if I should have changed the object of the sentence to "rodent." She was not amused.

One day I discovered the National Gallery. And there, at that great museum, my life changed. Forever. There on the walls were pictures that were exciting, stirring, disturbing, and puzzling. I needed to know what was going on in each of these paintings! I returned to the Gallery often. To this day when I travel to Washington, the National Gallery is my first stop and I seek out and say hello to my old friends who still grace the walls. On my last trip I noted that Dali's *Last Supper* had been demoted to the stairwell.

I returned to Oklahoma after my father died, graduating from the University of Oklahoma with a degree in history and philosophy. I fell in love, married, and after my husband graduated from law school in Arizona, we moved to Oklahoma City where he practiced law. We had three children, bought a little house that I remodeled myself, and adopted unruly standard poodles. I taught school and worked as a volunteer in the Junior League where I found myself leading the Arts Committee.

My volunteer work developed into a demanding project that needed full-time staffing. I went to New York to appeal for support from the Director of the Arts and Education Program of the JDR 3rd Fund. Director Kathryn Bloom visited Oklahoma

City and determined that our project with the Oklahoma City Schools, an innovative program to use arts organizations as the sites for Fifth Grade Centers (melting pots for the desegregation of elementary schools), was a good fit for foundation funding. But there was a catch: Kathryn would not fund the project unless I agreed to take the job as paid director.

So I went to work for the JDR 3rd Fund. I began my new career as an arts administrator, Director of the Opening Doors to Education Program of the Oklahoma City Arts Council, and found myself in a prestigious group of educators and artists across the nation who directed model projects funded by the Fund. The learning curve was steep and challenging. I was naïve and for several years thought that I would be able to make significant changes in the Oklahoma City schools. My goal was to make the arts central to the educational process in elementary schools. What I learned was that art in America is not valued in our schools for the great educational resource that it is. It will be used when it can provide solutions to crisis situations, or as an enhancement if budgets allow.

Although my project grew and prospered, I realized that I was at my best when I was building, not maintaining. I knew that it was time to leave. Kathryn Bloom understood and we remained close friends and colleagues until her death.

In 1976, I got a call from the Director of the State Arts Council requesting that I help him with a group of artists, arts patrons and educators who wanted a summer arts camp for talented high school students. They envisioned an Interlochen (an arts academy in Michigan) for Oklahoma. It was an exciting idea and after six months of discussion, and a meeting that I missed where I was elected Director, the group decided to seek funding for a pilot project.

We formed a new nonprofit organization, the Oklahoma Arts Institute, governed by a statewide board of directors. With seed monies from the Council, money was raised from the private sector to hire nationally recognized artists to come to

Oklahoma to teach for three days in the woods of eastern Oklahoma. Maria Tallchief agreed to come if I would assure her that she would be able to fly out of Oklahoma in time to join the Queen of England at the races at Ascot. I assigned her schedule to my husband who drove her to the airport and indeed she did appear at the races on time. Judith Somogi, Conductor of the New York City Opera, also agreed to teach, as did Donald Hall from New Hampshire, who in later years would become America's Poet Laureate.

Students auditioned and were selected to attend, and for three glorious days we had a pure community of students and faculty who lived art, theater, dance, music and poetry. The pilot was a great success and planning immediately began to expand the program for the next summer to two weeks and to include more artists and more students.

From the beginning, the Oklahoma Arts Institute has been a public-private partnership. In 1978, the Institute moved west to make its permanent home at Quartz Mountain in Lone Wolf, Oklahoma. Quartz Mountain was part of the lodge system of the Oklahoma Department of Tourism and Recreation, and together with support of the Oklahoma Legislature, generous donors and corporate sponsors like Phillips Petroleum, Quartz Mountain was transformed slowly over the years into an arts center. Public support matched with private contributions has been the cornerstone on which a strong foundation was built.

The Oklahoma Arts Institute at Quartz Mountain became the State School of the Arts. Student tuition was underwritten by scholarships from the Oklahoma Department of Education and matched with donations from the private sector. The quality of artists was another cornerstone. The best artists in the country graciously came to Quartz to teach for the Institute because someone, somewhere had been a mentor for them at a young age.

There were difficult times. In the 1990s, Quartz Mountain Lodge burned down. With substantial help of legislative leaders who had received thank you notes for years from our students, the old lodge was rebuilt as an arts and conference center. A museum-quality art collection of the work of faculty and students was installed, an award winning music performance hall was built and a library replaced the bar. At last, the facility matched the quality of the program.

On April 19, 1995, the Murrah Federal Building in Oklahoma City was bombed. It was a national news event, but in Oklahoma it was much, much more. Everyone had friends who died in the bombing. Actress Jane Alexander, one of our former faculty members who was then head of the National Endowment for the Arts (NEA), called me from Washington asking the Institute to do something, anything. The NEA would help.

The Institute responded. Six months after the bombing, survivors and family members of victims boarded buses in Oklahoma City for the trip to Quartz Mountain where they would participate in a weekend of workshops in the arts. We held workshops in poetry and essay. Participants made memory boxes and baskets. They drew, they danced, they sang. They produced objects of heart-breaking beauty that were later exhibited at the state capitol. It was an experience that gave witness to the healing power of the arts.

The years passed and each summer program for high school students and each fall season of adult institutes for teachers was an incredible learning experience for the students and for me. I spent time with my heroes. I experienced the standing stones of Stonehenge with photographer Paul Caponigro, the Hudson River with painter Don Nice, Shakespeare with actor Richard Thomas, Native America with painter Fritz Scholder and sculptor Alan Houser, poetry with William Stafford, dance with Marjorie Tallchief. Maria Tallchief and Donald Hall returned for anniversaries. Students went on to become artists, teachers, and arts patrons. Every year was an enlightenment.

But the day came when I realized that the building was done. I was now maintaining and I needed to leave. So in 2001, I retired from the Arts Institute after twenty-five years.

I developed arthritis and had to have hip replacements. While recovering from the first surgery, my friend Molly announced that she was going to take ballroom dancing lessons. I too wanted to take lessons and I limped into the studio with her to sign up. We both were hooked. She instituted a ballroom program at the University of Oklahoma and I became a competitive ballroom dancer. I am quite sure that my mother would have loved ballroom as much as ballet. At last, I had become a dancer!

I began to question who I was. As a younger woman, I knew my roles well. Personally, I was a wife and mother of three children. Professionally, I was President of the Oklahoma Arts Institute. But those roles had changed. I was divorced. My children were grown and gone. I had retired from the Oklahoma Arts Institute. What was my role now? I hadn't a clue.

I decided to make a pilgrimage. I chose to walk the French Road, the Camino de Santiago, from France across northern Spain to Santiago de Compostella and beyond to Finesterra, the end of the earth. I bought hiking boots, a sleeping bag, and a backpack and set off for Europe to begin walking. I crossed Spain alone on a four-hundred-mile journey of meditation that reconnected me to the arts and to myself.

Today, five years after my walk in Spain, I have returned to volunteering for my community. I am President of the Quartz Mountain Music Festival, Chairman of my municipality's Environment, Health and Education Commission, and I head the Cultural Committee of Creative Oklahoma. I know who I am now. I also know that I am changing and in the process of becoming. I'm comfortable with that.

The arts have been my guide and they will continue to lead me.

I am thinking of making another pilgrimage.

Mary Frates

KEY SUCCESS FACTORS: Passion, Relationships, Innovation

WEBSITES: www.oaiquartz.org, www.stateofcreativity.com

EDITOR'S NOTES: Mary Frates founded the Oklahoma Arts Institute and served for many years as its President. She now serves as the Culture Chair for Creative Oklahoma, Inc. Mary lives in Oklahoma City and has one daughter and two sons.

Remember always that you not only have the right to be an individual, you have an obligation to be one.

—Eleanor Roosevelt

FROM URBAN ENTREPRENEUR TO GLOBAL ADVOCATE: "YOU'VE COME A LONG WAY, BABY!"

Roxanne Mankin Cason—When I was coming of age, many brands of cigarettes were marketed to women. This was during the surge of feminism that marked the early 1970s, and the slogan of one particular brand—noting the contrast between that moment of rapid societal change and the suffrage era of a century earlier—served as a commentary on that moment of history: "You've come a long way, baby."

That statement, as dated as it is (cigarettes are blessedly out of fashion, and no marketer would think of calling a woman "baby"), contains a great deal of truth. Yes, women have made great strides since Gloria Steinem and her generation of leaders pushed for women's equality. Indeed, today many younger women take for granted the opportunities they have to pursue ambitious careers. But much remains to be done, here in this country and around the world.

My own journey to and through entrepreneurship illustrates both. And, because our collective journey as women is incomplete, my entrepreneurial experience and energies are today deployed to empower girls and women, borrowing a phrase from another ad campaign, to be all that they can be, and find their destiny.

Like most women of my generation, I grew up in a society where women, even those who were educated and qualified to work outside the home, were discouraged when it came to ambition.

I was fortunate in that regard. My parents, a physician and a former psychiatric social worker turned fulltime housewife, sent me to a private girls' school—a context now known, through research by New York University's Carol Gilligan and numerous others, to preserve and "grow" girls' voices and visions as they move toward maturity. My own parents went against the norm in encouraging me to find my voice and passion.

But the pull of stereotypes was strong. I was told I was the pretty daughter and thus could not be the smart one—that moniker went to my sister. Once out of the supportive context of my all-girls' school environment and into college, I faced a more typical social structure for that time, where almost all of my peers presumed they would marry and work inside the home and not in careers. If they were to work, it would be as teachers, nurses or secretaries. This was not my idea of my future, nor did it speak to my need for fulfillment. I left my college years full of knowledge, but clueless about how I would use it.

So I decamped to Aspen to ski and to figure out my next steps. I worked odd jobs and set myself the personal task of figuring out a way into an adulthood that would be acceptable to me, if not in keeping with the social norms of that time. Eventually, while in Aspen, I was recruited by a global entrepreneur to work as a personal assistant, thus exposing me to his high-octane world of real estate deals.

I loved everything about that job—from the intellectual stimulation to the sophisticated and refined lifestyle lived by the people who worked in international real estate. The opportunity, which fell into my lap, awoke me to a pathway. I recognized this and chose to walk that path, but the going would not be easy. As yet, I still had no clear vision for my future. I was inconsistent. I liked being serious as well as having fun. I was ambitious but sometimes timid. I had a good measure of confidence, but like most women during my coming of age—the 1960s and 1970s—I wasn't secure in my sense of self-worth.

In time, I returned home to the San Francisco Bay Area with no specific skill set except—and this is the key—what I had learned about real estate investment. My mother decided to tap that knowledge for the benefit of my parents' own investment portfolio and took me with her to meet a tax attorney who was respected nationally as one of the top experts in his field. My healthy skepticism of authority (these were the days of student protests around the nation, and young people were in full rebellion mode) led me to pepper the attorney with questions that were informed by my experience in Aspen and challenging enough to get his attention. He looked at me and asked, "Do you work in real estate investment?"

I said no, not anymore.

"You should," he answered back.

Neither of us realized it at the moment, but both of us would soon recognize that he would become a key player in my evolution as a businesswoman. He would become my mentor. Life often turns on small moments, and it is critical to recognize these moments when they come our way. Fortunately, I did.

But in those days it was unusual for anyone, let alone a man, to mentor a young, aspiring woman. I didn't let that stop me from returning to him, alone, for career advice. In those days—and this is still largely true—women in real estate worked on the residential side. However, my mentor knew a woman in commercial real estate working in San Jose, California, a bit south of San Francisco. She gave me my first real opportunity, and I did well enough so that, in time, I was ready to move to the "big leagues" in San Francisco.

By this time I had closed a number of deals and was making good money. I worked by day and, at night, I attended tax and finance classes, enriching my knowledge and investing in my own professional development. Often I would return to my mentor to seek his counsel. He would say, "This deal looks good, but if we changed some of the structure, your client would be in a much more favorable tax position." With his help I was able to structure some very sophisticated deals.

This established me as a competent and reliable real estate professional. Referrals quickly followed.

My big goal was to work for a large and prestigious firm. But at the time they didn't hire women for their commercial divisions. Nevertheless I was eager and optimistic, with budding self-confidence and no experience—not yet—with gender-based discrimination.

I began the process of interviewing at the big firms, and each interview invariably began with some version of, "What's a nice girl like you doing in a business like this?"

My standard response was: "I think I'm good at it, and I know I can make money at this and I know I can make money for you guys."

The invariable retort would be: "Don't you think a man would rather do business with a man?" I explained that I had male clients who were not only comfortable dealing with me, they were happy doing so, because I had made them a lot of money.

Another invariable retort: "But can you imagine a woman wanting to work with you?" Now this was an odd question, on its face, in the male world of commercial real estate. But I had also internalized many cultural norms about women, even while struggling against them. I conceded the point and the interview would end with my interviewer saying, "So that's why we don't hire women." And I would head for the exit.

In one particularly galling experience, the manager at a top firm had me interview with managers at ten local residential offices—and all men, of course. In our interview, the investment manager told me that the company was not hiring and that he was seeing me as a courtesy to my mentor. I commented that, through family connections, I had a substantial piece of property to sell—worth more than $12 million in today's dollars. Certainly, I thought, there could hardly be a greater incentive to hire someone than to have them come in with money to put on the table. Instead my interviewer suggested that I give him the assignment and get a referral fee of $40,000 as opposed to the standard commission of $720,000 adjusted for inflation. Fortunately, by then I had developed enough confidence to walk away.

As I walked down the hallway toward the exit, I passed a young man sitting at a desk who motioned me over. He was taking the commercial division entrance exam and was stumped. He asked me if I knew what a "capitalization rate" was. Indeed I did and I told him. He thanked me and shared that he had just been hired in the commercial division. This was the same division where the manager had just told me that they were not hiring. With a lump in my throat, I walked out.

That was a defining moment in my life. A man clearly less qualified than I was had just been hired, and I had been rejected. For the first time in my life, I felt the sting of discrimination. I felt a sense of despair at the unfairness of it all.

So I gave up on joining the "major leagues" in San Francisco and got myself hired at a smaller firm in a nearby suburb. I would soon come to see that doing well in the "minor leagues" would position me for the majors. One of my deals involved collaboration with an agent from one of those top firms in San Francisco. After we closed our deal, he asked me, "What are you doing working outside the big city?" He couldn't believe it when I told him I couldn't get hired by firms like his. He promptly set up an interview at his company, and I was hired. By now, I had lots of experience working on deals. Despite all my experience, the interview was full of gender stereotyping. But I managed to jump over the hurdles and got the job. They would take a chance on me.

At my new firm, I quickly became one of the top ten sales people and remained at that level year after year. Finally, I was flying high—working at the top of my game, very successful and enjoying huge remuneration. Frequently I would be in the process of a deal, and a client would get cold feet, sometimes called "buyer's remorse." Often, I would offer to partner with the client—that's how confident I was that the deal was good. Yes, there were risks involved for my client and for me. But learning how to manage risks was key to my success, and it's an important skill for all women in business. Year after year I made money for my clients and for myself—typically one hundred percent annual returns. I had built a brand for myself as a woman trailblazer in commercial real estate and real estate investments. Just as important, I was known for generating high returns for my clients.

My first foray into the world of entrepreneurship was organic. There was a need, a client lacked confidence, I supplied the confidence, assumed the risk and completed the deal. Soon, I was purchasing property for my own account and those clients invested in my deals and my syndication business emerged. My mentor was an essential advisor and my deals were exceptional. Partners were referred and my syndication business grew to include about two hundred investors from Europe, Asia and the United States. In this country, my investors included families, friends and whole neighborhoods. With my reputation for high returns, referrals and investment dollars poured in. Times were good. I had the equivalent of a long winning streak in baseball.

But eventually I learned another lesson, the hardest of all: reversals happen. By the 1980s, inflation in the U.S. was at record levels. The Federal Reserve aggressively raised interest rates to curb inflation. Rates shot up as high as twenty-two percent. My real estate investment business was at risk. I needed help to protect my investors and I found a way to do so. But my run as a high-flying entrepreneur came to an abrupt end.

Despite the frustrations of finding my way in a man's world, I had ultimately succeeded in doing so. In fact, I had succeeded spectacularly, living without a sense of limits. But during this extremely stressful time, a friend asked if this was my first experience with this sort of failure, and I realized it was. His response was something I'll always remember: "Roxanne," he said, "life usually hands people failures along the way. Failure can teach you a lot and toughen you up if you use it that way." Of course, he was right. I just had not had those opportunities.

I took on a partner to get through the tough times, and eventually the market changed and we liquidated the portfolio. But another obstacle arose: This time a health issue sidelined me. In fact, it forced me to retire from the rough-and-tumble world of real estate altogether.

I still had decades ahead of me and much to offer. How could I find a way to tap my skills—and by now my considerable experience—in a way that would be compatible with the new realities of my life? I would have to take charge of my own renewal in more ways than one. But the challenge felt like a jigsaw puzzle, the picture unclear and the pieces in disarray.

Gradually the pieces came together. As I had come into my own in my business life in the 1970s, I recognized that financial literacy and financial power were lacking among women. At my alma mater, UC Berkeley, I created the first women's financial literacy program in the nation. I assembled faculty of women practitioners in financial literacy and I began lecturing on the topic of women and money at Berkeley and beyond. Meanwhile, I co-founded the Bay Area chapter of the International Women's Forum both as a way to empower other women and also as a means of professional networking and growth for myself. My business success had been accompanied by my desire to lift up other women. This emphasis on women's empowerment had become part of my personal brand.

As I sought to put all the pieces together, I began to volunteer in leadership positions at my stepson's school. I found that the entrepreneurial skills I had honed were very useful in working with people, working on committees and eventually chairing them. I found myself invited to join several nonprofit boards, but I wanted not only an outlet for my skills but also for my passion. It's common to want to join the board of the ballet, symphony or art museum. But now it was clear: The new application of my entrepreneurial skills would be to help girls and women around the world meet with less resistance than I had, in their quest to be all they can be. Not only did I want females to have all the advantages of their male counterparts, I began to see—using business terminology—that women were underutilized assets in all aspects of life. If girls and women could function at their full potential, their families and communities and nations would flourish. Fortunately, this concept has become widely shared by many powerful individuals and institutions, but translating it into reality requires massive change on a global scale.

I learned about a group working to educate girls in developing countries in the belief that education is the key to the advancement of women and girls, reduction of early marriage, fewer babies born to them, better education for their children and better economies. If women and girls are not educated, subsequent generations place further strains on society both because of out-of-control numbers and because the cycle of poverty is perpetuated. The importance of educating girls touched me (surely my own rich experience in a girls' school played a role in sensitizing me), and I thought I could really make a difference in this arena. So I decided to devote myself to the cause and set out to learn everything I could. Subsequently, I was asked to join Save the Children, the well-known global humanitarian organization dedicated to create lasting, positive change in the lives of children in need around the world.

During that same time, I joined the Women's Leadership Board at Harvard's Kennedy School of Government and, subsequently, served as the chair for five years. In my position as chair, we built a global board of women who were leaders in their own right and who came together to advance women's initiatives and research at the Harvard Kennedy School, Harvard and throughout the world with Harvard's vast power for articulating and propelling change.

My work with Save the Children led me to Egypt, where Save the Children partnered with Exxon Mobil, a supporter of a program called Ishraq. The program enables girls who were not allowed to go to school to enter a program where they learn to read, to write and to do mathematics. The program also includes health and life skills education. More recently a microfinance component has been added. Microfinance is a program created by Nobel Laureate, Mohammed Yunus, to provide small ($120 typically) loans to women. Through our research, we've learned that when you give girls an education and teach them life skills, you ultimately empower them. I have been touched to see that fathers who were skeptical of the usefulness of educating their daughters are transformed into fathers deeply aware of their daughters' value to society as educated young women.

Through the Harvard Kennedy School, I led a delegation invited to Egypt by the finance minister. At a conference convened by the Minister of Finance and Egyptian academics, I was asked to address the conference as a keynote speaker. It was there that I met Egypt's First Lady, Mrs. Suzanne Mubarak. She asked me if Save the Children could provide her with curricula for small children to learn about peace and tolerance.

My subsequent inquiries, with Save the Children and with the Harvard School of Education, determined that no such formal educational programs existed. My entrepreneurial spirit kicked in, and I brought together a team from Harvard and Save the Children to create a pilot program. Just a few months prior to this writing, the pilot was launched. If the evaluations are positive—and we have reason to believe they will be—we hope to expand this program throughout Egypt and eventually throughout the Middle East.

While I have opened doors and have had remarkable opportunities, and worked to pave the way for women to work in a male-dominated field, I must nevertheless recognize that opportunities for women remain limited. In important ways, men are still in charge. Whole sectors of society—including our own U.S. congress, where women are a paltry seventeen percent in 2010, and most of the top echelons of business—remain men's enclaves. Yes, we've come a long way. But, there is much still to be done. Women can make waves and those that come after can ride those waves, and we must always remember that we all stand on the shoulders of those who came before us.

My past experiences, both good and bad, all important lessons learned, have led me to the most important work of my life. I am in a position now to truly make a difference. I have deep aspirations that the current and next generation of global women will experience a more level playing field, less violence, more opportunities allowing them to achieve their dreams.

Let us all find our passions, create meaningful lives and create a world where women can entertain possibilities and arise every morning with hope and expectations as they eagerly create their destiny and realize their dreams.

Roxanne Mankin Cason

KEY SUCCESS FACTORS: Passion, Work Ethic, Perseverance

RECOMMENDED BOOKS: *Career Warfare: Ten Rules for Building a Successful Brand and Fighting to Keep It* by David D'Allessandro; Peter Drucker books; Warren Bennis books; Horatio Alger and Ayn Rand books

EDITOR'S NOTES: Roxanne Mankin Cason has devoted herself to the empowerment of women and girls worldwide over the last twenty-five years. Now retired, she made her mark in her native San Francisco in the 1970s and 1980s in real estate syndication and development.

Cason's increasingly global philanthropic work includes funding girls' education projects in Upper Egypt; leading a collaboration with Save the Children, Massachusetts General

Hospital Center for Global Health and the Suzanne Mubarak Women's International Peace Movement to develop literacy curricula for early childhood education on tolerance and peace in Egypt launched in 2009.

Cason has served on the Global Education Advisory Board of Save the Children since 2003 and as chair of that body since 2009 where she has spearheaded girls education and SUPER (Save University Partnership for Education Research), a collaboration between Save the Children's Global Education Group and major universities to advance research. In 2005, she joined the Save the Children Federation Board of Trustees. She currently serves on the Advisory Board of Grameen America.

She is partnering with Judith Bruce of Population Council and Save the Children to hold seminars on investing in adolescent girls to advance best practices in programming for impact and quality as part of the Clinton Global Initiative. Also, she chairs the Heart (Healing and Education through Art) Endowment Campaign at Save the Children.

Several years ago, in New York, she co-sponsored the Save the Children collaboration with Queen Rania of Jordan for the advancement of girls and youth employment in the Middle East. Most recently, Women's eNews honored her with their 2009 "21 Leaders for the 21st Century" award and Harvard University acknowledged her leadership by naming a conference room in her honor at the Harvard Kennedy School.

Past board memberships include The Hamlin School, a private girls' school in San Francisco; the Saybrook Institute, a postgraduate degree institution; Women's Forum West; Women's Western Bank, the first women's bank; Occupational Medical Corporation of America; the Hearing Society for the Bay Area (now the Hearing and Speech Center of Northern California), serving as board chair from 1998 to 2006; Educate Girls Globally, where she served for two years as board chair: and the Women's Leadership Board of the Harvard Kennedy School where she served from 2003 through 2009 as chair.

Cason, an early supporter of economic empowerment of women, created and implemented at her alma mater, University of California, Berkeley, a program, "Women and Money—the Changing Consciousness of Money Management," which, in the 1970s, was the first program of its kind. She co-founded the San Francisco chapter of the International Women's Forum, known as Women's Forum West. She currently is a member of the Trusteeship in Los Angeles.

If you have knowledge, let others light their candles in it.
—*Margaret Fuller*

PORTRAIT OF
A PROFESSIONAL JOURNEY

Joy Reed Belt—Life makes sense in retrospect. Likewise, careers often only make sense in hindsight. Like a pointillism painting, the whole picture only becomes clear once you step back and let your eyes take in the whole thing. If you get too close, all you see are brush strokes. Of course the piece would be incomplete without each and every dab of paint and touch of the brush.

As a young woman, I remember always wanting to work. It seemed I couldn't wait to make my way in the working world. Perhaps my drive was influenced by my father. He was a minister, which if you think about it is a fairly entrepreneurial vocation. He moved from one church to another—each time a bigger church—throughout his career. Every move required winning over a new congregation. Seeing how he successfully navigated that challenge taught me about adaptability and persistence.

After obtaining my undergraduate and master's degrees, I taught at a junior college and enjoyed every moment of it. My favorite course was a humanities course that consisted of seven disciplines including: drama, music, literature, art, dance and architecture. It was what I used to call a *Reader's Digest* course in culture.

A lot of my students were young men who were returning from Vietnam and attending school on the GI bill. They wanted to move on with their lives, but some of them were very emotionally shut down. I wanted to start some enrichment programs to help them transition back into their lives, but the junior college didn't have much money. If I needed funding, I had to go out and get it myself. That led me to start writing grant applications, and I found I had a knack for successfully getting programs funded.

The National Endowment for the Arts (NEA) became interested in me after reading some of my grant proposals. In conjunction with the United States' Bicentennial in 1976, the NEA was in the process of selecting a program development person for every state. I was offered the opportunity to head up the Oklahoma program. Initially I turned them down; I loved the junior college, my students and teaching. I recognized it as a tremendous opportunity, however, and I was offered a trip to Washington, D.C., which was very seductive so I ended up resigning from my job to accept the position.

My job was to help people in the state write grants in connection with the Bicentennial celebration. We developed some really fantastic programs through grants that got funded, including cultural retention programs for local Indian tribes. Some tribes did not have a written language and had only a small percentage of living elders who could speak languages of the tribes. These oral languages were in real danger of becoming extinct. I worked with the Center for Applied Linguistics in Washington, D.C. and wrote grants to record the spoken languages so we could develop alphabets and teach them to future generations.

I also wrote one of the first grants in the country to use Comprehensive Employment Training Act (CETA) money for artists. CETA was designed for blue collar workers, but in reading the Federal regulations I found that artists had similar characteristics that should make them eligible. They were underemployed, lived below a certain economic level, etc. I was told it wouldn't work, but I wanted to try it anyway. We succeeded in funding seventeen full-time positions that first year.

While I was doing the grant work, I met a smart, interesting and very creative man. He was an attorney who served on the board of several arts organizations. When my two-year program with the NEA was up, I didn't want to leave the state—largely due to this developing relationship. I decided to move to Norman to get my doctorate in adult education at the University of Oklahoma (OU). I always wanted to get my Ph.D. because my father had one and quite simply, I thought that would give me time to pursue the relationship and complete my Ph.D.

While at OU, I had a very strong mentor who became the head of my committee. My degree was interdisciplinary and in a sort of trial phase, but the program appealed to me because I had such a varied background. Unfortunately, none of the faculty liked the idea of an interdisciplinary doctorate and I became the test case. It was difficult at times but I learned so much, not only about what I was studying but about getting people to work together for a common goal.

Initially I planned to continue teaching once I graduated. By this point in my life I had taught at every academic level including grade school, high school and junior college levels and I believed my career would be in academia. My mentor kept telling me, however, that I ought to be an administrator. The more my mentor prodded me, the more interested I became in pursuing something outside of the classroom.

At that time, OU had the largest adult and continuing education program in the world. All of the training for such government entities as the U.S. Postal Service and the FAA were offered through OU. Other organizations, like the American Bankers, would approach us to offer special training, short courses, or certification courses for loan officers. We were also the only program in the country that licensed nursing home workers.

When I graduated, I was hired by OU to advise organizations and agencies that contacted the university because they needed training programs for their employees or association members. I would talk to people and determine what resources we had at the university to help them. Then I would work with program experts to secure faculty and develop curriculum and training programs for the corporate client. While In that position, I was exposed to many industries and companies and got a fast course on assessing situations and solving problems.

By this time, I had married that interesting attorney and we were living in Oklahoma City, which meant I was commuting to work at OU. My mentor announced he was retiring on the same day I learned there was going to be a five-year road construction project on my way to work. If God wasn't telling me something, my common sense certainly was—it was time to move on.

While at OU, I had been approached by Oklahoma City University (OCU) to develop a similar program to OU's in continuing education. I had also received informal job offers from several different companies I had worked with through the university's programs. Rather than accept any one offer, I wondered if I could possibly accept them all by starting my own business and contracting my services out.

I built my business by calling on some of the companies I had worked with previously. I also declined the job offer from OCU, but signed them up as my first client.

In the early days of establishing my business, one of my clients, who was the president of an oil and gas company, approached me. He told me that he wanted to be chairman and needed to turn the day-to-day work over to someone else. The board had hired an international firm to conduct a search, but they hadn't liked the candidates very much. There was one candidate they did like, but they were hesitant about actually making an offer. They wanted to fly the candidate in to meet with me, and the board would listen to my recommendation.

I met with the candidate. He was charming, handsome and he had a lot of good experience in Europe. I asked him why he wanted to go into the oil and gas business. He replied that he believed it to be the industry of the future and that he wanted to be affiliated with an international company. I thought to myself, "International?" This company's drilling rigs were in Oklahoma, Kansas and Colorado. The only thing international about this company was that the executives all drove 450SLs. The company had one German investor and the executives would all go to Germany every year to buy their cars.

Upon further questioning I learned that the candidate had never visited a drilling rig. I knew his expectation was that he was going to work for an international company, and their expectation was that he could make them become an international company.

So I went in to the board and I told them, "You know, if I was ever going to have an affair, this man would be high on my list. He's charming, intelligent and speaks three languages. But if you want him to manage the day-to-day operations of your company immediately upon being hired, I don't think he is your man." My recommendation was to have a more honest talk with him, get below the surface personalities and have a serious discussion about the expectations of both parties. The CEO followed me into the elevator and told me that now I had to find them someone else for the position. So I did.

Once my candidate was hired, the CEO called me and said they had a lot of positions over the coming year and they wanted to engage me. I didn't know anything about searching, or the role of a search professional. I was also very proud of my newly earned doctorate, and frankly, felt recruiting might be beneath me. When I declined, he said, "Honey, you may be highly educated, but you're not real smart. Do you know how much we paid that search firm and they didn't even find our candidate? Do you know how much you billed us?"

I most certainly did know how much I charged them. I had recently taken my invoice to the post office and was afraid to mail it. I'd stick my hand in the box and then pull it back out because it was all the money in the world to me. I was chagrined to learn the CEO thought I charged a ridiculously low amount. So I started my retained executive search business and, as he and other clients started recommending me to others in the industry, my business grew.

A few years later, I started an outplacement company when I was asked to transition a long-serving, but underperforming employee away from a client and into a new position. The timing to start an outplacement firm was right—shortly after I started my company, the FDIC hired me when they were closing banks.

In counseling people who were laid off, I would tell them, "It's not a death. You're not being disowned. It's a corporate divorce. And it always smarts more when it's the other person who wants it. We all know people who go on after a divorce and have a better life. And that's what we're going to do with you. You're going to have a better life."

Whenever I meet with people, I try to give them hope and encourage them to believe in themselves. Hope is the main thing people lose after being laid off. And you can't do anything if you don't think you can.

In 1999, I was traveling a great deal, still doing searches, outplacement and organizational development. My husband came home one day and told me there was something he wanted me to do and he was going to pay for it. I thought, "Great, maybe he's going to send me to a spa." Nope. He wanted me to take painting lessons. The whole time we had been married, he had been buying up property in the inner city of Oklahoma City and had turned the area into The Paseo Arts District. He wanted me to take lessons from one of his tenants who was an artist. I had never painted before and thought it was a strange idea.

He said, "I think you would be great at it. You have such a good eye and are so good at interior design. I think it would relax you, and I'd get my creative wife back."

In spite of my initial hesitation, I started painting and found I loved it. I was still traveling for work, so when I'd go to Germany, I'd buy the finest pencils. When in Paris, I went to the very same store where Monet bought his pastels. If I had to attend a business meeting somewhere, I'd look online and find out if there was an art class that would coincide with my trip. And that really enriched my life and allowed me to keep doing what I was doing—without it I would have burned out. All you had to do to make me relax was say, "cerulean blue" or "alizarin crimson."

Eventually, I came to share a studio space with another artist. I didn't want to sell my art because it took me about nine months to paint one piece, and I felt like they were my children. I also didn't think they were that good. So I started hanging artists' work I liked in my studio. For years, as I was consulting and searching, I was staying in touch with the arts community and I was helping artists with their careers and buying art. I started hanging art in my studio and having openings every other month. The exhibits just grew and grew and grew.

Ultimately my husband bought a landmark building in The Paseo Arts District, and I convinced him to let me have it. I felt very strongly that the gallery would be my third act. It brought together everything that I have done: I started out in the arts, I helped people with their careers, I knew how to find artists and buyers. I felt like this is where my life was supposed to end up.

Now I split my time between my firm and my gallery fifty/fifty … actually, it's really seventy-five/seventy-five because I still work very long hours. At times the responsibility gets heavy. As a business owner, I'm responsible for other people's lives and incomes and that can be scary at times. I'm always on call.

In the consulting business, my name is on the door and the jobs came in because of me and my reputation. Naming the firm after me was a way to quickly get my business up and running. A downside to that, though, is that everyone wants to eventually talk to Joy Reed Belt of Joy Reed Belt and Associates, and I'm limited in what I can delegate.

Running the gallery is a glorious experience because I love selling someone other than myself. I didn't paint those paintings. If you like that painting, that is wonderful. If you don't, someone else will.

In my professional life, I was often called an influencer. Well, now I'm the chief influencer of an art gallery. And I can work here as long as I want to. I can come in a wheelchair or a walker and say, "Sonny, move that painting!" Spending my days looking at beautiful and interesting art work, talking with artists and collectors, while constantly moving furniture and changing the walls, is not a bad third act.

Joy Reed Belt

KEY SUCCESS FACTORS: Work Ethic, Resourcefulness, Creativity

RECOMMENDED BOOKS: An avid reader, I read books that relate to work and careers as well as books about art and artists and I absolutely love to exercise my creativity by reading fiction.

WEBSITES: www.joyreedbeltsearch.com, www.jrbartgallery.com

EDITOR'S NOTES: Joy Reed Belt is the owner of Joy Reed Belt & Associates, Inc., Joy Reed Belt Search Consultants, Inc. and Career Resources, Inc. A Career Strategist and Executive Coach, Dr. Belt is a partner and has served as Managing Director and Chairman of the Board of OI Partners, Inc., the world's largest career consulting partnership with two hundred offices in eighteen countries, sixty-eight U.S. cities in thirty-one states, providing executive search, executive coaching, career transition, change management, and customized human resource and career management services. She was recently selected as one of the top two hundred fifty recruiters in North America and is a Fellow of the Institute for Career Certification International.

A Licensed Professional Counselor and Supervisor, Dr. Belt earned her Ph.D. from the University of Oklahoma and has completed three years of post-doctoral training with the Karl Menninger School of Psychiatry Post-Graduate Psychotherapy Program. A successful career changer prior to establishing her firm, Dr. Belt worked as an administrator at the Oklahoma College of Continuing Education (OCCE) and was active in establishing and directing educational and cultural management programs for Indian tribes in Oklahoma. She is also credited with establishing the Center for Business and Professional Development at Oklahoma City University. She is currently a visiting professor for the College of Continuing Education at the University of Oklahoma.

Dr. Belt wrote "Career Strategies", a nationally syndicated newspaper column for over fifteen years and continues to speak to numerous organizations annually. She has served on the Executive Committee of Healthcare Systems of Oklahoma and on the Board of Directors of the Oklahoma City Chamber of Commerce. She currently serves on the Executive Committee of United Way of Metro Oklahoma City, and has served on the Boards of the St. Anthony Hospital Foundation, Healthcare Systems of Oklahoma, and the World Affairs Council of Central Oklahoma (WAC). She is a past Chairman of the Board of Advisors of the University of Florida in Gainesville, Florida. She was in the inaugural class of Leadership Oklahoma City and is a founder and member of Charter 35, a professional women's organization. A member of the International Coach Federation, Dr. Belt is active in the National Association of Counseling and Development, the American Association for Counseling and Development, the Society of Human Resource Management, the International Association of Career Management Professionals, and the Society for Human Resource Management. She is a founding member of the Senior Human Resources Forum of Oklahoma. She recently became a member of Art Table, the national leadership organization for professional women in visual arts and is on the Board of The Paseo Arts Association.

As her third act, Dr Belt, who has received the Governor's Art Award, established JRB Art at The Elms in December of 2002. The gallery's mission is to provide thoughtful and enriching paintings, drawings, sculpture, fiber work and photographs carefully selected from established artists for sale to individual and corporate clients.

CHAPTER 2

KIND, INTELLIGENT AND FEARLESS

*You gain strength, courage, and confidence by every
experience in which you really stop to look fear
in the face. You must do the thing which you think
you cannot do.*

—Eleanor Roosevelt

The future belongs to those who believe in the beauty of their dreams.

—Eleanor Roosevelt

Christine Paul—My father always said that I was the only college graduate he knew who turned a college major into a career. But then again, he was convinced my college degree was a B.S. in attending parties. My real major, however, was speech communications with a dual minor in psychology and public communications from Syracuse University.

My interest in event planning was spawned in Sydney, Australia, where I was enrolled in the Boston University Study Abroad Internship Program during my junior year of college. They only accepted twenty students from across the country and I was one of them. I was very fortunate that my Syracuse advisor worked with me and Boston University's curriculum so I received full credit and stayed on track for graduation.

Traveling to Sydney was a great decision. It is a beautiful city on the water; a place unlike any other I had ever seen before. Throughout my Australian adventures I began to learn the art of being fearless. I went scuba diving on the Great Barrier Reef, held a koala named Sweet Pea in Melbourne, learned to surf in Byron Bay, climbed the Sydney Harbour Bridge, and camped under the stars in Darwin. The country was magnificent. I felt alive.

In addition to a rigorous class schedule, Boston University placed each student in an internship based on his or her career interest. I was placed in the Public Relations Department of the Australian Rugby Union (ARU). I wanted to be a lawyer, so clearly there must have been a clerical error along the way. That error would alter the course of my life forever. It didn't take long to learn that this internship was a huge opportunity as the Rugby World Cup was quickly approaching and I was right at the crux of it all. The ARU is to Australians what the NFL is to Americans. The only difference is the rugby players don't wear helmets or padding and play twice as hard. They were totally fearless. Although only a green intern, I was determined to be fearless, performing each task with as much heart as the players displayed on the field.

By the time my internship ended, I had learned many secrets from the Australians. First, impress your higher-ups, but make sure that you are kind and respectful to those under you. Second, as the scouts say, "Be prepared." In fact, be over-prepared if you want success. Third, when you make a mistake, admit it. These attributes gave my boss at the ARU great respect and credibility.

At the ARU, I learned how to work with a team, as a team, and with passion and perseverance. I learned another important lesson there that I have carried with me throughout my life: Once a match is over, it's over. Whether it is with your assistant, colleague or boss, move forward and put some shrimp on the barbie, mate!

As my plane cut through the clouds on my trip home, I knew I had begun to grow the wings I would need to start my own business one day. First, I had to finish school. Senior year flew by. As every senior knows, when commencement day draws near the little voice inside starts to question, "Am I ready?" "Will I find a job that I like?" "Will I find a job at all?" Then I remembered the lessons I learned in Sydney and realized the answer to all of my questions was simple; the answer was, yes! Of course, my parents weren't so quick to agree with my plans to forego law school to plan parties.

They said, "Talk to us after you find a job."

I started networking. I contacted everyone I knew: family, friends, and friends of friends. Did you know that only two percent of jobs are landed online and ninety-eight percent are landed through someone you know? I learned this at a networking course Syracuse University required their students to take before being allowed access to the alumni database. I guess they thought we might attack the alumni like a pack of hungry tigers ravenous for food. And let's face it, they were probably right. In this course I was told another secret; do not ask for a job. I will say it again; do not ask for a job. Everyone knows you need a job—ask for advice, guidance and their story. Why? Because everyone loves to talk about themselves. Build rapport with them, get to know them, forge a relationship. It is human nature to want to help people with whom you feel a connection. Not only will you obtain valuable inside information about your future life path, you may just land yourself the job of your dreams! And that is exactly what I did.

The week after I graduated from Syracuse University, I was offered an interview for an internship with a top financial firm working as an administrative assistant to the Head Event Planner. It is important to mention that I had been working to land this interview for the past six months. They were originally looking to hire an unpaid intern, but after meeting me they offered me a paid temporary position for the summer in the Event Planning Department at their corporate headquarters in New York. My soon-to-be boss asked the classic question, "When can you start?"

I responded with the right answer, "Tomorrow."

My boss said, "Good, be ready to hit the ground running!" Of course I had no apartment or any basic necessities, but that was okay because I was twenty-two years old and had a job at one of the top financial firms in the country and I would figure it out. And I did. I felt fearless.

Over the next three months I was thrown into a world of beautiful events, travel, very long hours and hard work. I implemented the lessons I had learned in Sydney and I did whatever was needed of me that summer. I followed directions, offered suggestions when asked, and did what was required of me to get the job done. Running errands, sealing envelopes; no job was too big or too small. I worked diligently and was exhausted as night fell or dawn approached, no matter what time zone I was in.

By the fall, my detailed work and positive attitude had been noticed. I was offered a full-time position. I continued to excel, planning events at the caliber required by my perfection-ist boss. Working with a demanding boss didn't seem like a blessing at the time, but years later I realized she was the best mentor I could have asked for. My training didn't end there, though. Learning to work with vendors and improving my bud-geting and time management skills were also critical to my development. And of course, working with clients and creating an event they would enjoy was a priceless reward.

For the next two years I worked meticulously at the firm. One of the most important things I learned at the firm was that suc-cess in event planning was based on intricate scheduling and intense attention to detail. I discovered that it is often helpful to visualize the event and imagine every aspect going per-fectly according to plan. During this walk-through visualiza-tion, you will see things you forgot. This technique allows me to troubleshoot and help flag potential problems in my plan and gives me time to re-work the strategy. In event planning, as in any business, Plan A is never enough; Plan B is a must and sometimes C, D, and E are essential too.

During this time I experienced an unexpected twist of fate. I had the pleasure of meeting a celebrity singer's daughter who had seen my work and invited me to help with her upcom-ing wedding. I soon found how exhilarating wedding planning could be. This was the start of my great love affair with wed-dings and private events. It was from these experiences that I began to realize I could not only execute events, but also execute them amazingly well with diligence and heart.

As time went on I became less enthralled with corporate Amer-ica. Behind the glamorous events, I discovered a world of ugly. I knew there was a better path, an ethical path, a happier path, and I was right. Making the choice to leave a job without having another one in place is not a decision I would recommend in retrospect, but live and learn.

Following my resignation, I searched for a job as an event planner in New York City. Although I was young, my experience spoke volumes. I was told over and over again that I was over qualified and should start my own business. Me? Start my own business? The idea started to become more comfortable as I took stock of my strengths and weaknesses. I knew I could do this and succeed. I took a loan from the Bank of Mom and Dad and took a leap of faith. Two months later my company, Christine Paul Events, was born! She was beautiful, healthy, happy, and all mine!

I was fearless. I spent mind-numbing long hours researching what I needed: insurance, contracts, lawyers, website, advertising costs, and that was just scratching the surface. I enlisted the help of family and friends to start the buzz. It is very important to remember that no person gets from point A to point B by himself or herself. The support of my parents and grandparents has been fundamental to the success of my business. Encouragement is nectar for any entrepreneur.

One of my very first clients was a gorgeous New York City couple who hired me to plan a spectacular wedding for them in Paris, France. This presented me with two major challenges. First, I had never been to France. Second, I didn't know how to speak French! I refused to let this opportunity pass me by because I was too afraid of the unknown. So, I decided I would figure it out. I traveled to Paris three times within a few months and researched the venues, the people, and of course, the mouth-watering cuisine. I learned to speak French. I wouldn't call it fluent French, but I was pretty good. Lastly, I hired a French-speaking assistant. Fast forward one year later and I say with great pride that my company put on the most breathtaking Parisian wedding you have ever seen. To this day when I remember this great feat, it brings a colossal smile to my face. J'adore Paris!

Since starting Christine Paul Events, I have traveled all over the world hosting fetes in exquisite locations. I have had the great pleasure of working with celebrities, politicians, philanthropists, and outstanding volunteer organizations such as New York Cares, where I sit on the Junior Committee. I have been featured on *Good Morning America*, *Martha Stewart Radio*, and have planned and designed events for *The Knot* magazine and the *Wedding Channel Couture Show*. My alma mater, Syracuse University, recently invited me to speak at the Lubin House, their New York City headquarters. There I spoke to the students from the heart and I shared with them a few life-changing words: be fearless and make some noise!

Christine Paul

KEY SUCCESS FACTORS: Originality, Intelligence, Kindness, Resourcefulness, Fearlessness

RECOMMENDED BOOKS: *Public Speaking for Success* by Dale Carnegie, *Who Moved My Cheese* by Spencer Johnson, *The Art of the Deal* by Donald Trump, *Good to Great* by Jim Collins, *The 7 Habits of Highly Successful People* by Stephen R. Covey, *Think and Grow Rich* by Napoleon Hill, *You Can Work Your Own Miracles* by Napoleon Hill

WEBSITE: www.christinepaulevents.com

SOCIAL MEDIA: Twitter—CPEventsNYC, Facebook—Christine Paul Events, Inc., LinkedIn

EDITOR'S NOTES: Based in New York City, Christine Paul is a Certified Special Events Planner and the owner and Principal Planner/Designer of Christine Paul Events, Inc. The company provides professional event planning services for any type and size of wedding, party, corporate event, bar/bat mitzvah, and just about any other social occasion. Christine Paul Events also specializes in destination and green eco-friendly events.

The more you praise and celebrate your life,
the more there is in life to celebrate.

—*Oprah Winfrey*

REFRESH, REJUVENATE, REVIVE AND REPLENISH!

Debra D. Murray—Super Blue Stuff became a household name after the company became the best-selling product promoted through an infomercial in 2001. Super Blue Stuff has now been joined by other pure and natural products that really work and meet the needs of our customers, but the road to success has been less than smooth.

I grew up in an entrepreneurial family, including my great grandparents who homesteaded land in Oklahoma. A strong work ethic and sense of responsibility was expected. I had car payments before my driver's license. My dad was a true entrepreneur; charismatic and passionate. While selling barbeque at the state fair next to a booth where emu oil was sold, he learned some of its benefits. Intrigued, he purchased some and began mixing it with off-the-shelf products to produce a product that could be used for pain relief. After taking it to a specialty lab for extensive testing, he had his product: Super Blue Stuff!

At the time my dad developed this product, I was in the Washington, D.C. metro area working as a sales and marketing consultant for home builders. My experience in Washington prepared me for what was about to happen. Dad called and said, "I don't know what to do with the company." Although I was not aware of the extent of the problems, I knew instinctively that I was supposed to return to Oklahoma. Dad had created products that helped a lot of people and he knew how to spread the word, but dealing with the FDA and FTC was another thing. The company was in financial trouble because of millions of dollars of fines and law suits. The company was insolvent and he was forced to surrender assets to the bank and file personal bankruptcy.

Having a history of turning companies around, I knew I wanted to take on what would be both a challenge and an opportunity. The bank advertised the company for sale, but the lawyers told me to walk away from it. This served as motivation for me and after long negotiations and introducing investors into the picture, the deal was made. The focus at this point was on cleaning up and rebuilding.

I brought in key Blue Stuff employees, those doing all of the hard work and getting little credit, and opened the company as Blue Spring International. I cashed in everything and with my family's support, paid off the investors within a few months of starting my company. This allowed me to run my business with control and peace of mind. Some of my strategic business moves that have led to the success of Blue Spring International are:

- Evaluating the product line, eliminating some of the products and adding new products.
- Achieving Over-The-Counter (OTC) status for our Super Blue Stuff Pain Relief Cream by increasing one ingredient to meet FDA requirements.
- Branding the name through premium packaging and a consistent message based on our values.
- Focusing on customer service and feedback.
- Obtaining Certified Woman Business Enterprise status through the Women's Business Enterprise National Council.
- Networking with like-minded people.
- Hiring people who have strengths I don't possess and referring to their occupations as "positions" not "jobs."

Blue Spring International is now a comprehensive health and wellness company with over one hundred offerings. We provide the "Bridge to Wellness," making our customers feel good enough to take the steps needed for health. Our product lines include nutrition and wellness, spa and salon, pain relief and muscle comfort, and homeopathic medicines. Quality ingredients, outstanding customer service, and guaranteed results all underscore our commitment to innovation and ongoing improvements.

Blue Spring distributes products globally through retail and wholesale outlets. Our balanced health and wellness approach truly helps our customers "rejuvenate, replenish, refresh and revive." We always ask ourselves the following question: "Is this the best thing for our customer?" Entrepreneurs also have to keep in mind that to be sustainable a company has to make money. We practice strategic philanthropy and give what we can when we can. We always keep in mind, however, that our customers are those who pay for the products!

Having a quality product and complete confidence that a product delivers are the keys to building a return customer base. We know our products work, so I have always offered free samples through our website as part of our marketing efforts. A satisfied customer recently posted this fact to social media and within a few hours, our offer was hitting websites faster than we could track. After receiving thirty thousand requests for free samples within three short days, I now know the power of social media! Unprepared for this high and quick demand, I had to decide how to best handle the situation. Honesty is always the best policy, so I sat down and carefully wrote a detailed letter explaining what happened and our current inventory situation. I sent this letter via e-mail and explained that we were unprepared for the tremendous response, but would fill the requests as quickly as possible at a rate that would satisfy everyone within a few months. If they were in immediate pain, however, we would give them our most popular 4.4oz jar FREE if they would just pay the reduced shipping rate of $5.00.

We had never done anything like this before, but knew it was important to deliver on our promise. We had those who opted for the $5.00 offer and others who opted to wait for the free sample. Only a couple of people were disrespectful to us regarding our generous offer; many more became new customers! Now we give free samples for $1.00 shipping and handling and the customer gets a great coupon for their first purchase.

My advice to entrepreneurs and aspiring entrepreneurs is to see the landmines and act strategically, don't confuse fear with strategy, never give up, create the ability to take care of yourself, and know that you'll figure it out. And as you make the journey, refresh, rejuvenate, revive, and replenish!

Debra D. Murray

KEY SUCCESS FACTORS: Customer Service, Networking, Perseverance, Teamwork

RECOMMENDED BOOKS: *Good to Great* by Jim Collins, *The World is Flat* by Thomas L. Friedman, *God Wants You To Be Rich* by Paul Zane Pilzer, *The Art of Profitability* by Adrian Slywotsky, *Ready, Fire, Aim* by Michael Masterson

WEBSITES: www.bluespringwellness.com, www.bluespringwellness.com/freesample

SOCIAL MEDIA: Twitter—bluespring, Twitter—emuoil

EDITOR'S NOTES: Debra Murray is the President and Managing Member of Blue Spring International LLC, and its parent company, HealthStyle International LLC. Ms. Murray has over twenty-five years of sales, consulting, and management experience in real estate, retail, and the health and wellness industries. As an active member of Women Impacting Public Policy (WIPP) and the National Association of Women Business Owners (NAWBO), Ms. Murray works to further opportunities in the world of business for women.

Debra is an accomplished public speaker, with many prestigious awards, achievements, and invitations to speak worldwide.

- Spoke at the Middle East/North Africa (MENA) Business Women's Summit in Abu Dhabi, United Arab Emirates
- One of eleven women chosen by NAWBO/State Department for a Trade Mission to Belgium/Holland (Benelux)
- Recipient of numerous awards from DiversityBusiness. com, including being among the Top 500 Diversity Owned Businesses in the USA
- Chosen as one of four American business women to teach Sales and Marketing at Dar Al Hekma College, the first college for women in Jeddah, Saudi Arabia
- Invited to present with Dr. Naeema Farooqi at the International Society for Business Education (ISBE) conference in Glasgow, Scotland
- Hosted and mentored business women from Afghanistan in her home and at her business, and accompanied them to Washington, D.C. for WIPP conferences and other events focused on "Peace Through Business"
- Recipient of numerous Platinum Awards for millions of dollars in sales from the National Sales and Marketing Council
- Member of International Women's Forum (IWF)
- Member of Women Presidents' Organization (WPO)
- Privileged to be chosen to represent the United States as a businesswoman at an international press conference in the United Arab Emirates and kick off breast cancer awareness in the Middle East with Under Secretary of State for Public Diplomacy and Public Affairs, Karen Hughes, and Nancy Brinker, founder of the Susan B. Komen Breast Cancer Foundation

*Happiness is a conscious choice,
not an automatic response.*

—Mildred Barthel

HAPPY DAYS

Gemma Cocker—It's 4:30 a.m. in a frosted field. The sound of ABBA cranking from a car stereo at over one hundred twenty-five decibels is banging against my delicate ear drums. I'm in my gym gear with my pajamas still on underneath. I'm freezing, muddy and less than pleased about being forced to take part in an aerobics class with my new colleagues who are acting like they're center stage at Carnegie Hall. And this was only day two of the team bonding, induction exercise of my highly sought after graduate job where I was positioned to climb the ladder to "unimaginable heights." Looking back, it's not hard to see why that morning left me with the sickening thought that the corporate world wasn't all it was cracked up to be.

Fast forward through exactly one year of being undervalued, dealing with extreme in-house politics, corporate bureaucracy, deaf ears, egotistical and brash middle management, condescending communication, the water-cooler-gang gossip and finally, what was nothing short of psychological bullying, I walked out of a senior partners' meeting of that global corporate firm with an ear to ear smile having just handed in my notice ... and the smile's been there ever since.

So let me rewind a bit for you. I come from a middle class family in Dunedin, New Zealand. I have an older sister and a younger brother. No, I don't suffer from middle child syndrome. To the contrary, I've always been ambitious and confident. I grew up across the road from a beautiful white sand beach called St. Clair—yes, it was as awesome as it sounds. As a kid I represented my province in swimming and surf life saving competitions. My parents have lived in Australia since I was sixteen, which was probably the catalyst for my decision to leave high school early and go straight to University.

After five years of study, mixed together with some musical theater shows, dancing, singing competitions and concerts, as well working as a full-time event manager and volunteering at the local law support center, I walked away with a double degree in law and science, majoring in psychology. I'm also a qualified Barrister and Solicitor of the High Court of New Zealand and a tech geek/Internet enthusiast to boot.

I'm currently a London-based singer, dancer and actress. I am also the Director and co-founder of Tweetie and the Brain, a service to help build and manage presences on Twitter. Sure, I take on a lot of commitments, but I hate turning down opportunities. And if you love your life and work, you'll be surprised by how much you can do, and how quickly you can turn big goals into reality.

So looking back to that fateful day when my smile decided to stick—my "turning point" so to speak—I can't help but grin, because that was the day I decided that from then on in, I would be happy every day.

Be Happy Every Day

A surprisingly simple statement, but one that so few people ever truly understand or live by. But if there's anything I've learned in my short time on earth so far, it's that regardless of what people try to tell you about life, study, having a job, getting that self-important career (and worst of all—money), I absolutely guarantee you, that none of those things means anything unless you're happy.

So why isn't happiness the goal of every man, woman and child's daily routine then? Why is the focus on happiness lacking in our general thought process? And why do so many people live through sixty years of a nine-to-five job only to be saddened by regrets at the end of all those years? It's because happiness is undeniably and unashamedly elusive.

And why is it elusive? Well to be honest, I don't really know. I have more than a few theories—most of which are focused around our environments, our fears, and the social conditioning we've all been subject to in some form or another early on in life. But, I'm not going to talk about how elusive happiness is. I'm simply going to give you a list of concepts I live by that help me be happy every day.

1. My happiness lists: I write these lists twice a year, once before my birthday, and once before Christmas. It's simply a list of tangible or intangible things I'd like to happen that will make me happy. It's important to realize that these lists are not about material possessions (although they can be included). These lists are all about helping me focus on what will make me happier than I am at the present time.

2. Goals: I set myself short-term, medium-term and long-term goals. Without direction and purpose in my life, I'd just be wandering away the days, weeks, months and years. Life's WAY too short for that!

3. Laughter: I make myself laugh every single day—a big belly laugh if possible. And some days, if I can't find anything to laugh about, I force out laughter anyway, and within seconds I'm genuinely laughing—sometimes until I'm crying! I can't remember who taught me this, but it's a GREAT way to lighten your mood!

4. Meditation: Meditation is an incredible way to find inner peace and to re-energize, as well as to cure annoying thoughts, stress and fatigue. A five minute meditation session, twice daily, does wonders for my spirit.

5. Energy and influence: I surround myself with positive people and avoid being influenced by those lacking positive vibes. I think a lot about the energy I both

receive and give to others. It's amazing how different every situation can be depending on the energy you bring to the table.

6. Being thankful: I was lucky enough to have been born into a society where everyone received an education. Taking that thought back a step further, I was lucky enough to have been born into a home where I had food, water, clothing, and a bed to sleep in at night, as well as supportive family and friends to share my life with.

7. Less excuses: In comparison to a lot of the world, I have a lot to be thankful for and comparably nothing to complain about. I do my best to leave the "ifs, buts and maybes" behind and take advantage of the opportunities presented to me. If the opportunities that I'm after are difficult to find, I dig deeper until I find them.

8. Take control of my own destiny: I always make decisions with my goals and happiness lists in mind.

9. The 80:20 rule (also known as "Pareto's Principle"): I try to keep the 80:20 rule at the forefront of my mind on a daily basis, and choose to work smarter, not harder. There's no point in working twenty hours a day when I can produce eighty percent of those results in four hours. What was I doing during the other sixteen hours?!

10. Don't wait: If I ever find myself in a situation where I think I'm going to be unhappy about something that's within my control, I only have to remember my awful year at the corporate firm for two seconds before I do my darnedest to change it. Never again will I let myself be unhappy for an entire YEAR of my life before taking action.

11. Be kind: This is the final point, but so important. A genuine kindness towards others is so important both for them and for you.

And that's all there really is to it! None of it's a secret. No magic dust. No trinket box locked away in an ancient crypt. Just a number of simple concepts and decisions I choose to live by—all of which have led me to true success. I choose to be happy every day, and I provide my own terms and direction for gaining that happiness. I'm not saying it'll work for everyone, but if you try it, and it does work, well, wouldn't that be an amazing life to live!

Gemma Cocker

KEY SUCCESS FACTORS: Motivation, Determination, Replace "You Can't" With "Why Not," Think Outside the Box, and Think Big!

RECOMMENDED BOOKS: *The Power of Now* by Eckhart Tolle, *The 16 Laws of Success* by Napoleon Hill, *The 4-Hour Work Week* by Tim Ferriss, *The 7 Habits of Highly Effective People* by Stephen R. Covey

WEBSITES: www.gemmacocker.com, www.tweetieandthebrain.com, www.gemmaleighcocker.com

SOCIAL MEDIA: Twitter—gemmacocker

EDITOR'S NOTES: Gemma is currently living in London where she juggles singing, dancing, and acting with her online businesses. She's a serial social butterfly and you can engage with her on Twitter.

You may be disappointed if you fail, but you are doomed if you don't try.

—Beverly Sills

DESIGNING A BUSINESS, CREATING A LIFE

Dindy Foster—It's my mother's fault, really. After all, she was the one who taught me that changing furniture around could provide a different feel and look in a room. Instead of just sharing the requisite fairy tales, she read me a book on the wonderful antebellum homes of Louisiana. She introduced me to beautiful things. Because of her, I can't really remember a time when I didn't think about design and architecture.

Having now been in interior design for twenty-eight years, I think it is safe to say my mother's to blame and I couldn't be more grateful to her.

I actually got my college degree in fashion design. A lot of interior designers start out that way. Learning about fabric—its texture, movement, patterns—is as integral to interior design as fashion design. When I was in school, I wasn't quite sure what I wanted to do. I suppose I had dreams to go to some big city and apprentice under a fashion designer, but I didn't take any steps to make that happen. Instead, I did what most of my peers were doing at that time: I got married.

Shortly after our wedding, my husband, who was in the military, was stationed in a village just south of Venice on the Adriatic Sea. We were in the Palladian country for two years and soaked up the experience. The sights, sounds, and smells of that amazing area greatly influenced this small town girl.

When we moved back home to Oklahoma, I settled into the life of a housewife, but always knew I needed to be doing something ... creating something ... dreaming of something creative. I started out by owning a retail clothing shop for ten years. I loved fashion, and the skills I obtained in school translated to retail well. Experiencing that setting and learning how to run a business was a fantastic education for me.

I also found a way to express my interest in interior design by putting a little design studio in our clothing store. We were in a small town, and people kept coming by to see what I was up to. Word of mouth can be a powerful thing.

When my husband and I moved to another town, I took my samples with me and operated out of my basement. I learned just how important networking can be when my drapery contact invited me to do a designer showcase house in Tulsa. I was so green I didn't know the industry lingo. I kept hearing the term "color board," but didn't know what it was. I educated myself and completed the house. I can remember being afraid of failure, but I knew if I didn't at least try it, how would I ever know if I could do it?

Out of that showcase came the offer to share space with another designer in Tulsa. I'm a firm believer that when opportunities present themselves, you have to be willing to take them. I moved from my small-town basement to a work space in Tulsa.

I began to build my business on that blessed word of mouth and a reputation for quality and hard work. Initially, I had trouble knowing how to properly value my services. In that respect, I think it would have been beneficial to have worked, or at least interned, for another designer. Having the exposure to another designer's method and the inner workings of a business would have been a great lesson.

As it was, I flew by the seat of my pants. I started out charging too little, but I knew that I had to build a reputation and earn it. There's a fine line, though, in that if you don't charge what you're worth, people won't think you're worth it.

I learned that being a designer and being a business owner are two separate things. In this business, it is necessary to be very detailed in order not to lose your shirt. If you don't keep track of all the little things, you can really damage yourself financially. You've got to have a business sense on top of your capabilities as a designer. So many designers don't have that combination of business and artistic acumen.

I also learned to continue to take the opportunities that presented themselves. When I had the chance to do my first out-of-town job, I almost turned it down. I felt overwhelmed by the logistics and being outside of my normal environment. Then I remembered the lesson I learned with the showcase house: if I didn't at least try, I'd never know what could have been. So I went for it, and it was the best experience of my life. The people I worked with were wonderful, and I made friends and contacts that led to other jobs.

In the early days, I worked alone. That helped me really find out who I was and gave me confidence to sell myself and my skills. I have now learned to rely on others and have added a partner. It was difficult to let go of some things initially. Now I can see the benefits in sharing the load, and I enjoy working as a team.

Recently, we had a three-week job in Aspen. The house had three levels and fifteen thousand square feet. We provided the client with everything: the furniture, the art on the walls, the accent pieces, the floor coverings. We had to move the furniture up and down the stairs. Of course, negotiating the logistics of finding a receiver in Colorado and making sure everything was delivered to the house was just as laborious.

When I had just started the business, a job like that would have been too overwhelming. I would have run from it. But that's why a business needs to evolve as you do ... a little more and more and more ... until finally you're in a position and have enough experience that you know what you're dealing with and how to make it work.

One thing I love about the design business is that I learn something new every single day. If I was to know everything about this industry, I wouldn't like it. It is constantly changing and evolving. That is what makes it interesting for me. It's not all picking out wallpaper and paint and fabric. It's a lot of behind-the-scenes office work and dealing with delivery problems. We really don't do the same thing twice and are always reinventing the wheel and dealing with hundreds of different vendors. We may work on a very traditional house, then move to a contemporary house, and then move to a Mediterranean house. We're constantly challenged to think about the bones of the house and the people in the house and their lifestyle, because we want the houses to reflect the people who live there. As designers, we are basically the resource to bring it all together in good taste.

I've been very fortunate in that I've had mostly good clients. A great client relationship is one in which the client is open, and I'm able to discuss why I'm doing what I'm doing. I love listening to my clients and learning about their lifestyles and how they want to live in their homes. I am always honest, upfront, resourceful, and very responsible with my clients' money.

Of course, there have been a few clients who have tested me, but that's true with any business. In certain cases, I have had to withdraw from a project. I haven't done it very often, but I have done it. Now, I don't like to give up and I firmly believe where there is a will, there's a way—but in some instances it is necessary to walk away. I'm charging by the hour, and I don't want to do that when we can't get someone to move forward with a decision. You will lose money spending time with someone who is stagnant when you could move forward with another client who is ready to make decisions. Walking away is not ideal, but it can be empowering and necessary.

I've been operating my design business in Tulsa for eighteen years now, and I absolutely love what I do. I have freedom, and I like doing my own work. I have control of my business and live by my decisions. I like that. Of course, it can be frightening not knowing what the future is going to be and being solely responsible for your business.

So far, I have been fortunate and blessed in my career. I have greatly enjoyed meeting people and taking the opportunities that presented themselves. While I hope to scale things back in the next few years, I imagine I'll always be rearranging furniture.

Dindy Foster

KEY SUCCESS FACTORS: Honesty, Resourcefulness, Business Acumen

RECOMMENDED BOOKS: *Ghosts Along the Mississippi* by Clarence John Laughlin, *The Decoration of Houses* by Edith Wharton; *The Draper Touch: The High Life and High Style of Dorothy Draper* by Carlton Varney

EDITOR'S NOTES: Dindy Foster has been an interior designer for twenty-eight years. She lives in Tulsa, Oklahoma, with husband, Floyd Foster, and their two Brussels Griffon dogs, Tillie and Simon. They have a son, Gilbert, and a fourteen-year-old grandson, Gage.

*A woman is the full circle. Within her is the power
to create, nurture and transform.*

—*Diane Mariechild*

AN INTERNATIONAL EDUCATION

Ruth Leebron—I was lucky. Opportunities came along, and I wasn't afraid to take them. When I was growing up, women my age were afraid to venture off by themselves. I wasn't. I always spoke my mind—if I felt something needed to be said, I said it. I was never a shrinking violet, and as they say, I got out among 'em. That attitude served me well whether I was traveling the world as an Army wife, or teaching accounting to students in China.

I was born and lived in a small town called Carnegie in southwestern Oklahoma. My parents and uncle owned a department store in town. My uncle, in particular, was a very savvy merchant. During World War II, there wasn't enough cotton duck material to make the cotton bags needed during cotton picking season. So my uncle traveled to New York City and found some little factory that was making what he needed. He bought the material for two cents a yard and was able to sell it at the store in Carnegie for five cents a yard. No one else around could get cotton duck and people came from all over to get it. Between him and my father, the store did very well and even outlasted the national chain competition.

My mother was a very outgoing person and was the head of the women's department in the store. She was born and brought up in Europe and spoke fluent German, French and Russian. Within a few years of arriving in the states, she spoke fluent English.

Carnegie was in the middle of Indian Territory, and in fact, housed the headquarters of the Kiowa tribe. Within a few years, Mother was speaking the native tongue to the Kiowa. She had an ear for language.

When I was thirteen or fourteen, I was put to work in the store trying to sell, but my sales ability was nil. I would give products away before I could sell them. So my parents moved me to the office, and I guess that's how I picked up on accounting.

Every summer my parents would take us on a driving vacation someplace. Our first trip was up through Canada down the Hudson River to New York City and back to Oklahoma. The next year we went to Colorado. The next year it was California. By the time I was twelve, I had been to almost every state in the union.

When we would travel through the mountains and go around those hairpin curves, I was intrigued by how those roads were built and how the bridges were constructed. Those trips opened my mind to the possibilities of my future.

I did very well in school, and believed I could do what I wanted in life. I knew that there weren't many career paths open to me then; women went into teaching or nursing. Of course, some women were lawyers and a few were doctors. It became my dream to become an engineer and build those bridges and roads that fascinated me as a child.

When I went off to the University of Oklahoma, my father talked me out of pursuing civil engineering. I would have been the only woman in the program, and my father was concerned about my safety. So, I ended up majoring in accounting, even though I was one of very few women in the program.

After graduation, I took a job in Oklahoma City with the largest private firm at the time. I was the first female accountant ever hired by that firm. When I wanted to go out on an audit, my boss told me that the clients would think he was crazy if he sent a woman. In spite of such common attitudes at the time, he took a chance on me. It didn't hurt that I was at the top of my class and I had good recommendations.

I got married my junior year of college because my husband was going off to the war. When my husband came back, I quit my job and followed him around in the Army. We lived in post-war Japan and Germany and had many, many posts in the United States.

The entrepreneurial lessons I learned growing up were helpful to me as an Army wife. At each new post, I had to make do with limited resources, create a home for my husband and children, and adapt to new cultures. I also volunteered quite a bit during that time.

In Germany, I was President of the Parent Teachers Association of the American school, which was for Army kids with classes taught by American teachers. At one point, we had an exchange with the German school board where its members met with the teachers of our school. Now, the American students were taught like most American children; the teachers were fairly loose about their discipline, but it was an orderly class. One of the Germans said the American teachers must have better nerves than their German counterparts because the Germans would never allow their children to get up and move around. That comment angered me somewhat because I knew our children were well behaved. So I responded that we believe it is important to give our children freedom. Because of that freedom and the way we teach our children to think for themselves, we will never have a dictator taking over. The Germans didn't say anything else. They got the message.

When I was at Fort Sill, my husband was not a very high ranking officer at a post with lots of generals. The generals' wives decided they needed a younger woman to be the president of the officers' wives club, and apparently, I was that woman. I never had such a miserable time in all my life trying to please three generals' wives and get five hundred officers' wives involved in volunteering on the post.

When my husband retired from the military, he was offered an investment banking job in Oklahoma City. So, we moved back home, and I began teaching at Oklahoma City University (OCU). I enjoyed teaching accounting and found it to be an exciting time at OCU.

Starting in 1976, thousands of Iranians were sent to America to study because the Shah wanted to educate his people. OCU got several hundred students. We had classes of Iranian students, and later Saudis, Libyans and Jordanians. I found teaching students from different countries to be extremely interesting. My students were studying for their masters in accounting, and we had to integrate their background into our curriculum.

The mid-1970s were somewhat tumultuous personally. After thirty-two years of marriage, my husband and I divorced. I could take care of my checkbook, my household and everything because I had a background in accounting. But most of my friends who were also separating or divorced had no experience with personal finance. I had one friend in particular, who had a tremendous amount of money, but didn't know the first thing about managing it.

I decided to set up a program of about seven courses, and I called it Survival Course for Women. I taught basic finance (What are stocks, bonds? How do you buy them? Whose advice should you take?). My premise was that you've got to learn how to manage your own money because no one will manage it as well as you. Even your kids won't manage it as well. They don't have the same feel for it since it's your money. I also taught basic accounting (balancing checkbooks). I had a plumber come in and talk about basic house maintenance. I had an insurance man come in and talk about all the different products. I even had a policeman come in and talk about security.

To promote the program, we sent out postcards to various organizations in the community. We had a great response. I did about four or five different sessions. In fact, a bank heard about it, and they had me conduct courses for people who held trusts with them.

I also taught a class on entrepreneurship at OCU. I brought in speakers who made their own money without inheriting it. I included entrepreneurs who didn't have their M.B.A.s, because I wanted our students to know just because you get your M.B.A. doesn't mean you'll automatically be successful. I also brought in one person who never finished high school to show the students that they'd be competing against people who have entrepreneurship in their blood.

In the 1980s, OCU had a very innovative president named Gerald Walker. He developed an M.B.A. program for Pacific Rim countries. A group of trustees and professors went to Beijing in 1985 and signed an agreement with the government of China to put our M.B.A. course at the University of Commerce in Tianjin, China. The program was eventually expanded to Taiwan; Hong Kong; Kuala Lumpur, Malaysia; Singapore; and Wuhan, China.

For the second time in my life, I headed overseas and gave my first class in Tianjin in 1985. When I got to China, I was given an apartment that was so old, it looked like something out of Carnegie, Oklahoma, in 1929. We had hot water one hour in the morning and one hour in the evening. I had to decide whether I wanted breakfast or a shower in the morning. It wasn't possible to do both. So I'd cook breakfast in the morning and shower at night.

I was appointed Dean of International Programs. After living overseas in Japan and Germany, I was used to being with foreign nationals and I knew how to overcome language barriers and embrace new cultures. So heading up the program was very natural for me.

In addition to scheduling the courses and selecting and managing the professors for the program, I was also teaching classes. We would complete a whole semester's work in ten days—that meant lecturing four hours a day for ten days straight.

In 2001, I taught my last class. I was in China on September 11, 2001, and had a very hard time getting home. Having lived in Japan in 1948, I had visions of something happening that would prevent me from returning home. My then husband was eighty-eight years old and had health problems. After twenty-eight trips to Asia, it was time for me to retire.

In retirement, I haven't slowed down too much. I'm currently working with the Executive Service Corps (ESC), a volunteer organization for people who have some kind of executive background or professional expertise. We work as a team to help non-profits.

Through ESC, I assisted a charter school that needed to get a grant. They were initially declined due to their outdated accounting systems. I got them updated and they got the grant.

I'm working now with a young woman who is the Executive Director of an organization called Smart Start, which focuses on reading to young children before they're three so that when they go to preschool, they already have a command of the language. We have an awful lot of young teenage mothers in Oklahoma, and we're trying to encourage literacy among this demographic. The Executive Director of Smart Start has her Ph.D. in early childhood education, but she has no experience in accounting. As an Executive Director, she has to be able to prepare statements, and she has to be able to read them to know what her organization is spending money on. I taught her basic accounting.

Looking back, I can say I've had a good career, and I've enjoyed it all. Engineering might have been more fun, but accounting has taken me all over the world.

Ruth Leebron

KEY SUCCESS FACTORS: Fearlessness, Intelligence, Integrity

EDITOR'S NOTES: Ruth Leebron lives in Oklahoma. She is retired from Oklahoma City University where she taught and became the Dean of International Programs. In retirement, she enjoys sharing her knowledge of accounting with non-profit organizations.

*People grow through experience if they
meet life honestly and courageously.
This is how character is built.*

—Eleanor Roosevelt

SEEKING WISE COUNSEL

E. Claudine Long—As more and more women began enter-ing the workforce in the 1980s, it was not possible for a woman to hit the glass ceiling hard enough from below to break it herself. No matter how smart she was, or how hard she worked, she needed someone above the glass ceiling to help her break it. With the help of my mentors, and as I stood on the shoulders of those women who came before me, I was able to break the glass ceiling in my industry—banking—to become the first female Senior Vice President of a major bank in Oklahoma and eventually start my own business.

As the sister to six brothers, I was comfortable in a man's world. Our parents had impressed upon us the importance of the gender-blind Golden Rule: treat others how you wish to be treated. Children often believe adults play well together and that the Golden Rule is always followed. I came to learn adults don't always follow the Rule.

Things started off fairly well. I began working for a supply company in the oil field. Females were something of a rarity among the "rough necks." After I'd worked there for a while, the Treasurer from the main office came to our little town to visit me. They were going to name a person I liked very much as a store manager, because, as the Treasurer said, "You are here." That was very flattering and a successful strategy. I learned my first professional lesson: know your value to your company—that's your negotiating point.

My second lesson was harder learned. Fast forward: I was working for a different company and met the Chairman of the Board when he flew in for a meeting. I had spoken with him on the phone in advance of the trip, so I was somewhat acquainted with him. I was not expecting, however, the very sexual suggestions he made to me when we finally met. I smiled and sent all the gentlemen into the meeting, got them coffee and shut the door. I then cleaned out my desk, went home and called the HR manager with my resignation. The lesson I learned is: know how to pick your battles. Although this was a clear case of sexual harassment—and trust me, you know it when you experience it—I couldn't fight the Chairman of the Board. I knew no one there was going to fight for me. I also knew I couldn't condone that behavior by continuing to work there. As the country western song says: "Know when to walk away."

My next lesson came from the experiences of other women. When I was the manager of the Women's Division of Manpower, I began to see lovely ladies in their late thirties and early forties who had never worked before. They'd come in wearing their best Sunday dresses and shoes, but there was an air of desperation about them. Due to their current circumstances, they found themselves in an alien environment and completely unprepared. Most had gotten married right out of school and because their husbands decided they didn't want to be married or decided to move on without them—whatever the reason—they were forced to enter the working world. Unfortunately, they had no marketable skills. Manpower ultimately developed a training program to help these women renew their skills so they could become employable. I learned from them the importance of not allowing oneself to become obsolete. Keep up with whatever is going on because you never know when or if your circumstances will change.

My glass ceiling lesson was learned as I worked in the banking industry. Banking was most certainly a man's world. I worked for two gentlemen who came to know and respect my abilities and thus became my strong mentors. Unfortunately, at that time, only women whose families owned banks tended to have titles. Rank and file had very little room for advancement. In fact, my bank had a policy that no clerical worker could ever become an officer. I had worked my way up in the clerical ranks to become the highest paid female at the bank, but my head was banging up against that darn glass ceiling.

While attending a retreat, I learned that to break through I needed to assess my goals and make moves that would change my life. I was asked to write down what I hoped to eventually earn. My goal was so ridiculous I was a little embarrassed to put it down on paper. Indeed, when I came home I shoved the paper to the back of my desk because I didn't want anyone to see such an unrealistic figure. Whether or not I reached that ultimate goal, I knew there were changes I needed to make. Most importantly, I knew I needed more education. So I made the decision to pursue my education while I continued to work and care for my family.

This opened the door at my bank so I could eventually become one of the first female Senior Vice Presidents of a major bank in Oklahoma. I worked hard and enjoyed banking very much. I also became a mentor to women in all professions. Women in Oklahoma City now knew there were fewer limits to what they could do.

In the mid-1980s I was reminded of the lesson I learned at Manpower. The banking and brokerage industries changed due to deregulation. It was also the advent of the 401Ks and the ability of savings and loans and brokerage firms to offer financial products, along with checking accounts. In my thinking, a bank had to change if it wanted to compete. It could do as it had always done, of course, but it would be left out of the larger financial picture and become obsolete.

After completing the College of Financial Planning requirements, I became a Certified Financial Planner because I felt banks should be able to provide comprehensive financial services and I wanted to keep up with the changes in the field.

In retrospect, I was probably a majority of one with this opinion. Perhaps though, time has proven me correct. About that time the bank had an upheaval in its management, and I was asked to establish a financial planning department for one of the Big Eight accounting firms. I also began teaching financial planning at Oklahoma City University as an adjunct professor. Sharing my knowledge with students was a delight.

By the early 1990s it was becoming clear because of family responsibilities that it was time to venture out on my own and start a private practice as a financial planner. I had been able to build a client base through teaching, a good reputation in the community through my twenty plus years of banking, and the inherent fears and timidity we all have concerning our money. I hoped that combination would enable me to get my business off the ground.

Within five days of opening my office, the Oklahoma Securities Commission knocked on my door. I knew they would be coming—they regulate my industry and have certain legal requirements that must be met. I just didn't think I'd have to deal with them within my first week! Fortunately, I had set up my practice with those requirements in mind and I received a quick approval.

At that time, I believe I was the only financial planner in the state who was solely fee-based. I sold no product … no insurance, stocks, bonds, mutual funds. It was difficult if you did not sell a product, but my feeling was that I could establish a company based on charging by the hour as lawyers and accountants do. I could tell at the first meeting approximately how much time it would take for me to assist my prospective clients in meeting their goals.

That first year was spent developing a relationship with each of my clients, along with a detailed plan. I offered recommendations. I held hands. I went with my clients to visit their brokers, their attorneys, their accountants. I assisted in the implementation of the recommendations my clients accepted. My goal was to educate them during that first year so they would feel comfortable making decisions about the different aspects of financial planning, budgeting, investing, estate planning, tax planning and insurance and retirement planning. I built my business based on those personal relationships. My clients always knew I would speak what I perceived to be the truth no matter how difficult. I knew it was important to do so to develop trust. Integrity is essential in my business—if your clients know you're dedicated and committed to working in their best interests, you don't have to be perfect, but you have to have integrity.

Through my working years, I have been both an employee and a business owner. I've come to believe that what distinguishes entrepreneurs from employees is that entrepreneurs cannot accept anything less than their best. If entrepreneurs are competing, they're competing against themselves. It's an inner drive that motivates them to always do their best. That drive followed me from my first job to building my business. I always had to know that I was doing my best.

A few years ago I was cleaning out my desk and came across that piece of paper. As I looked at that proposed earnings figure I had felt was so unrealistic, I was stunned to realize I had long ago reached that goal. I had been so busy building my business and working on behalf of my clients, I hadn't even noticed reaching that milestone. Don't misunderstand, money is important, but there are many things more important.

If someone is considering starting their own business, I would encourage him or her to seek counsel. I think it is imperative to seek advice from those who have gone before you, those around you—even your competition. Be open to what they have to say. If you find a flaw in your plan, be willing to revise and rethink things. I think it is also essential for women to support other women. I have spent a great deal of time mentoring women in Oklahoma because I believe when one woman advances, we all advance.

The glass ceiling is still firmly in place in certain industries. I am happy to know that in some fields it is indeed shattering. The more we work together, support one another and expect the best from each other, glass will come raining down.

E. Claudine Long

KEY SUCCESS FACTORS: Integrity, Dedication

RECOMMENDED BOOKS: *The Richest Man Who Ever Lived: King Solomon's Secrets to Success, Wealth and Happiness* by Steven K. Scott, *A Cup of Cappuccino for the Entrepreneur's Spirit* book series, fiction for entertainment

EDITOR'S NOTES: E. Claudine Long helped Oklahoma City women see that there were fewer limits when she became a Senior Vice President of The Liberty National Bank and Trust Company. She built on this success and served her community as a financial planning executive and educator and also as a board member of Downtown Now, the Oklahoma Arts Institute, and her local YMCA. Additionally, Claudine co-founded and served as President of the Oklahoma City Public School foundation and was named "Outstanding Volunteer" by Fund Raiser Executives.

When not busy with her clients or community organizations, Claudine likes to spend time with her four children.

CHAPTER **3**

DREAMERS, BELIEVERS
AND ACHIEVERS

*Don't limit yourself. Many people limit themselves
to what they think they can do.
You can go as far as your mind lets you. What you
believe, remember, you can achieve.*

—*Mary Kay Ash*

Every great dream begins with a dreamer.
Always remember, you have within you the strength,
the patience, and the passion to reach for the stars
to change the world.

—Harriet Tubman

EVERY DREAM HAS A STORY

Jo Lynne Valerie—Ten years ago, if someone told me that within the next decade I would create and initiate literary projects and community events that would positively impact my entire region including three cities, and that those projects would fall under the umbrella of a corporation I would form, well, to be honest, I would have believed it. I bet you thought I was going to say, "I *wouldn't* have believed it." Well, it is true that some of what has taken place during the past several years has certainly been unbelievable. But for the most part, I must admit that I was not surprised when amazing things began to happen in my life. I never once considered that my dearest dreams might not materialize, that the accomplishments in life I held most dear might not become my reality.

Take a walk back in time with me to the year 1999. After stints in New York City; Dallas, Texas; and Scottsdale, Arizona; I was back living in my hometown of Rochester, New York. I had two children and was expecting another. I worked part time as a freelance writer, penning features for such publications as *Woman's Day* and *SageWoman*. Eventually, I began my own newsletter on holistic health, which I offered free to local health food stores and specialty shops. My modest newsletter reminded me of the larger, more inclusive local magazines on holistic health and alternative medicine I'd enjoyed in some of the other cities I'd lived in.

I wrote fiction at night while my children were sleeping. Stories have always meant the world to me. I was the only child of a single parent, raised in an environment rich in culture and academia, but not always brimming over with happiness. Books—stories about people living in a different place, going about their lives in a different way, seeing the world through a different lens than my own—were very often the lifeline that got me through tough times. I dreamed of doing just one thing with my life: becoming an author.

Back in 1999, I was confident in my writing, but I was not naïve. I knew that to be an author required the kind of writing chops that classes, a string of feature articles, and a self-published newsletter usually couldn't provide. I believed then as I do now that life experience makes the best authors. So I wrote my newsletter, articles, and short stories. And I bided my time.

But have you ever heard the saying, "Sometimes life hands you a project?" Early into 2000, that is precisely what happened to me. I noticed that my city did not have the kind of free holistic health magazine other cities did. I thought that was sort of silly, as I knew for a fact there was holistic culture, and a then striving to grow holistic community, in Rochester. Without much more thought than that, an idea formed in my mind. Not twenty-four hours later, I laid a foundation for starting my own full-fledged publication. That foundation consisted of my own brainstormed ideas, research I conducted and printed from the Internet, notes from a conversation with a magazine editor in California I knew, and a pretty impressive list of the columns, departments, and features I wanted my magazine to have. I really had no idea what I was doing, but I was absolutely certain of one thing: my magazine was going to be the most outstanding local publication my city had ever seen, and I was going to make it happen!

In just forty-eight hours, the plan that would produce the magazine's first edition was created. I was still very much in that initial two-day planning phase when I spoke with an old high school friend. After graduating college, she moved to Los Angeles and immersed herself in the print and media industry. She asked me, "Who will your graphic designer be?" When I said that I'd find somebody, she replied, "Oh, please. Send me your ideas and I'll create a mock up. This magazine is going to be the *&#%."

I was thrilled to have her on board. We'd been through a lot together as kids; if there was anyone I could trust to contribute as much passion and gusto as I intended to, it was her. My friend began to design a mock up of the magazine so I could pitch it to prospective writers and advertisers. But there was one very important piece of information she needed in order to do that: she had to know the name of the magazine. To this day, I cannot tell you where the name came from, but I knew immediately what it was. My magazine was to be called *Nature's Wisdom*.

I was surprised at both the number of supporters I instantly had, and the number of folks who didn't think the magazine could get off the ground. I paid the naysayers no mind. I was not interested in the potential downfalls; I wanted to hear about how I could side-step downfalls, learn from the mistakes I knew I'd make, and maximize opportunities and potential. I never considered any other outcome but success. To that end, I chose to seek out and surround myself with people who were as excited about *Nature's Wisdom* as I was. My feeling was that joined together, our mutual excitement would become a force. I believe that is exactly what happened.

The early days were exciting; I gathered one of the most fantastic teams an editor could have by visiting or telephoning area holistic professionals I admired or who were very well known for their excellence. *Nature's Wisdom* hit the ground running and quickly became a sought after publication. I realized promotion was vital, but as I had no budget for publicity, I fell back upon my literary training, writing copious amounts of press releases, and calling and e-mailing television stations and newspaper reporters to pitch a story on the magazine or myself. Within the first four months of being in print, I managed to be featured in three newspapers as the region's newest independent magazine publisher and editor, and I was featured on five television news broadcasts as the subject of a feature story.

I became known as a local holistic expert and began receiving invitations to do live television spots, explaining a natural remedy or therapy. Area natural health centers and stores began calling me to ask if my writers or I could be booked for speaking engagements. That led to the creation of what became known as *"Nature's Wisdom* Events"—first networking evenings, then later day long lecture series, and eventually full scale two-city holistic expos. This was when my background in journalism and radio served me—I promoted and emceed these events personally. Soon, nearly every single event my magazine hosted regularly sold out.

I loved the *Nature's Wisdom* Events; that was when I got to meet the people who read and loved my magazine face to face and advertisers and writers got to meet the readers. It was also at these events that I got a very clear sense of the different kinds of people who read and loved my magazine. Some were natural health and green living enthusiasts like me. Others were merely interested in considering alternatives. Still others came from a more serious, urgent place. There were many individuals in my own city, I learned, who valued the information in my magazine because conventional treatments or foods did not work for them. I realized to my great dismay that there was a significant number in my own community who could not afford the specialty whole or organic foods their health conditions dictated they have.

In response, I formed The Natural Food Cupboard, New York State's first, and to date, only natural and whole food pantry. The Natural Food Cupboard took donations from the community and from *Nature's Wisdom* Events ticket sales in order to provide food and natural personal care products to needy families and individuals for the holidays during November and December.

When WNED, the PBS television station in Buffalo, New York, wanted to create a holistic television show, *Nature's Wisdom*

Television, I was invited to be on the team of writers. Eventually I co-hosted the show on camera. I cannot tell you how many times, while driving from Rochester to Buffalo to work on the show, while pulling an all-nighter preparing a new issue of the magazine for press, or while packing up food baskets for a needy family, that I smiled to myself and thought, "Wow. This all started out of my living room while my kids were in school, or while they were sleeping at night!"

But I will never forget what I said to my friend from Los Angeles when she asked me what my long term plans were for the magazine, after she pointed out that we had progressed to that delicate threshold where the magazine either had to push ahead, expanding perhaps into another state or onto the national level, or maintain its presence as a regional publication. My response went something like, "I have to be honest ... I still want to write books. I'm hoping all I've done with the magazine will give me the foundation to do that."

But when *Nature's Wisdom* was at its height, I did not begin to write my first book. Rather, I launched a second magazine. Why would I do that when the addition of a second publication would move me no closer to my dream of becoming an author? Simply and honestly put, because as Editor in Chief of *Nature's Wisdom*, I had come to dearly enjoy every interaction I had with our readers. I regularly received post-it notes attached to subscription checks, and touching cards sent in the post or via e-mail. I loved meeting readers and the professionals whose practices were promoted or sustained through their article or ad in my magazine. I loved reading the "participant feed-back" forms I always asked folks to fill out at the end of one of our networking events or expos. I listened to what our readers said. They wanted more. More than holistic health, environmental awareness and green living, they wanted information that had only been touched upon occasionally and lightly in *Nature's Wisdom* magazine. The readers wanted insight on all manner of spirituality. So, once again without much thought or preparation, I launched a second publication.

From the start, *Full Moon Rising* magazine was known as my "wild child." Unfortunately, while *Full Moon Rising* debuted to an enthusiastic readership, it did not receive the financial support required to publish beyond two issues. Still, something key happened after that first debut issue. Something so significant, in fact, that I often wonder if the purpose of *Full Moon Rising* wasn't really to gently steer me in a new, very much longed for and very much anticipated direction.

As any good magazine editor will tell you, when a publication premieres to rave reviews, there is one task that becomes imperative: to follow up that first issue with a second issue that is as good as, if not even better than, the first. Because *Full Moon Rising* was a "wild child," I could push boundaries and run features that I could not in the more conservative *Nature's Wisdom*. I knew right away that what the second issue of *Full Moon Rising* needed was—fiction! Yet, with an imminent deadline and writers already hard at work penning columns and features, there was no time to call for submissions. I knew that if I wanted a short story—and boy oh boy, did I ever—the task, *the assignment,* would be my own.

The long and short of it is, I got to work. I wrote—incredibly fast—a short story that is still read and listened to on the *Full Moon Rising* website. Readers loved it, and I loved hearing their feedback. But with the writing of that story, I became aware that my wait to become a writer of fiction was over. Just weeks after the publication of the short story that graced Issue Two of *Full Moon Rising*, I began penning the initial ideas and beginning paragraphs of what would later become the spring story in my book, *A Tale For All Seasons*.

Lots of people have asked me how I came about the idea of writing a book containing four novella length stories, one for each season. I suppose it's because when I wrote that initial short story for the autumn edition of *Full Moon Rising*, I set the tale in autumn. It wasn't difficult for me to capture the look and feel, or the rich sensibility of autumn; I've always been very aligned with nature. I wanted to do that for each of the other seasons, too. I wanted to weave the intricate energies and nuances of spring, summer, and winter into the lives of characters in truly luminous tales.

Contrary to my training and the method many very successful authors employ, I did not create story outlines or organize brain-storming sessions with other writers or potential readers, and I did not develop on paper the plots for any of the tales in my book. Rather, I opened myself to the inspiration that had guided me every step of the way as I created and published *Nature's Wisdom*. That same inspiration had helped me write and co-host *Nature's Wisdom Television* for PBS and many other literary endeavors. Most of all, I trusted my gut, my intuition.

I thought—and hoped—the end result would be four short stories that would be uplifting, touching and perhaps inspirational. What I wrote were four novella length works that, I have been told, get under the skin of the reader, introducing a new kind of modern day literature. I know that sometimes my stories provide the flame required to spark renewed faith or hope in a reader, and sometimes my stories ignite the fire required for a reader's own transformation, or for believing again in their dreams or passions.

I realized just the other day while driving (and I said it aloud!) that I wrote the kind of book I myself would love, if I were to discover it on a shelf in some bookstore. I have written the kind of characters I'd like to meet in real life; people I would like to have as friends. Just as I believe *Full Moon Rising* came into being to put me on the path to becoming an author, I believe I wrote the stories in *A Tale For All Seasons* to uplift readers' hearts, expand their realm of possibilities, and renew their faith in the world and what humans are capable of ... what they themselves, might be capable of. And something tells me, this new leg on my personal journey has only just begun!

Jo Lynne Valerie

KEY SUCCESS FACTORS: Passion, Faith, Confidence

RECOMMENDED BOOKS: *A Tale For All Seasons* by Jo Lynne Valerie

WEBSITE: www.JoLynneValerie.com

SOCIAL MEDIA: Twitter—JoLynneValerie

EDITOR'S NOTES: Jo Lynne Valerie has been a writer her entire life since she began making books from paper and crayons when she was a child. She received a bachelor's degree from SUNY Brockport in journalism and creative writing and enjoyed the publication of her essays, articles, and poetry in many mainstream publications including *Woman's Day* and *SageWoman*. In 2002 she created her own publication, *Nature's Wisdom* magazine, a regional magazine that provides information on natural health, environmental awareness and the mind, body, spirit connection. Her latest work, *Full Moon Rising* magazine, allowed her to blend all of her passions and skills, as well as her chosen spiritual path. She resides in upstate New York with her husband, three children, classic Witch's cat and blue-eyed Northeastern Husky. When not cooking or reading, she gives psychic readings to clients and takes on occasional Craft apprentices. Jo Lynne is also a Certified Herbalist, Licensed Holistic Aromatherapist, and Reiki Master. She taught Aromatherapy, Numerology and Meditation and is currently the facilitator of a WitchCraft Learning Circle of Discovery in her hometown. *For a glimpse into the world of the characters in A Tale For All Seasons, to listen to audio excerpts or to read teasers, visit Jo Lynne's website at www.JoLynneValerie.com.*

*I think education is power. I think that being able
to communicate with people is power.
One of my main goals on this planet is to encourage
people to empower themselves.*

—*Oprah Winfrey*

DREAM AND BELIEVE, LEARN AND ACHIEVE

Freda D. Deskin—"Dream and Believe, Learn and Achieve" is written across the home page of The Advanced Science and Technology Education Charter Schools' (ASTEC) website. That simple philosophy sums up the way I have lived my life. These same words have also provided the inspiration for countless learners to discover that regardless of background or ability, they can reach their highest potential and experience a meaningful life while practicing personal accountability.

I was born in Pasadena, California, and spent time in Arizona and California before moving from Hollywood, California, to a farm in Lexington, Oklahoma. I had just finished seventh grade and, as you can imagine, this move provided quite a change in scenery and lifestyle. When my dad bought chickens, cows, and pigs, I initially was intrigued by the novelty of the animals and I gave each one a name. Quickly I learned I didn't want to drink cows' milk and I was afraid of the chickens.

Dad was always an entrepreneur. He invented a piece of equipment for the Bureau of Reclamation to help clean canals. Mother, one of eleven children, understood the value of hard work. My parents instilled a strong work ethic always demonstrating problem solving, discipline and responsibility.

I had a fabulous teacher in sixth grade, Mr. Phillip Wilson, who made a difference in the lives of his students. Mr. Wilson's influence made me want to someday make a difference in the lives of those younger than me.

After marrying my high school sweetheart, Bob, we moved to Edmond, Oklahoma. Less than one year after we were married, Bob was sent to Vietnam and was MIA for several weeks. These were difficult times, but he returned and we were married for thirty-one years.

Knowing that education was important to my success, I obtained an elementary education degree with a minor in physical education, math and English from the University of Central Oklahoma. I went on to earn an M.A. in secondary education and a Ph.D. in curriculum and instruction from the University of Oklahoma. I was also fortunate to study at Harvard University in the Strategic Management program.

In 1978, I started a program in Oklahoma called "Odyssey of the Mind," an international program that teaches and rewards creative problem solving for students in kindergarten through college. Team members apply their creativity to solve problems that range from building mechanical devices to presenting their own interpretation of literary classics. They bring their solutions to competition on the local, state, and world levels. Thousands of teams throughout the U.S. and from about twenty-five other countries participate in the program. Over thirty years later, this program is still thriving.

In 1985, I was selected as a finalist in NASA's "Teacher in Space Project," becoming one of only one hundred individuals in the world with the official title of "U.S. Space Ambassador." The Teacher in Space Project began as a NASA program announced by President Ronald Reagan in 1984. The goal was to inspire students, honor teachers, and create interest in mathematics, science, and space exploration. Over eleven thousand teachers applied for the program and I was fortunate to be among the final twenty. This was an exciting time for the entire nation that ended in the worst nightmare possible when Christa McAuliffe and six other astronauts died in the Space Shuttle *Challenger* disaster in 1986.

The shock and sorrow of this event served as motivation to inspire and educate children in science and space exploration in other ways. In 1986, under my leadership, Oklahoma's first aerospace summer camps were launched. More than twenty years later, the program has grown to include tens of thousands of participants including outreach programs and teacher training throughout the United States. NASA and the Challenger Center continue to work closely, providing materials and ongoing trainings for the Space Ambassadors. I was fortunate to have served in the capacities of Curriculum Developer, Advisor, Consultant and National Faculty Member to the Challenger Center for Space Science Education.

As an educator, I taught for fifteen years at the pre-collegiate level and nine years at the university level. I served for six years as a university dean before founding ASTEC in 2000. This was Oklahoma's first "startup" charter school and my answer to better prepare youth for responsible citizenship and success in the work force of tomorrow. Today, nearly one thousand students are enrolled in ASTEC.

My latest endeavor has included study to earn an advanced level certificate as a consultant from the American Feng Shui Institute. This inspired the launch of my most recent company New Day Feng Shui with products to balance the energies of any given space to assure the health and good fortune for people inhabiting it.

To be successful, it is important to believe in and trust yourself. The late Oklahoma Chief Justice, Alma Wilson, served as my mentor and taught me how to trust myself and how to negotiate personally and professionally for a "win-win." It is also important to give back. We teach this to our students by supporting a number of non-profit groups. Because I "Dream and Believe, Learn and Achieve," I have been blessed with great success.

Freda D. Deskin

KEY SUCCESS FACTORS: Passion, Relationships, Tenacity, Integrity, Perseverance

RECOMMENDED BOOKS: *Love is Letting Go of Fear* by Gerald Jampolski, *The Seven Spiritual Laws of Success* by Deepak Chopra; *Good to Great* by Jim Collins; *The 7 Habits of Highly Effective People* by Stephen R. Covey

WEBSITES: www.astec-inc.org, www.newdayfengshui.com

SOCIAL MEDIA: Facebook

EDITOR'S NOTES: Dr. Freda Deskin has been honored with many awards including "Woman of the Year" for Oklahoma by the Girl Scouts and the Newcomer of the Year award from the Last Frontier Council of the Boy Scouts. She is a two time honoree of "*The Journal Record's* Fifty Women Making a Difference" in Oklahoma. She received the Frank G. Brewer Award for the Southwest Region from the U.S. Air Force for outstanding contributions in aerospace education and the prestigious "By-liner" award by Women in Communication. Freda was named the Outstanding National Educator from Women in Aviation in 2007. She also received the Marita Hynes Award for Excellence from the University of Oklahoma for her lifelong encouragement of women and girls in sports. Because of her work with curriculum development and Microsoft's Flight Simulator, Dr. Deskin was invited to a small dinner party and dined with Bill Gates in his office. Freda has one son named Sam and two toy schnauzers named Alma and Wilson.

I've been absolutely terrified every moment of my life—
and I've never let it keep me
from doing a single thing I wanted to do.

—Georgia O'Keeffe

COURAGE IS NOT
THE ABSENCE OF FEAR

Karla Driskill—Courage is not the absence of fear—it is taking action in spite of fear—moving against the resistance engendered by fear, into the unknown and into the future. This is now my philosophy of life. But it has not always been this way.

Prior to September 2003, I was afraid of success. I did not allow myself the luxury of dreaming. I had traded dreaming for survival. I was married to a minister and homeschooled our four children. I had no degree, no work experience, and seemingly, no options. We drove a seventeen-year-old conversion van and did not even live paycheck to paycheck, we lived paycheck to two days after payday and then I panicked. However, when the pain of remaining the same is greater than the pain of change, you change.

I found myself in this position in the fall of 2003: my desire for a different life for myself and my family was greater than my fears. This is when my sister introduced me to an amazing business opportunity with an Internet-based health and wellness company. I loved the products, but more importantly, I loved the idea that I could make money by sharing these products with my friends. I had not worked outside of the home in seventeen years and did not in any way consider myself a business woman, but I was tired of wishing and hoping for a different life, so I decided to create one.

With nothing but raw enthusiasm and a firm belief in our products and company, I jumped in with both feet and started building a business in January 2004. I talked to anyone who would fog a window. I asked everyone I met for referrals. I had so many coffee dates with people to share my vision that I am surprised I didn't overdose on caffeine. I believed this was a once in a lifetime opportunity, so I made the necessary short-term sacrifices to ensure my business would succeed. I began to dream of more than just grocery money and a nap. I began to "dwell in the realm of possibility," as Emily Dickinson said. And I began to see the opportunity to take others with me on this journey towards freedom.

Through much perseverance and with a team of dedicated visionaries, we tripled my husband's salary in less than a year and we traded in our van for a white Mercedes Benz. I will never forget when we pulled up to the Mercedes dealership to pick out our new car. My husband turned to me and said, "Karla, we are not Mercedes people."

To which I replied, "Speak for yourself! I am now!"

We are living proof that anyone can change their life if they have a big enough dream and a no-quit attitude. I believe that if your dreams are big enough, the facts don't matter. I once read that you only live once, but if you work it right, once is enough. I see my business as an opportunity to serve others and give them an opportunity to live abundantly in every area of their lives ... from their health, to their wealth.

I would encourage you to have the courage to take an honest look at your life and ask where you see yourself in five years. Do you see yourself driving the same car, living in the same house, stuck in a dead-end job, struggling to make it until pay-day? Or can you picture a better quality of life for you and the ones you love? You can create the life you want by having the courage to look past where you are to where you want to be and then allowing your dreams to be the fuel that propels you past the obstacles that are on the journey towards success. It takes courage to change, but I believe it is worth every effort to embrace the life you were created for.

Although I have experienced many ups and downs on this journey, I still get up every morning excited about the possibility of positively impacting someone's life through my business. I am not the same person I was when I started this business and for that I am thankful. I have a desire to reach my full potential and to encourage others to do the same. I believe that as a result of my commitment to serve others, I will leave a legacy that will benefit those I come in contact with. My business gives me the opportunity to pursue excellence in every area of my life and for that I am eternally grateful.

Karla Driskill

KEY SUCCESS FACTORS: Courage, Determination, Vision, Belief

RECOMMENDED BOOKS: *The Success Principles* by Jack Canfield, *Dare to Dream and Work to Win* by Tom Barrett, the Bible, *The 8th Habit* by Stephen R. Covey

WEBSITE: karladriskill@myarbonne.com

EDITOR'S NOTES: Karla Driskill is an independent consultant and Executive National Vice President for Arbonne. She lives in Stillwater, Oklahoma, with her husband Ron and four children, Lane, Laurel, Alyse and Tyler.

The power of a book lies in its power to turn a solitary act into a shared vision. As long as we have books, we are not alone.

—Laura Bush

VISUALIZE, BELIEVE, SPEAK AND DO

Fiona Ingram—I have enjoyed a charmed existence. I have always been successful at whatever I tackled and don't have a "born in poverty" hard-scrabble story (although my parents were very poor when I was growing up). Changing my career midstream was the biggest step of my life, gave me a slap in the face and made me rethink the value of life in the face of death.

With a brilliant academic track record, I earned scholarships that paid for a fantastic education, enabling me to study abroad in Europe and gain wonderful life experience. I came back home to South Africa and had no trouble establishing myself in the world of journalism. It was all very easy—too easy.

One day I decided I wanted something more out of life. I'd read loads of John Kehoe's Mind Power books and had taken many courses, so one day I said to myself, "I really want to be a world famous, published writer. Let's see if it happens." I had no idea what kind of book I would write, I was just tired of writing articles and correcting other people's work. I reminded myself of my goal every day and waited ... until it happened: I wrote a children's book and my life changed.

Writing a children's book was an unexpected step, inspired by a recent trip to Egypt. In fact, I should say I owe it all to my mother, who read about a tour to Egypt in a family magazine. I wasn't sure about Egypt—Europe is more to my liking—but Mother was insistent, and so I went along with her whim. We took my two nephews along for the ride, and they became the models for the two young heroes of the book, Justin and Adam Sinclair.

My book, *The Secret of the Sacred Scarab*, began life as a little anecdotal tale for my nephews (then ten and twelve). When we got back to South Africa and had admired the photos and sorted out the souvenirs, I wanted to give them something special to remember the trip. I picked up a writing pad and a red ballpoint pen. Then, without even thinking about it, I wrote the title and the first word, "Egypt!" The rest just seemed to flow. I used the actual trip as the basis, recounting the many unusual things that had happened to us and infusing them with more exciting meaning. My reminiscences grew into a children's book. By the time I finished the book, I realized that the children couldn't possibly save the world in one book ... they'd have to carry on. So, that first book has now become the first in the adventure series, *Chronicles of the Stone*.

In my naïveté, I already saw myself at the top of the tree, so to speak, in the world of writing. I resigned from my job and finished the book. Then came a wake-up call. My mother, who had encouraged me and been a financial and emotional tower of strength, fell desperately ill. I had planned to go to London to see literary agents to sell myself and my book series. I cancelled the trip when my mother's surgeons told me that she might die. There was no question about it—I could not leave her for the sake of the book.

I sat in the intensive care ward, feeling very sorry for myself. She couldn't die, not yet! I wasn't ready to lose her; there were so many things I had not shared with her, so many things we had not done together yet. Then it struck me—how selfish could I be? If I wasn't ready for her to die, how much more was *she* not ready to die? The book and all thought of my own desires flew out my head and I realized I would give it all up in exchange for her life. Boy, did I pray! She pulled through and I took her home and nursed her back to health, although she is now in a wheelchair.

Undaunted (and still naïve), I decided to submit my manuscript to thirty-five British literary agents. In my innocence, I already saw myself as the next J.K. Rowling, with agents clamoring to represent me. What a blow! Thirty-three sent back letters that hinted they hadn't even bothered to read the material. Two kind and generous agents told me what I needed to know: that I could certainly write, the action was good, the characters nicely defined, and that I should cut the book in half and persevere. I took their advice and now have my first book under my belt, having finally found a publisher in the United States. I dedicated the book to my mother because without her it would never have been written.

Although it hasn't been easy, I learned an incredible amount in a very short space of time. As a technophobe, I've had to embrace a new world, shake myself out of the warm cocoon of "being a writer," and get to grips with making it happen for myself.

Even though I knew nothing about book publishing, apart from the actual writing, I found an artist to illustrate the book, designed a website, and nursed the book through the editing and rewriting processes. I plodded through the whole marketing route in the face of overwhelming competition, given the number of books published every day in the United States. Now I have loads of material on the web about my book series and have achieved a lot of publicity.

I am not world famous nor rich yet, but I have faith in my work. Without my mother telling me to pull myself together and "just get on with it," I would have given up many times. I have also successfully used the mind-power techniques I have learned. Whenever I felt that cold wave of despair, that feeling of "I'll never make it, why am I even bothering" begin to envelop me, I would close my eyes and visualize my success (usually me signing loads of books, waving to ardent fans and seeing my book covers plastered in shop windows). The help and advice I have received from marketing and other literary experts has also imbued me with such optimism and instilled a belief in the generosity of others. I know it's important to give back that help and advice to others and have written three articles on publishing and marketing one's work—all the tips needed to get out there and make it happen!

Fiona Ingram

KEY SUCCESS FACTORS:

1. Visualize what you want to achieve, even in the face of overwhelming odds.
2. Believe with your heart and soul you can achieve what you want.
3. Speak aloud every day what you want to achieve (a short, pithy mantra).
4. Do something about it.

RECOMMENDED BOOKS: Any Mind Power books written by John Kehoe, *Think and Grow Rich* by Napoleon Hill

WEBSITE: www.secretofthesacredscarab.com

EDITOR'S NOTES: Fiona Ingram is a full-time children's author and is working on the second book in her series, *The Search for the Stone of Excalibur.* She lives in Johannesburg, South Africa, with a menagerie of interesting animals, her eccentric and very-much-alive mother and her adopted daughter. Fiona has finally mastered the intricacies of online marketing! Her book, *The Secret of the Sacred Scarab,* is available on www. Amazon.com. The first chapter of her second children's book is available on her website. *The Secret of the Sacred Scarab* was a finalist in the 2009 Next Generation Indie Book Awards (Juvenile Fiction), a finalist in the 2009 National Best Books Awards (Children's Fiction) and a winner in the 2009 Readers' Favorite Book Awards (Preteen). The book was voted Number Two in the Children's & Teens Book Connection Top Ten Favorite Books of 2009 for Kids, Tweens and Teens.

How wonderful it is that nobody need wait a single moment before starting to improve the world.

—Anne Frank

TURNING A DREAM
INTO REALITY

Julie Gilbert—Are you insatiably curious and do you ask a lot of questions? Are you dissatisfied with the status quo? Are you a bit of a rebel, a risk taker, thick-skinned and self-assured? If you answered yes to these questions, you may just be an entrepreneur whether you realize it or not. You may be working within a large company and people call you the "change agent" or "fixer," but really, you're an entrepreneur. You may be dreaming of starting your own company or you might be content to work for others. Regardless, you've got entrepreneurial wiring.

I was predetermined to be an entrepreneur. My parents were business owners in a very small South Dakota town. While everyone else's parents farmed, my folks built a gas station, owned a restaurant and ran an auto repair shop. I was working for my parents from the time I was very young. They deliberately taught me to be comfortable with risk and to be aware of what was necessary to build a business: hard work, vision, intellect. As a result, I was quite a risk taker.

I was always piloting projects and trying to get our whole town involved—whether it was organizing a parade or raising money for a family that was struggling. The urge to create something out of nothing, which is what I believe entrepreneurship is, was starting to develop in me at a very early age.

I wish I could say I've ended up where I am through foresight and planning. Actually, I benefited from letting things fall into place. In college I majored in marketing and finance. I got to my junior year and needed an internship for the summer to pay the bills. I went to the jobs' board and was dismayed to see the jobs that were applicable to my degree were not what I had in mind.

I literally took two steps to the right to look at the job offers on the accounting board and saw the selection was a whole lot better looking in terms of the companies and the pay offered. I walked into the career office, changed my major and signed up for accounting internship interviews.

I was hired by Deloitte. I then went to summer school and doubled down in accounting classes to get my degree in my new major.

After graduation, I worked at Deloitte full time as a CPA in corporate tax. Deloitte was intellectually stimulating and felt like a very intense, complex ballgame. I was looking at taxes, treatises, international laws and rules, and exceptions. The books are deep and the issues complex. I was initially very intrigued by that, but it wasn't too long before I started to get restless. I was looking for loopholes in the tax law because I was trying to figure out how we could help companies in ways they hadn't considered.

I should have just been content to do my work, but I really couldn't help myself and I started innovating a new business for Deloitte. Unfortunately, the culture there was more about conformity than innovation. There I was, a twenty-six-year-old tax accountant, proposing the start of a new business that frankly was outside their realm. I couldn't even get time with the senior leader of Deloitte to tell him about my idea. Rather than be dissuaded, however, I just got more creative.

I noticed the senior leader always carried the same coffee cup when he came into work. So I figured out where he was buying his coffee and knew his walk from the coffee shop to the office would be my best opportunity to pitch my idea.

I positioned myself at that coffee shop at 6 a.m. and waited. When he showed up, I presented my idea to him. I told him I believed in it so much that if it didn't work in three months, he could keep my entire bonus for the year and fire me. After a lot of convincing, he agreed, saying, "We win, no matter what."

My idea worked. That business was a success and it gave me the credibility to build out other businesses for them.

After nine years at Deloitte, I moved to Best Buy where I headed up the home theater division called Magnolia Home Theater. My initial role was to serve the high–end male consumer. To conduct my research, I actually went into customers' homes on the weekends and I would watch home theaters with them. Surprisingly, I found the person I would talk to most wasn't the man I was sent to observe, but his wife. I became very interested in the way she would engage me and how she came up with problems and solutions. It was obvious in retrospect—women were starting to earn and spend a lot more, having significant influence on purchases—but retailers weren't yet focusing on this evolution.

Another turning point occurred when I visited a store in California. The male employees would greet me, but instead of shaking my hand, they'd shake the hands of my male colleagues. They would treat me like I wasn't even there. In spite of the fact I had been working long hours to build this business and it was on pace for a tremendous success, the reality was that the culture of the company didn't allow me to be seen as the leader because I came in a different package—I was female. It wasn't that they were intentionally disrespecting me. Culturally, there was a block for them. It was disheartening.

Conversely, the women who worked in the store would hug me. That familiarity was as weird as not getting a handshake from the men because I didn't know the women who embraced me. On one particular day, I actually asked one woman about it and she told me the female employees thought of me as a role model because they never saw any female executives come through their door. They certainly never saw any that were driving business and had such success.

Many entrepreneurs probably have had something that really ticked them off and provided the passion to drive what they were doing. For me, that "something" was when a male colleague told me I was respected by my colleagues within the company except for one group—the female executives. I was stunned because I had never even met them; I traveled a lot and was rarely in the corporate office. When I sought to understand why they hated me, I was told it was because of my success.

When I took a look at how I and other women employees and customers were treated, it made no sense. Women were going to be our future consumers and yet women of the company didn't feel like they had a voice. The women executives seemed unwilling to participate; yet I needed them to help build the business. This paradox angered me.

That night I didn't sleep well, but I ended up dreaming about what would become my company, my vision, my passion— Wolf Means Business. The idea for my company came to me in one fell swoop. Wolf would be a platform to get the voices of all employees and customers innovating in a structured way to create growth for the company in various areas. Wolf provided a way to engage employees at all levels, as well as customers, regardless of gender, to grow a business in areas that represent those people who are involved.

It was still the middle of the night when I woke up from my dream. I immediately mapped out my idea for Wolf. Within a week I had started piloting it. Other businesses are typically built top down when senior executives are brought on board. In my case, I knew I needed to go to the bottom of the company and build teams ("Wolfpacks") and teach them how to be entrepreneurial and help them build the company.

I spent the next six months innovating Wolf in the night while leading the scale of Magnolia Home Theater, which I had built with the premise of getting the voices of employees and customers engaged. I was motivated because I could see the potential to transform companies all over the world and also create mass social change in addition to providing financial results for companies, women and for human beings. I knew that Wolf's impact would move well beyond Best Buy.

When my boss at the time gave me the lowest ratings I had ever received on my performance appraisal (despite Magnolia, my baby, being the most successful business grown internally in the history of Best Buy) with no rationale for "why," I resigned. I was destined to take Wolf to a broader scope.

Three days before I was to leave Best Buy, the CEO, Brad Anderson, met with me. He tried to convince me to stay, but I was determined to leave at that point. He asked me what three things Best Buy could do to ensure the program would be a success after I left. I told him my successor should report to him and the position should be a full-time job.

Most importantly, my successor needed to be given an upside to balance out the tremendous risk the position presented. I told him that anyone who is crazy enough to accept the position will be passionate about it, but they are taking all of the risk in terms of it failing. When it fails for a whole bunch of reasons, their own personal brand will be tarnished and they'll have to find a new job. I told the CEO that if he was going to ask someone to take that risk, he had to be willing to give them all the rights, including intellectual property, to what they created and the freedom if they wanted to leave and do this for other companies.

He agreed to all three suggestions and then said to me, "So, what do you think?"

I told him if he was really serious and was willing to write up a legal contract, then he had his person. I would stay and launch it at Best Buy. At some point when I felt that it was scalable, I would leave and do it for other companies, but Best Buy would always be known as the place where it first started.

So Wolf was developed and rolled out at Best Buy. The support of Brad Anderson was instrumental in ensuring the success of Wolf. His commitment to provide the necessary resources made all the difference. Among our results:

Revenue

- $4.4 billion increase in revenue from female customers (eleven percent increase in total company revenue)

Market Share

- Highest ever female market share in company history
- Females became the majority of the most "valuable" customers

Brand Reputation

- Largest increase in brand perception in company history

Network

- Passionate, global, viral customer networks growing market share and innovating new business offerings
- Over forty thousand members in forty-plus countries

Performance Outcomes

- Five percent reduction in female turnover resulting in a minimum of $25 million in savings
- Eighteen percent increase in the number of female employees.
- One hundred percent increase in females in the most profitable business unit

- Forty percent increase in female General Managers & General Managers in Training
- Sixty percent increase in female Operations Managers
- Thirty percent increase in female Customer Experience Managers

While still at Best Buy, I moved from Minneapolis to New York City. My boss was not happy about it, but I felt it was important to move because I knew I wanted to build Wolf to be a business with global impact, and so I had to have a network around me that was global in nature and very diverse. If you have tons of passion, but no network, you're probably not going to get very far. If you have a huge network, but no passion, you're just going to have really good parties. The trick is to get both lined up. If you can get both together, you're going to have one heck of a success, especially in the world of entrepreneurship.

In December of 2009, when buyouts were offered to all corporate employees, I knew it was the right time for me to leave. I had built a foundation and proven the financial results in a very short period of time. I had two leaders in place who I felt were very competent to take the reins at Best Buy.

About one year ago, I launched Wolf as a free-standing, independent company. It became clear to me almost immediately that Wolf was what I was meant to do as a human being. In the past I would build a business, get bored and begin transitioning it into maintenance so I could go on to the next idea. Today, I don't have any restlessness because I'm constantly innovating. There are no barriers to that innovation at all.

As a corporate entrepreneur, I was very limited by what the company was willing and not willing to do and how far they'd take my ideas. My own company is limitless.

Over the years I've learned many lessons about entrepreneurship. As an entrepreneur, I've found that you have to be willing to do it all. I came from a humble place. If I wanted something, I had to go build it. If you're not someone who came from that place, I imagine it would be very hard to put in the amount of work it takes to get a project moving.

When first starting out, entrepreneurs have to actually thrive on being the chief dishwasher and decision person and finance person and HR person. I thrive on that diversity of roles because I'm curious and I love to learn new things. I'm not afraid to clean the toilet and also go make a presentation to a board of directors. I love the variety and challenge.

Also, being told "no" is something you have to get used to. You have to be ready to be told no at least twenty times a day. Instead of getting down about it, you have to thrive on it. In fact, it helps if you actually see it as a challenge. That will give you even more conviction to prove the naysayers wrong. But it is important to listen to why you're being told no. There might be some wisdom in the "no" that would be helpful to you and speed up what you're trying to do.

You have to try to seek to understand what your true passion is. What is the thing you're really, really good at? What drives you naturally? What do you *love* doing? For me, I was sitting in a cube and going through boxes to do a tax restructuring when I kept finding myself trying to figure out who I could call to get insight into why we were doing what we were doing.

The truth was, I needed human contact. I'm very curious about all different kinds of people and I love being in the middle of a group of people, getting to know them and their essence, and figuring out a way to reposition them so they can do what it is they love to do all the time. I wasn't being fulfilled doing tax returns. That led me down a path of seeking to understand and learning who I was as a human being.

Another important piece is having a really broad, authentic personal and professional network of people around you—those who are very different from you, those who get who you are, those who are invested in you and want to help you, and those you can help in return. They will open doors for you that you would have no ability to do yourself. I figured this out later in my career when I stepped back and realized that there were some things that would have been impossible to accomplish by myself.

Finally, speaking the language of business by having a strong understanding of finance is imperative. It's quite difficult to be successful if you don't have at least a fairly solid foundation on how you make money in business. I just don't think that's something you can delegate to a CFO, especially in the early days.

Stepping out on my own has allowed me to be me. When I worked for other companies, I changed or morphed who I was to fit the culture. As a result I restrained my ideas, my questions—the very essence of who I was—because at some point you have to conform to survive.

As an entrepreneur, I'm rewarded for my ingenuity and creativity. Now I'm able to focus on what's important—changing the world!

Julie Gilbert

KEY SUCCESS FACTORS: Curiosity, Background in Finance and Accounting, Looking for the Paradox

WEBSITE: www.wolfmeansbusiness.com

EDITOR'S NOTES: Julie Gilbert is the founder and CEO of Wolf Means Business. Initially rolled out at Best Buy, Wolf increased Best Buy's female market share by over $4.4 billion and reduced female employee turnover by more than five percent each year. In 2009, Julie left Best Buy to bring Wolf to other companies.

In her sixteen years in corporate America, Julie's other business successes included the launch of Magnolia Home Theater at Best Buy, Virgin Mobile's launch in the U.S. (in partnership with Best Buy) and tax consulting business for Deloitte & Touche.

This year, *PINK* magazine named Julie one of the Top 15 Women in Business in the United States. Other honors include the EPIC "Circle of 10 Award" from The White House Project, one of Minnesota's Women to Watch (by the *Twin Cities Business Journal*), Top 25 Business Leaders in Minnesota (by *Minnesota Business Journal*) and one of the 100 Most Successful Women in Business by Profiles in *Diversity Journal* magazine.

Julie serves on the board of directors for the Harvard Business Kennedy School Women's Board and The White House Project. She also is active with Susan G. Komen, the world's preeminent organization dedicated to raising awareness and funding to find a cure for cancer.

A South Dakota native, Julie earned her master's degree in strategy and marketing, and her bachelor's degree in accounting, both with highest distinction, from the University of Minnesota Carlson School of Business. She has taught courses and workshops at New York University and the University of Minnesota. Julie is also a CPA in the state of Minnesota.

An avid writer, Julie regularly blogs for The Wolf Pack Den, *PINK* magazine and the Harvard Business School. She has been published internationally and is writing a book about the power of finding, exercising and listening to the voices of people (their ideas, knowledge and insight) at all levels of organizations to re-invent business and grow as individuals.

CHAPTER 4

FUN, FABULOUS AND FOCUSED

If you obey all the rules, you miss all the fun.

—*Katharine Hepburn*

The world is round, and the place which may seem like the end may also be only the beginning.

–Ivy Baker Priest

TRAVEL GIRL MAKES GOOD

Renee Werbin—If you want to ride atop an elephant in Tibet or plan a group dinner at the Sistine Chapel in Rome, I can arrange that for you. If you want to know the best places to buy a little black dress in Paris, New York, Milan, Frankfurt or Wichita, I know where to send you; that's my job, I'm the Travel Girl. I've traveled the world and parlayed my knowledge into successful businesses. The most important thing about me, however, is that I'm first and foremost a wife and mother. The joys of my life are the people I love. Everything else is just icing on the cake.

Family has always had a big influence on me. My mother, Fannye Galanty, was a teacher whose students admired her. They went on to become doctors, lawyers and judges—in no small part due to my mother's impact on their lives. My sister, Ellen Williams, is a mega talented and award winning writer who has always been a loving sister and incredibly supportive of me. My father, Irving Galanty, taught his daughters that we could be anything we wanted to be and do anything we wanted to do. He adored my sister and me and had the most wonderful values in life. He instilled a wonderful work ethic in me and always taught me to do the right thing. When you have a parent who believes in you and teaches you that you can achieve your dreams, you go far in life. Indeed, what I wanted to be, I became.

In college I majored in education and after graduation, I taught for two years. When I had my children, I stayed home to raise them. I adored being a mother and threw myself into the role wholeheartedly. I learned to bake challah loaves for the Sabbath, strip and paint cabinets, plant vegetable gardens and drive carpool. I was the room mother for each of my three children every school year. Whatever needed to be done, I did. As my children grew up and needed me less, I realized I needed to find something to do with all my energy.

When my youngest child was five or six, I went to see the travel agent we frequently used and I told him I wanted to go work. He looked up at me, sensed my potential and said, "Welcome aboard." I started working part time as an outside sales travel agent. I brought in my own clients and ran them through his agency. Before too long, I had more work than I knew what to do with. It was time to open my own agency.

I launched SRI Travel in 1987. I named the agency after my three wonderful children: Stuart, Robyn and Ian. All three of my incredible children are honorable adults, each hardworking and involved in helping to make this world a better place. My devoted husband, a lawyer and judge, gave me office space and his wholehearted support. I started with one employee, my personal knowledge and word of mouth. The business took off from there.

SRI is successful because our agents are extremely well traveled and knowledgeable in what we do. Wherever our customers want to travel, we know how to help them make the most of their journey. We can arrange cooking classes in Paris, archeological digs in Israel, private tours of the Sistine Chapel, hot air balloon rides in Switzerland and dog sledding in Alaska—anything our clients might want to do. We've developed a network of exceptional local guides, and our focus is on customized travel. We have agents who specialize in different areas. When you come to us, you're getting advice from informed travel agents along with our personal tips on sightseeing, restaurants, shopping—even how to pack.

We've also learned to adapt to the ever-evolving travel industry. The Internet is our biggest challenge—commissions, especially with the airlines, are completely gone. When I opened SRI Travel our business was eighty percent corporate travel, we issued scores of airline tickets, booked hotels, arranged transfers and reserved rental cars. When the airlines began instituting commission caps, I turned my business around to focus on leisure travel. When airline commission completely disappeared I reinvented my business and ventured into the wholesale arena by developing relationships with hoteliers and resource people around the world. I developed a wholesale division of SRI Travel, created an informative brochure and took my "show" on the road to meet with travel agencies around the U.S. It wasn't easy but it was fun—in the business world one always needs to reinvent herself. Our wholesale product is doing well. It's quite upscale and offers four and five star hotels, private tours, transfers and guides.

My next business venture developed when CNN's *Travel Now* show invited me to their offices to discuss making arrangements for a three week shoot they were going to do in France. CNN executives had scheduled twenty minutes to meet with me but the meeting lasted two hours; thankfully they realized I was quite knowledgeable about France. We were hired to handle the travel arrangements for that show and I developed a wonderful friendship with the host of *Travel Now*, Stephanie Oswald. We enjoyed our time in France together. In fact, we like to say that *travelgirl* magazine was born on the streets of the Champs-Élysées in Paris.

After September 11th, Stephanie and I were having dinner in Atlanta, and we were discussing what she was going to do next, CNN had put travel shows on hold believing the current focus should just be the news. Stephanie is an accomplished broadcast journalist and had been CNN's travel correspondent for thirteen years. I was running SRI and working as travel editor for another publication. I said, "Why don't we launch our own magazine?"

Stephanie looked at me and said, "Sounds great."

We decided then and there to launch a women's travel magazine together.

Stephanie's nickname at CNN was Travel Girl, she was traveling weekly in search of new destinations to present on air. Coincidentally, everywhere I went, I was also called Travel Girl. It seemed obvious what to call our publication, but there were doubters. We were advised to change the name to "Travel Woman" or "Travel Lady" since our target demographic did not include the teen market. We were told repeatedly that our chosen name wouldn't cut the mustard. We refused to give in and instead dedicated ourselves to making sure our audience understood the name. To us, "*travelgirl*" brings out the essence of youth, and everyone wants to feel young. We cherished the name and fought to keep it. We learned in the process that sometimes you hear a lot of good advice from people you respect, but you ignore it and things work in your favor anyway.

We went to see my husband, Sam, who incorporated *travelgirl* magazine. I invited one of my closest friends to join our team and Michael Morris became our savvy financial partner and business wizard. We're like a brother/sister team. I'm most proud of our fourth partner who stood by my side when we founded *travelgirl*. My very capable and lovely daughter, Robyn Werbin, is *travelgirl*'s associate publisher. Robyn's multi-talented; she writes, edits, and handles *travelgirl*'s accounting.

The magazine business is basically an ad game. It doesn't matter how good your magazine is, how qualified your writers are, or how many awards you win; if you don't sell ads, you're going to close your doors. Your publication is dependent on the advertising dollar. In the beginning most magazines, in order to sell ad space, create a mock publication to show potential advertisers what it's going to look like. We didn't bow to conventional standards. Instead all four of us knocked on as many doors as we could. If we had connections, we used them. Each of us had a lot of friends and knew a lot of people.

Stephanie's network connections and our wonderful publicist were able to get us on national television to promote the magazine. We put our first issue on the newsstand nationwide and never created a mock version.

When you enter into an arena like publishing, there are a lot of men involved and one has to be tough. To compete in this field where there is so much competition you need good decision making skills and a strong constitution. You need to stand up for yourself, stand by your beliefs, and make sure your publication offers competent and insightful editorial. You must have excellent writers, great editors, and wonderful creative people. When we launched, every good old guy told us we'd never make it. That fortified my determination. I like to say—Don't ever tell me I can't do something because then I'm determined to show you I can. Can't isn't in my vocabulary.

On June 26, 2003, our first issue hit the national newsstands. We were the first travel publication to launch post September 11th. *travelgirl* is a magazine that helps our readers navigate the modern world of travel for business and for pleasure. In addition to travel, we cover topics important to women such as family, finance, health, humor, spirituality and fitness. *travelgirl* magazine's mission is to improve the quality of life for women by helping them find their own private oasis while vacationing and in their daily lives. We can help you plan an exotic honeymoon, tell you about a spa treatment that you can do at home and offer tips for taking the kids to London. We have developed a niche market and have never tried to become a mega publication. Eighty percent of our readers are women and their median age is forty. Our website, www.travelgirlinc.com is an integral part of our corporation and we offer articles published only on our website.

Stephanie was the cover model for the first two issues until my very smart daughter, Robyn, convinced us to start putting celebrities on our covers. *travelgirl* magazine is not about celebrities, but celebrities sell magazines and Robyn felt that putting a famous face on our cover would jump start our newsstand sales. She was right. Our third cover featured my friend, Kathleen Kennedy Townsend (Robert Kennedy's daughter who has been the Lieutenant Governor of Maryland). From there we went to Jane Fonda, who lives in Atlanta and couldn't have been more gracious. Some of the other celebrities who have graced our *travelgirl* covers are Tony Bennett, Bette Midler, Liza Minnelli, Reba McEntire, fashion designer Oleg Cassini, Cher, Christina Applegate, Jane Seymour, Carol Alt, fashion designer Diane Von Furstenberg, Niki Taylor, Lauren Hutton, Robin Roberts, Joan Rivers and Carlos Santana. I interview all of the famous people who grace our covers.

Instead of simply focusing on the fact that these personalities are celebrities, we focus on how they've used their celebrity to provide a positive impact. We wrote about Jane Fonda's non-profit organization G-CAPP, which helps young women in Georgia prevent adolescent pregnancy. Cher was fabulous to interview and shared that when she made the movie *Mask*, she was contacted by the Children's Craniofacial Foundation. She became so involved with that organization that a portion of the proceeds from all of her concerts goes to these very special kids. Tony Bennett built a public school for the arts in New York called the Frank Sinatra School of the Arts. Tony's an icon and an incredibly generous and humble man. He named the school he founded for his best friend Frank, not for himself. I interviewed Robin Roberts on the set of *Good Morning America*. I adored her; she's a marvelous person and has had a profound impact on breast cancer awareness. She blazed a trail when she offered on-air insight into her own battle with the disease.

One of the most important tenets of our magazine is that each and every single article is written by experienced writers who go out into the field to research the article in person. When you read about a new facial treatment or Botox, please know that one of our writers experienced the Botox injections. When you read an article about Helsinki, Finland, our writer was there traveling around Helsinki firsthand. Our writers are impressive; among their ranks are Pulitzer Prize winners, Emmy award winners and staff writers formerly with *Time* and *Newsweek*. You can trust what you read in *travelgirl* magazine.

I also write for the magazine. Writing is something I've always loved to do; it's a quality effort between me, my computer and my heart. I call it as I see it and hope that my journalism has a great impact on people. When I'm writing about a destination, I try to see the destination from the aspect of someone sixty, forty and twenty-five so there is something for all interests and ages. When I research something that can improve the lives of our readers, I feel a great responsibility to pass on that information usually through my publisher's letter which appears in each issue.

We are now in the process of enhancing and enlarging the *travelgirl* brand. The *travelgirl* luggage collection was launched on QVC in December and our product is just now arriving at department stores. We will soon be offering a clothing line as well. It is so exciting to see the business take off. It's our baby, it's been a joy to develop and we want to make sure we take care of it.

As President of SRI Travel and Publisher and co-founder of *travelgirl* magazine, I am involved in every aspect of running both businesses. They say when you own your own business, you get to pick which twelve hours you want to work. I'll let you guess how many hours it takes to run two businesses. I don't know if everybody can do as many things as I do in a day. It's just natural to me to do ten things at once and, for the most part, do them competently. When it's your business, you do what needs to get done.

One of the most important things I can tell someone starting a business is to learn to adapt. Don't sit back and complain about how things used to be. That's no way to get ahead. Adapt, change your focus, regroup and reinvent yourself. Those that can adjust will succeed.

It's also important to learn to listen. My mother always taught me that if God wanted you to talk more than he wanted you to listen, he would have given you two mouths and one ear. I listened more than I talked, and I learned. Entrepreneurial skills are probably within everyone. It's just necessary to hone in and develop them. Read the books you need to read, do the research you need to do. When I took on *travelgirl*, I certainly wasn't the best writer in the field, but I can tell you I became one. I spent the time learning what I needed to know. It's a joy to experience new things; always try to seize and appreciate the opportunities that come your way.

It's not difficult to start or own a business. What is difficult is to manage your business well. It's most important to treat people properly and learn to change with the times—that's how you'll become successful. Make work a team experience. I always tell our staff that no one works *for* me, they work *with* me. We work together and we try to keep the atmosphere fun.

I am the luckiest mother in the entire world because my daughter works by my side as my partner. She's much smarter than I am with mathematics, and she handles all the accounting. I haven't signed a check in years. How lucky I am to see her beautiful face every day.

My best piece of advice is to make good choices in your life. My husband of forty years has supported me in every endeavor I've ever had and I am still head over heels in love with him. The single best decision I've ever made in my entire life was marrying my husband.

By doing what I love, I've been able to make my clients' travel dreams come true and meet some of the most famous people in the world. I've traveled the globe and led a truly remarkable life, but I like to think I'm grounded. Most Fridays you'll find me at my favorite spot: at home baking two challah loaves and looking forward to spending the Sabbath with my family.

Take care of your home first and make your husband or partner and your children the most important parts of your life … as they should be. And then work hard, surround yourself with qualified, kind and honest people and make sure you can see your way through. Then take the risk and remember, don't take "no" for an answer.

Renee Werbin

KEY SUCCESS FACTORS: Determination, Risk Taker, Won't Accept "No"

RECOMMENDED BOOKS: *The Year of Magical Thinking* by Joan Didion, *The Last Lecture* by Randy Pausch

WEBSITES: www.sritravel.com, www.travelgirlinc.com

SOCIAL MEDIA: Twitter—travelgirlmag; Facebook—*travelgirl* Magazine; www.travelgirlinc.com for our *travelgirl* blog

EDITOR'S NOTES: Atlanta native Renee Werbin knows the ins and outs of the travel business. She has successfully navigated the industry for twenty-two years as CEO and President of SRI Travel and Werbin LTI Tours, LTD. Her clients include Fortune 500 companies, screen legends and CEOs from some of the most prestigious companies around the world. Her companies have organized trade missions for governors around the globe.

Werbin's travel expertise has influenced network news organizations, multi-million dollar corporations, politicians and foreign dignitaries. She has been a guest many times on CNN, FOX and CBS. Her traveling companions have included celebrities, television crews, and publishers and editors from some of the most distinguished publications in the country. She is requested often as a keynote speaker at women's events, journalism schools, news organizations and company events, lending her expertise on travel to people across the United States.

In 2002, Renee parlayed her journalistic skills into her most recent entrepreneurial endeavor, as co-founder and Publisher of *travelgirl* magazine. *travelgirl* is the culmination of her dream to share her vast knowledge of travel and her zest for life with others. Seeing the country face the tragedies of September 11th enforced her goal to help others navigate this new world of travel. She is passionate about travel, flying weekly for business in search of a story or a new take on a previously visited destination.

Werbin is a *magna cum laude* graduate of the University of Georgia. She serves on nine charitable and advisory boards and has been recognized numerous times for her civic and charitable endeavors. She is involved with the Crohn's and Colitis Foundation of America (CCFA) and has served, along with her husband, as honorary chairman for fundraising dinners. She works steadfastly for the Georgia Commission on the Holocaust, the American Israel Chamber of Commerce, the Hazel K. Goddess Fund for Stroke Research in Women, charities for children, breast cancer and cystic fibrosis charities and the Jewish National Fund, among many others. She is also a proud member of the International Women's Foundation.

Renee's most cherished role is that of wife and mother. Her children are her pride and joy, each an accomplished adult. Renee is proud of their dedication and integrity.

Live and work but do not forget to play, to have fun in life and really enjoy it.

—Eileen Caddy

IF IT'S NOT FUN,
DON'T DO IT!

Jeanna Gabellini—Using a positive mindset to make dreams become reality is something I believe in whole-heartedly. By focusing my thoughts in a constructive and passionate way, using the Law of Attraction, I have been able to draw positive people and positive results to me. I can say with conviction that the Law of Attraction has influenced my life and shaped my career.

It was 1996 and my friend had just called to let me know that he had seen an ad for the Coaches Training Institute (CTI). He knew that I had been coaching people on their lives and business goals through a personal growth seminar company for years … for free! Unfortunately, up to that point I had no idea that coaching was an actual profession where you could get paid!

I followed my gut and registered for the first CTI workshop. I fell in love with coaching and decided that I was going to become a certified co-active personal and professional coach. Not wanting to waste any time, I opened my business, Masterpeace Coaching and Training, that next week.

Not many people knew what coaching was back then, so my daily mission became to educate people about my vocation. It was simple to talk to potential clients because I was one hundred percent passionate about the benefits of using a coach. As I'm naturally a social person, my entire marketing plan was based on networking events. My agenda was never to obtain clients at the events. Instead, I focused on creating relationships and spreading the word about coaching.

My passion led the way to a full coaching practice in record speed. I was new to marketing and did everything backwards. I didn't have a brochure or a website until I was already making a living from my new profession. My ignorance worked in my favor, however, because I was not focused on selling and didn't fear rejection. My connection to the benefits of what I was offering was very attractive to the people I met. My business expanded into teaching classes, both in person and over the phone, on topics I was passionate about. There's that word again ... passion.

A few years later I met Eva Gregory, another coach, at a year-long leadership program. We began meeting in a Mastermind group to brainstorm about our businesses every week. We were both successfully using the Law of Attraction to teach our clients how to focus on and quickly achieve their goals in satisfying ways. Inspiration hit! We thought that we should teach a class on the subject. It sounded like pure fun. Our first class sold out. Again, our marketing was not brilliant, but our excitement about the Law of Attraction was contagious. This led to a business partnership that is now ten years old and still a blast. People always ask us how we found such a perfect business partner. We respond that we weren't trying. We just followed our inspiration. Our motto is, "If it's not fun, we're not doing it!"

As an entrepreneur, I have enjoyed being in control of all parts of my business. One downside has been that it was sometimes easy to become overwhelmed since I didn't have a team to whom I could consistently delegate tasks. My business was growing and so was my standard of living. I began to get out of balance in my life. Work became my only focus, as I feared that my profits would decline if I stopped moving full speed ahead.

Thank goodness I had my own coach! Baby step by baby step I let go of my fear of losing business if I relaxed more. I did something that felt very drastic at the time ... I began taking Fridays off. It became my "Pure Pleasure Day." I did whatever I wanted that brought me joy. At first it felt scary. I felt guilty for not working, but I stuck with it.

I noticed something strange happening. I began making *more* money. Whoa! I decided to rethink the whole way I ran my business. What if I totally re-designed the entire business to suit my needs? I went for it! I decided Mondays would also be non-appointment days. If I felt like working on the business, I did, or I took four-day weekends! Then I raised my coaching rates so that I could work with fewer clients in a more intimate way.

I still had butterflies in my belly with each change I made. I learned that by following my "joy-o-meter," things only got better. I tripled my income that year and felt no stress. This was how life was supposed to be … fun!

Several years later I entered and exited a very negative relationship. I stopped focusing on what made me happy and began to live in fear about the now ex-boyfriend who was harassing me. My creativity and inspiration came to a screeching halt. I wasn't paying attention to building new classes or projects. After a year, I said, "ENOUGH!"

I began to focus again on things in my business that felt good. Slowly, inspiration wove its way back into my brain. I began creating new classes that I was jazzed about. The classes attracted new clients. At the same time, Eva and I signed a book deal with the famous *Chicken Soup for the Soul* guys. A year later we got to see our book, *Life Lessons for Mastering the Law of Attraction*, in major bookstores everywhere. I doubled my income that year and became completely debt free.

I've learned that when I focus on things that feel fun, my life and business are easy. Trusting in this process as a business owner can seem counter intuitive. You're taught in business that you've got to work long and hard if you want to be successful. I've come to know that if I focus on the clients and projects that feel good, my work feels like play and abundance abounds.

Jeanna Gabellini

KEY SUCCESS FACTORS: Be Excited about What You're Doing, Relax into Profits, Work with a Coach, Focus on the Benefits of What You Offer, Above All Have FUN

RECOMMENDED BOOKS: *The One-Minute Millionaire* by Mark Victor Hansen and Robert G. Allen, *The CashFlow Quadrant* by Robert T. Kiyosaki, *Think and Grow Rich* by Napoleon Hill, *The 4-Hour Work Week* by Timothy Ferriss, *Leadership and Self-Deception* by The Arbinger Institute

WEBSITE: www.MasterPeaceCoaching.com

SOCIAL MEDIA: Twitter—jeannagabellini

EDITOR'S NOTES: Jeanna Gabellini lives in a small town in northern California with a perfect view of the bay. She walks her talk by using the Law of Attraction to manifest all the fun stuff in her life. She's an adventure junkie who met her mate while skydiving. She works from home three days a week and takes an abundance of breaks to play with her baby boy, Lucky.

*Life is a succession of moments. To live each one
is to succeed.*

—*Coria Kent*

FEEL THE MOMENT

DeDe Murcer Moffett—Life is a series of moments and events. The best moment, my best moment, is right here, right now with you. Feel this moment.

I haven't always lived in the moment, or wanted to feel the moment. Much of my life, actually twenty-four years, I numbed out moment after moment with alcohol. The first time I drank, I blacked out. In fact, most of the time when I drank, I blacked out. Many would say I had an allergy to alcohol. I say I had an aversion to seeing the truth in myself. Fear and insecurity ruled my thoughts and my days.

As a child, I would spend hours in my room listening to Streisand and Johnny Mathis, dreaming and acting out the part of an entertainer. At the age of thirteen, I began a decade of sharing my love of singing and entertaining at churches, my school, and many other local and national events. Eventually my singing abilities earned me a vocal scholarship to Oklahoma City University. Unfortunately, doubt and fear were my dominating thoughts and feelings, and I left school to go out in the world and make money. After all, that's what appeared to bring one happiness and fulfillment in life! Right?

My grandparents were entrepreneurs and the founders of Walker Stamp and Seal, a printing company that also sold notary seals and stamps in downtown Oklahoma City, Oklahoma. I learned about entrepreneurship by working in their business with several other family members.

After leaving college, I thought it would be a good idea to go into sales since that's where the money was. So off I went to find my fortune and happiness. I spent a number of years working as a salesperson for companies such as Estee Lauder, Waste Management and Toyota Motor Company. These jobs took me from Oklahoma to California to Texas, where I now reside and where I was a partner in a company that provided an investment service to credit unions.

Although I was successful in all of these jobs and was making big money, I wasn't happy. I wasn't living a life of my dreams. Something was missing. That something was me, the real me. There I was, forty-three years old, doing a job I didn't want to do, playing the part of a successful businesswoman. I was killing myself with alcohol so I could continue doing what I didn't want to do simply because I thought that's what I should do. I was attempting to live what I perceived to be the American dream!

Everything changed when I woke up from a blackout after thirteen glasses of wine at a business conference. I looked at my fiancé's face and saw all of the pain, fear and disappointment I held inside reflected back to me. Through the gift of one of my worst days, I began to wake up to the desires I had buried so long ago. The beginning of the end had begun. Hallelujah!

I quit drinking that day in April of 2007 and I haven't desired a drink since. I haven't had to white knuckle it, get on any kind of medication or stay involved in a twelve-step program. What I realize today is that when you do what you love with those you love, you begin to heal. You no longer want to numb yourself or miss a moment of this wonderful life. When you compromise yourself for the approval of others (be it your spouse, parents, friends or priest) you are going to lose. And very often lose big. When living your life for everyone but yourself, you will not live fully or find the joy you seek. Your desires are there for a reason. Listen to them. They will heal you and lift you up to a joy beyond words, building a ladder for others to follow.

Today I am the CEO and founder of Snap Out of It Women's Group, the *Snap Out of It* radio show and the Snap Out of It Radio Network. In July, I finally united with my authentic self and released my debut CD, *I Believe.* Through my Snap Out of It ventures, I teach and inspire others through workshops, conferences and singing. I help people wake up to their true, authentic selves and recognize and shift out of their limiting beliefs to live lives of their dreams with passion and joy.

Today, as I combine singing and public speaking to deliver a message of hope and transformation, I am truly fulfilled and enjoy each and every interaction and event fully and without compromise. I now listen to the soul and the voice of inspiration.

Entrepreneurship means living every day doing what you REALLY want to DO and NOT doing what you really DON'T want to do! Those simple but profound words were shared by a wise and dear teacher who overcame a terminal cancer diagnosis by living what he preached. He also told me that I could do what he did, I just hadn't learned how to yet.

It is your choice whether or not to live your passion, but life will support you on your journey. Others will be there right when you need them most, and you will heal yourself and others through the passion, joy and inspiration of doing what you really want to do. This life is always just a decision away. Take it, risk it, do it.

DeDe Murcer Moffett

KEY SUCCESS FACTORS: Passion, Inspiration, Authenticity

RECOMMENDED BOOKS: *The Soul's Intent* by Ernie Vecchio, *Fear Proof Your Life* by Joseph Bailey, *The Essential Laws of Fearless Living* by Guy Finley

WEBSITE: www.dedemurcermoffett.com, www.snapoutofitradionetwork.com

EDITOR'S NOTES: DeDe Murcer Moffett combines her inspirational speaking and singing to deliver a message of hope and transformation after overcoming a twenty-four-year alcohol addiction. She also coaches women around the country on redirecting their beliefs and thoughts that immobilize and disempower. DeDe is the CEO and founder of the Snap Out of It Radio Network where she is the host of a popular online Internet show also called *Snap Out of It,* geared toward helping others release limiting beliefs that keep them stuck. In 2010, DeDe will produce and organize the first annual Snap Out of It Women's Conference and Expo to be held in Dallas, Texas.

We are each gifted in a unique and important way.
It is our privilege and our adventure to discover
our own special light.

—Mary Dunbar

GIVE ME THE BRIGHT
LIGHTS ALWAYS

Linda C. Haneborg—The youngest of three children, I was born in Chicago where my father was an executive with the White Motor Company. When I was two, the company asked him to move to Houston to build the division there as he had done in Chicago. Described as a rare combination of Archie Bunker, Ronald Reagan and John Wayne, Dad was charismatic, yet had a down-home, colorful way about him.

The job in Houston didn't sit well with Dad so he told them to "take this job and shove it." He left the corporate life, moving the family back to his boyhood Nebraska farm. It was there I started my school career in a one-room country school house, Pleasant View District 89.

When I was in sixth grade, we moved to Wichita, Kansas, and I was placed in a Catholic grade school. This was a huge transition for me, going from thirteen total students in several grades to more than forty in one grade alone. Not to mention they were all dressed to the nines. Fortunately, we wore uniforms because all I had were hand-me-downs, and most of those included plaid shirts and lined jeans with a pair of lace up shoes that I called high-tops. (No wonder I am such a shoe-aholic today.)

High school was a peach compared to grade school. At Mount Carmel Academy, I formed friendships that have lasted a lifetime. I think that's because in an all-girls' school, we found the time to establish better relationships. It was also during high school that I learned my love for work and what doors it could open for me. Since my parents both worked (my mother taught school and my father started a new business ... at age forty-nine, I might add!) and my brother and sister were soon off to college, I realized I could help supplement the family income and provide for all my extras by getting a job. At age twelve, I started babysitting and before long had a long list of customers.

As soon as I turned sixteen, however, I went to work in a dress shop, Thurston's, which carried the most beautiful women's clothes in Wichita. I was in heaven and quickly began putting more tickets in the drawer than my paychecks could cover. Fortunately, I was able to work at Thurston's all through high school and whenever I would come home from college. I finally had the wardrobe to rival any college coed, and it gave me a great start for the professional world after college as well.

Starting my college career at Newman University, in Wichita, for the first semester, followed by Wichita State University for the second semester, allowed me to stay at home and continue to work. I really wanted to go away to college. My parents agreed as long as I attended a Catholic school. So, I went to Creighton University for one year in Omaha, but then transferred to Colorado State University where I got my degree in sociology and anthropology.

At the same time I was falling in love with Colorado, I fell in love with my future husband, Steve. We got married and I accepted a job with Xerox in Denver. Starting a job with such a prestigious company was like heaven on earth for me ... until I found out what my job really entailed. I would be a customer representative and teach people how to use the copy machine and other equipment. This meant I would stand in front of a group of people and teach classes that were two to four hours long. The number one fear in America is public speaking and I had it!

In high school when I had to give a speech, my mother would make me memorize it because of my phobia. I once tried to give the speech "The Challenge of Citizenship" in which I repeated the title three times and could come up with nothing else. Consequently, at the end of the semester, I had five speeches that I had to make up. I received an incomplete on my report card because I could not again get up in front of others after the aforementioned fiasco. When I shared my concern with my supervisor at Xerox, he told me that I could do it. Because of the respect I had for Xerox and for him, his encouragement made me believe in myself. Having someone else value me and show confidence in me made the difference.

My husband went to work for Adolf Coors Company and life was wonderful. As Steve was promoted within his company, I was able to transfer with Xerox. We had the perfect life in Colorado. During that first year of marriage and jobs, however, Steve came home one night and announced he was getting a promotion, but we needed to move to Oklahoma City for our new home. My dream of living in Colorado was indeed short lived.

Our first baby was born in Oklahoma City. She was a perfect child in every way except for her heart. Heather Kristin bravely endured four heart surgeries over her nearly three years. Her short time on this earth was an extremely tumultuous time in our perfect life with our perfect family. After three surgeries at Children's Hospital in Oklahoma City, the fine doctors there recommended we take her elsewhere for the next surgery as they had done all they knew to do.

We searched the world to find similar cases with positive outcomes and decided to take her to the hospital where more heart surgeries were performed than anywhere else, St. Mary's Hospital in Rochester, Minnesota (associated with the world-renowned Mayo Clinic). Although she lived a few days after doctors installed a pig valve in her heart, we lost our beautiful Heather. There is nothing in life worse than losing a child.

We began to try to put our lives back together. Steve's job with Coors transferred us back to Denver. I had great opportunities offered to me by Xerox, but at this point decided to do something different. I went into real estate as Director of Marketing for a development company. We started out using an outside advertising agency and with my recommendation we formed our own agency. It was a fabulous job that gave me a reason to get up every morning. I had a private office, was the first woman in a management position with the company, and I was content. In the short year that I worked for Medema Homes, we went from two hundred homes to twelve hundred homes. It was a fast and fabulous ride.

Steve came home one evening and told me he had an opportunity to move to Iowa with the company, which meant another promotion. I resisted the idea since we had moved into a new home and I so enjoyed my new job. I was beginning to feel somewhat whole again, but in the end we moved. I quickly realized I could not stand in the way of his future. We moved to Cedar Rapids on December first and the following March, Julie Brooke was born and she was perfect in every way.

This story has a pattern: When Brooke was three months old, the Adolf Coors Company now offered Steve a position in Oklahoma City or Dallas. We talked about it and knew we loved Oklahoma, so Oklahoma it was. I went to work for *Oklahoma Living* magazine and quickly moved through the ranks there.

Four years after moving to Oklahoma, our son Douglas was born and I worked part time so that I could spend more time with our children. I soon took a job with Channel 34 as Director of Public Relations, which allowed me to learn a lot about television. This job was offered to me by a young lady who had worked for the magazine. This is a good example of how relationships are critical in business and should always be viewed as mutually beneficial.

While at Channel 34, Gean Atkinson, a friend and mentor who I had met years earlier, called and said that he would like for me to work for Express Personnel Services as the Assistant

Director of Corporate Communications. I interviewed with the founder and CEO, Bob Funk, and was delighted to have the opportunity to work with another fast-growing company. I later accepted the position of Director of Communications, brought in new advertising agencies and bought into Mr. Funk's mission of growing the company into an international franchise.

I never turned down an interview to build the company's brand. From the *Today Show* to *The Wall Street Journal,* to radio interviews all over the world at all hours of the day, to getting Express into a number one best-selling book, I was living the life of a so called "corporate celebrity." During my twenty years there, Express grew from seventy offices and $15 million in revenues to more than six hundred offices and $2 billion in revenues.

I was an "intrapreneur" (an entrepreneur within a company). The franchisees were the entrepreneurs. I had passion, worked a lot of hours, and enjoyed the excitement as if it was my company. Throughout two decades there, I garnered six hundred awards for Express and my departments and worked my way to Senior Vice President. All good things must come to an end and so, in my twentieth year, I decided to retire and move forward.

Retirement from Express opened other doors for me. I gave my life to God and the message I got was *sit down, shut up and listen!* My life has taken the most phenomenal road since. A lady I worked with at Express brought me a sample of anti-aging serum. I tried it and loved it. I asked her what was in it and where it came from. She explained that a doctor had created a cream for cancer patients going through radiation via the Oklahoma University Research Parkway. As a result of seeing what it did for cancer patients, an entire skincare line was created with a formula for babies and adults.

What I soon discovered was missing in my exciting corporate life was the lack of connecting one-on-one, making a difference in people's lives. Even such a role as representing this new skincare line, Therametics, and introducing it to cancer patients and doctors would get me back to touching others' lives and making a difference for them. Since this is not my company, however, I realized I still had a yearning, even after all these years, to do my own thing. So-ooooooo...

After having individuals come to me for consulting or counseling, I decided to start a marketing consulting business—Linda Haneborg Associates. Since I have been dubbed the "Maverick Marketing Maven," I figured the more than thirty years of experience I have in the business of marketing could be extremely useful to others. Our tagline is "We build brands. We build boards. We weave dreams ... for individuals and companies." Now in my new life, I am having the time of my life helping others achieve their dreams.

Having served on nearly forty boards, one of my passions now is to help more women get on corporate boards. I am researching this topic and have a goal of writing a "how to" book for eligible women to serve on corporate boards. I also desire to establish an Oklahoma Chapter of Women Corporate Directors. Although I have collaborated on five books previously, I am now writing my own, *What Are You Waiting For?*

My message is loud and clear: It's never too late to change careers, or to be an entrepreneur. You have to believe in yourself and not be afraid to take action. My greatest achievement is overcoming my fear of public speaking. I now speak all over the country and say, "Give me the bright lights ... always."

Linda C. Haneborg

KEY SUCCESS FACTORS: Confidence, Passion, Taking Action

RECOMMENDED BOOKS: *The Breakthrough Company: How Everyday Companies Become Extraordinary Performers* by Keith R. McFarland, *Bounce: The Art of Turning Tough Times into Triumph* by Keith R. McFarland

WEBSITE: www.lindahaneborg.com

EDITOR'S NOTES: Linda C. Haneborg received her bachelor's degree at Colorado State University and completed graduate studies in liberal arts at Southern Methodist University. She is a frequent speaker at universities and professional conferences across the nation and has authored a number of national articles.

Active in numerous national professional organizations, including the International Women's Forum (IWF) and the White House Women's Information Network, Haneborg was one of only forty women internationally invited to a women's issues conference sponsored by the Harvard School of Business at the White House.

Haneborg has long been involved in her community, serving on nearly forty boards, including serving as Past President and Board Member of the Oklahoma City Chapter for the Association for Women in Communications (AWC). A member of the Women's Leadership Board at Harvard and the national board of AWC, she currently serves on the National Women Business Owners Corporation board, whose mission is to certify women business owners. She has received the National AWC Headliner Award and Matrix Awards and the Oklahoma City AWC chapter's Byliner Award for the communications category. Additional awards include the Girl Scouts' Woman of the Year, *The Journal Record's* Woman of the Year and Oklahoma City University's Woman of Excellence. In 2008, Haneborg was the recipient of the Lifetime Achievement Award from *The Journal Record's* Woman of the Year program. This award was particularly meaningful on the eve of her retirement and the fact that she was only the third person to receive this award in the twenty-six-year history of the program. Haneborg served as the 2009 Co-chair of the American Heart Association's Go Red for Women® for Oklahoma City and will serve as the 2010 Co-chair of the Allied Arts Campaign.

When Linda is not traveling, she enjoys her homes in Oklahoma City and Santa Fe, New Mexico, with her husband, Steve.

The soul should always stand ajar,
ready to welcome the ecstatic experience.

—Emily Dickinson

LIVING LIFE BEAUTIFULLY

Aimee Gold and Marcy Chekofsky—With keen senses of determination and aspiration, we combined our passion for fashion and art with our heightened sense of health consciousness, and designed a new product named JAM Bands. For the last year, we worked tirelessly to fulfill a dream to create a beautiful, elegant product that would make a woman feel healthy and relaxed as she goes about her day. In other words, we created art that makes you feel good.

We collaborated before. Ten years ago we set out to write a how-to party planning book. It was the height of black tie gala events and we were inspired by the first book we ever bought on Amazon.com, *Colin Cowies' Weddings*. We envisioned our book as a stunning coffee table book as well, rather than a how-to paperback guide recommended by the many editors we queried. Rather than change our vision, we accepted defeat and let our book fall by the wayside.

Marcy moved to Tulsa, Oklahoma, two days prior to September 11, 2001. She had to take two planes to come home to the New Jersey/New York area. If you are a poor traveler, as she was, it helps immensely to have something to rely on that helps combat motion sickness. Like many of our generation, we believed there was only one over-the-counter product, but it left us drowsy and dazed. Knowing there had to be a better way to travel, we soon discovered acupressure bands and never used the over-the-counter medication again.

As is not uncommon once your children are grown and living their own lives, mid-life can create a sense of dissatisfaction with one's place in the world. We watched our six children— three for each of us—head off onto their own successful and independent paths. For years they were our mission, and we did well; our children had become financial wizards, marketing majors, digital advertising creative types and a singer/ songwriter—each one with a passion and a gift. Yet we were left feeling as if we hadn't reached our potential—and it sat heavy on our minds and hearts.

Twenty-five years after leaving a career as a health care management consultant in New York, Aimee saw the possibility of getting back on the fast track to be dim. The excitement and unknown potential of entrepreneurship called. She had spent the last seven years being the mom/manager for her youngest child. She knew how to network and build a brand.

Marcy dabbled in real estate before realizing her true calling and returned to her career as a speech pathologist, a career she enjoys today. Always thinking creatively, Marcy tried her hand at screenwriting, devoting five years to a comedy script patterned after her own life in New Jersey.

We each felt we needed to do more. An idea that we spoke of for years began to take precedence during all our conversations. We found ourselves constantly coming back to the same fascinating product idea: an acupressure band that was beautiful and hip yet as functional as what we wore hidden under our sleeves when we traveled. More importantly, we wanted to help manage the woes of women across the world.

We didn't just talk—we read, we researched, we questioned, and we learned that the potential and benefits of acupressure were being grossly ignored. Acupressure bands would not only relieve the symptoms of nausea for the poor traveler, but also for the pregnant woman suffering from morning sickness, the woman in labor, the woman receiving chemo and radiation therapy, and the woman suffering from nausea following surgery.

We also learned that acupressure bands can be used as a relaxation and coping technique for manageable stresses. It seemed to us that every woman could benefit from wearing acupressure bands, or at least knew someone who could!

In 2009, we decided to bring a very unique and colorful acupressure band to life. The first step was to create a prototype of the product. There were so many ideas—should it be leather, should it be metal like an expandable watchband, or could it be made of ribbons? We cut and sewed for weeks. Hesitant to share our idea with too many, we spoke mostly between ourselves.

Then Aimee, an avid reader of *The New York Times*, saw an advertisement for a women's belt. Thinking our band could be a bracelet version of the belt, she did her due diligence and found the manufacturer. This led us to the garment district of New York City. What a wonderful world exists in those few, condensed and busy streets.

One meeting led to another and every conversation led to a new idea. We gathered time and again for brainstorming sessions with different manufacturers and finally decided on silk ruched, elastic bands for comfort and beauty. We spent hours agonizing over the right size pearl that would activate the pressure point but not be uncomfortable to wear. We examined the details of the stitch count and searched for the right hardware manufacturer. Not wanting to commit too early to any one style, we remained open and allowed ourselves to mix things up.

The result of that research is JAM Bands in an array of beautifully colored silk charmeuse patterns and solids with complementary rhinestone buckles offered in different shapes and colors. Each pair of bands come in a matching silk pouch with drawstring; perfect to toss in your purse and beautiful to the touch.

Designing our product was only one part of what needed to be done. We understood that naming and branding a product and company is as important to a product's success as the product itself. We wanted our product's name to be iconic and expressive and spent days struggling to find the perfect combination. We finally came up with a name we felt was representative of it all, only to find the name was registered just the day before! That was meant to be, however, for with just a little more brainstorming, JAM Bands came to mind and is now our registered trademarked name. The meaning behind the name is clear: JAM Bands jam the signals that trigger nausea and stress in the body.

Vivant Vie Ltd. was not decided upon easily either. We scoured dictionaries—*Webster's* as well as French and Spanish dictionaries. We wanted a company name with meaning. In concert with our product, the French words *vivant vie* translate into living life in English. We were more than thrilled and extremely proud when our attorney called to say the legal search was complete and we could incorporate under Vivant Vie Ltd.!

Now that we had our product and company names, logos, artwork, web design, banking, credit and insurance, more legal details needed to be attended to. We wanted to do everything right; success was all we could think about. Yet all the while we tried to contain our development costs.

Things fell into place as samples from overseas were getting closer to our specifications, but our work was just beginning. We now needed to spread the word about the power behind our bands. The pearl-like button, located on the inner-side of the bracelet, applies gentle pressure to the Pericardium (P6) Neiguan acupressure point in the wrist. Stimulation at the P6 point activates the central nervous system to release certain chemicals known as neurotransmitters such as serotonin, dopamine and endorphins. These neurotransmitters are natural mood elevators that interrupt other chemicals that cause anxiety, nausea and vomiting. We needed to get women talking.

Believing in the power of social media, we decided to use the social networking site Facebook as our website. Through Facebook.com/jambands, women will have the opportunity to share their unique and common experiences and learn from and help each other.

We believe in Karma and we are idealists. We believe there are fashionistas everywhere who will welcome JAM Bands onto their wrists. Optimism is a gene we both inherited, and encouragement from everyone we speak to, unrelenting support from our families and the strong belief in our idea has propelled us forward. Being a start-up company, we have pulled from all our in-house resources—our finance team, our photographer/artist and Facebook designer, our e-commerce marketing guru, our literary editor, our medical consultant, all of whom are family members—and we thank them. They helped make our product what we dreamt it could be.

We are proud to say that we have caught the attention of nationwide network television personalities, an international chain of maternity stores, a premier department store, as well as the travel department of a Fortune 50 Blue Chip company, to name a few. We are determined to bring acupressure to the forefront of women's consciousness and to build Vivant Vie Ltd. into an international company, with our product made available for women around the world.

Aimee Gold and Marcy Chekofsky

KEY SUCCESS FACTORS: Passion, Perseverance, Optimism, Inspiration

RECOMMENDED BOOKS: *The Tipping Point* by Malcolm Gladwell, *The Back of the Napkin* by Dan Roam, *The Girl's Guide to Building a Million-Dollar Business* by Susan Wilson Solovic, *Small Is the New Big* by Seth Godin

WEBSITE: www.vivant-vie.com

SOCIAL MEDIA: Facebook—jambands

EDITOR'S NOTES: Aimee Gold lives between New Jersey and New York, back and forth so often, she sometimes awakens unsure of where she is. She's raised three loving and successful children, Adam, Dina and Jodi, and all that she has achieved and hopes to achieve is owed to their unconditional love and support. She has devoted the last year of her life to a start-up company she co-founded with her sister. Their dream for the company encompasses all the good things life can offer for all involved and all those they will reach with their product. Foremost, she wishes everyone health, happiness and a wellness state of being.

Marcy Chekofsky divides her time between New York City and Tulsa, where she resides with her husband, Ken. Marcy and her sister Aimee co-founded Vivant Vie Ltd. This venture has been a very rewarding and emotional experience. Marcy wishes to thank her husband and children, Joshua, Jason and Jenna, for their guidance and support. Marcy is passionate about nutrition and health. She loves to share her knowledge and findings. This passion has fueled her start-up endeavor to develop a natural, personal wellness product.

They have a number of upcoming media events to showcase their product.

CHAPTER 5

POSITIVELY PASSIONATE

*When work, commitment, and pleasure all become one
and you reach that deep well where passion lives,
nothing is impossible.*

—Nancy Coey

You are unique, and if that is not fulfilled then something has been lost.

—*Martha Graham*

AN AMERICAN DREAM

Muriel Siebert—In no other country could my story have been possible. I was a girl from Ohio who moved to New York. At a time when women were primarily wives and mothers, I was looking for a different life, excitement, a career. For ten years, with the exception of only a couple of months, there were thirteen hundred sixty-five male members of the New York Stock Exchange and only one woman—me. It's only in America where I could have done this.

My mother was the youngest of eleven children—all born in Hungary. Her family owned a tannery on the outskirts of Budapest and eventually came to America in three waves, settling in Cleveland, Ohio. My father was a dentist, but he also had a degree in engineering. During what should have been his peak earning years as a dentist, he volunteered his engineering expertise for the war effort. After developing cancer in his fifties, he died broke because he had needed around-the-clock nursing care. Before my father's illness, we worked hard and lived well. I had seen what it was like to have a little bit of money, and I knew what it was like to lose it all.

One of my only trips out of Cleveland was a quick vacation to New York City and a visit to the Stock Exchange. I was struck by the excitement on the floor and thought there was probably no better place to be. After my high school graduation, I attended college for two and a half years before I moved to New York City where my sister already lived. I applied to the United Nations, but because I didn't speak two languages, I was not offered a position.

I got a job as a trainee in the research department of Bache & Co., a brokerage firm. I was grateful for the opportunity, and I worked hard even though I was basically just a runner for the senior analysts. I used that experience to learn about stock analysis and why certain companies were attractive for investors. I was thrilled when I got my first $5-a-week raise because that meant I could spend 20¢ more on lunch.

I began to make a name for myself as an analyst focusing on the airline industry. I switched firms four to five times in ten years and worked my way up to become a partner. I was making my firm and clients lots of money, but I was earning less than my male counterparts. While I was making a good living, this disparity was infuriating.

The idea to buy a seat on the Stock Exchange came from one of my clients, Gerry Tsai, who used to run Fidelity Capital and started Manhattan Fund. I had asked Gerry where I could be paid equally because I was making half the money my male colleagues were making, and no one wants to be a second class citizen. Gerry said to me, "Don't be ridiculous. Buy a seat and work for yourself."

I responded, "Don't you be ridiculous. A woman on the Stock Exchange?"

He explained that he didn't think there was a law against a woman owning a seat. So, I read the Stock Exchange constitution and confirmed that a woman should be able to buy a seat ... in theory. Practice, however, is often more complicated than theory and it wasn't that easy.

The Stock Exchange wanted a letter from the bank saying in the event they accepted a bid card from me that the bank would give me a loan. The bank said in so many words that I would have to get the seat to get the loan. I was in a catch twenty-two. I called a friend who worked with Chase Bank and said, "I guess I'm not getting the seat." He called me back in fifteen minutes and said I'd get the loan. I later understood that David Rockefeller signed the loan application—my request was unusual enough that it got all the way to Mr. Rockefeller. And I got the seat.

It was a risk to buy the seat. I had nobody to bail me out if I failed. And I wasn't the only one who could have been negatively impacted—I was also supporting my mother at that time. I felt that if worse came to worst, though, I could go back to simply being an analyst.

Fortunately, my talents were recognized and I was able to make a go of it. Sure, not everyone liked me nor having a woman show up in a previously male-only venue. I was not greeted with open arms. But I was finally controlling my own destiny. When I had the seat, I could make the same amount of money as my peers. If I wanted to be paid equally, it was up to me to earn it.

Initially, my only employee was a male secretary. Two years after buying the seat, I added two partners and changed from being simply a seat holder to a brokerage operating as Muriel Siebert & Co., Inc. We did research and were paid a commission if companies followed our advice and bought stock I was recommending. When new laws in the early and mid 1970s abolished fixed-rate commissions for New York Stock Exchange members, I knew a drastic change was required in order for the firm to survive. I ceased my research operations and on May 1, 1975, we became a discount commission house. I was on the front page of *The Wall Street Journal* the next day. The transition worked, and Muriel Siebert & Co. not only survived but thrived.

In 1977, I was appointed the Superintendent of Banks for the State of New York. Governor Carey had made promises during his campaign to hire more women. He told Phyllis Wagner, the wife of a former mayor of New York City, that he wanted to hire a woman to regulate the banks, and he showed her a list of names. She said, "If you've got Mickie Siebert, stop there." And that's how Governor Carey happened to call me. I had never worked for him before. I had never even contributed a dime to his campaign.

It was a difficult time in my life. I had been supporting my mother who was ill. As long as I was working, I could control my own earnings and continue to pay for my mother's care, which was expensive. The governor's offer was enticing, though, because New York City had major financial problems and I felt I could make an impact. The appointment also posed a tremendous challenge because no woman had held that post before.

At that point, I'd had the seat on the Stock Exchange for about nine and a half years. I thought I had established enough of a reputation that if I left it for a while to accept the appointment, my accounts would continue until I came back.

When Governor Carey offered to hold the position open until my mother's situation stabilized, I accepted. Sadly, my mother passed away on July 6, 1977, and I signed my oath on July 7, 1977. I put Muriel Siebert & Co. into a blind trust and spent the next five years as the "SOB." The term was initially only for two and half years, but the savings banks were in very serious trouble and I was asked to stay on.

At the time, regulating New York State banks was very important. We regulated the Chemical Bank, Manufacturers Hannover and JP Morgan. We also had the savings banks and savings and loans. One-third of the industry was going broke because the interest on mortgages was only yielding eight and a half percent (we didn't have securitization of mortgages and assets at that point) and the banks had to pay ten to twelve percent for money. So you don't have to be a genius to realize there were major problems. I forced banks to merge and encouraged stronger banks to take over weaker banks. I worked hard and was respected in my position. During my tenure, no bank in New York failed.

Under the blind trust, I was not allowed to have any contact with my firm while I was the Superintendent. When I returned to my firm in 1983, I found it in a state of decline. Only one person remained who was there when I left. I had to re-acclimate myself to the changes in the industry and rebuild my business.

Perhaps I should have come back to my firm earlier. I can't judge that because it's not possible to turn a clock backwards. I certainly would have made more money had I not left my firm for five years, but I benefited in other ways. Being Super-intendent helped me to have a much broader outlook. And I'd rather have broader knowledge than have more money.

Today I'm happy to see that women have made remarkable gains as entrepreneurs. There are more women starting busi-nesses now than men—they've gone into businesses that have not been considered traditional women's businesses and they're doing well. I think it's fascinating to see the way women are making strides and being accepted today. It's no longer, "My wife's got a job to buy little things." Now it's "She's got a job because it's necessary to pay the bills, to pay the mortgage"—it's a fact of life.

When I'm advising aspiring entrepreneurs, I always tell them to consider the best and worst case scenarios for starting their own business. If they can't handle the worst that can hap-pen, they probably shouldn't move forward. In my career, I've experienced both the best and worst that were thrown at me and have had a much richer life for it.

On the fortieth anniversary of my election to membership of the New York Stock Exchange, I rang the closing bell to cele-brate. I wear an American flag ring as a reminder that it's only in America where I could have had the chance to pursue my dreams. I couldn't have done this anywhere else. We're very lucky here. We are really very lucky.

Muriel Siebert

KEY SUCCESS FACTORS: Work Ethic, Luck, Risk

WEBSITE: www.siebertnet.com

EDITOR'S NOTES: Known as the "First Woman of Finance," Muriel Siebert has been a leader and innovator for many years. Starting as a Wall Street brokerage trainee, Muriel rose through the finance industry to start a brokerage firm that still bears her name—Muriel Siebert & Co., Inc. In 1967 she became the first woman to own a seat on the New York Stock Exchange.

In the 1970s, Muriel took advantage of deregulation in the brokerage industry and led her firm's change to a discount broker. Later, she created Siebertnet, one of the first computerized stock trading venues. She also answered the call of civic duty and served as Superintendent of Banks for the State of New York where, among other achievements, she rehabilitated New York's Municipal Credit Union.

Muriel believes that giving back is more than an obligation; it's a privilege. She co-founded the New York Women's Forum thirty-five years ago, and through her efforts and others', its affiliated International Women's Forum is today a thirty-eight hundred-member leadership association with sixty locations in twenty-one nations. A passionate advocate for personal financial literacy, Ms. Siebert established the Muriel F. Siebert Foundation whose goal today is to improve the lives of young people and adults by disseminating the vital knowledge contained in the *"Siebert Personal Finance Program: Taking Control of Your Financial Future."* For her efforts, among numerous other honors, Muriel has been made a member of the National Women's Hall of Fame, inducted into the Junior Achievement U.S. Business Hall of Fame and has received eighteen honorary doctorate degrees.

Never underestimate the power of passion.

—Eve Sawyer

MOJO ON THE PRAIRIE

Jo Khalifa—The human condition is something that cannot be ignored or taken for granted. Some of us, not by choice, are thrown into life without much of a chance or opportunity. If I can make a difference in the world, I will have accomplished much.

In 1991, the company my husband was working for transferred us from small town America, Minot, North Dakota, to Michigan. At the time, I had a floundering cookie business and welcomed the move. Rather than re-starting my business in our new home, I decided to go to college to pursue a psychology degree.

After two years of city life, we were looking for a more rural lifestyle to raise our seven children. In June of 1993 we were lucky enough to find a small farm back in North Dakota. Once we settled into our beautiful little piece of paradise on the prairie, I enrolled in the college system and resumed my studies.

Needing a break from my studies, I tried to figure out what else I could do. Since moving back home I was faced with the dilemma of not being able to find a good cup of coffee. I mentioned this to my husband and he suggested that I try roasting my own beans. As nuts as that sounded to me at the time, two months down the road I was doing just that.

I decided perhaps I should open a coffee shop that would focus on quality and freshness. I began roasting coffee in a cast iron frying pan and moved on to various home-roasting machines. One summer morning as I was sitting out on my deck watching the sunrise and roasting our morning coffee, I had an epiphany. Coffee roasting was what I was going to do for the rest of my life; I had found my core passion. In May of 2005 we restored an out building on the farm and MoJo Roast, INC was born. We were the first coffee company certified organic in the state of North Dakota.

I have always had the entrepreneurial spirit within me and have dabbled in several different business start ups. I don't think that a person says or consciously thinks they will become an entrepreneur, it just happens. It's a spirit within that drives certain people to become entrepreneurial.

I have never looked at adversity as a failure or loss. It's just a temporary hurdle to get through. Knowing this, I have had my best growth through difficult times. Time can also be a detriment. Growth never seems to happen at the rate one wants it to!

Finding a niche was important to me. Looking at what I felt was the obvious checklist of successful business criteria, I quickly realized that consistent product quality and personal service was missing in many of the markets I was becoming familiar with.

Thus was born the concept (and niche market) of personal coffee roasting. I know my product well and present it with the passion and knowledge that each individual deserves. MoJo offers product education, top quality product, and personalized roasting for my wholesale and retail clients. I also keep client profile folders on each customer order, ensuring the same roast every time.

In the first six months of being in business I was in a roast-off competition with two hundred and fifty roasters from around the globe. My team came in third. This verified to me that this is, correctly, my chosen field.

Word of mouth is powerful and has been instrumental in growing my business. I look back to the short time that I have been

roasting coffee and see that power. Accolades and achievements vary from being invited to create a gift basket for President Obama on his inaugural day, to designing a signature
coffee for Fort Abraham Lincoln in Mandan, North Dakota.
The fort now serves the very same coffee that Custer and
his 7th Calvary would have been drinking in the late 1800s to
tourists from far and wide. My coffee is served in restaurants,
coffee bars and specialty shops across the country. Out of
the top ten most interesting local news stories for 2009, MoJo
Roast, INC made it to number three.

I know that I have been given a great gift and that it is my obligation to give back. My passion is fueled by the coffee grow-
ers and their stories of poverty, hunger, anguish and abuse.
I'm involved in the Café Femenino Foundation that helps with
education and domestic abuse in several coffee producing
countries. The women who grow the coffee for me are paid
at least their countries' minimum wage. Some of the monies from this foundation are also donated to a local domestic
abuse center. I'm also involved in cancer foundations.

Consumer education has been very important to my business.
Many people do not understand coffee and how it impacts the
world. Helping them to understand has helped my business
grow. With every business endeavor that I pursue, I have two
questions in mind: who will it help and who will it benefit? My
future goal is to help unite people throughout the coffee world.

My customers and the wonderful supportive friends that I have
chosen to surround myself with help to rekindle my passion
on a daily basis. It's not just a business for me; I truly believe
I make a difference in lives by bringing awareness, hope and
of course, a great quality product. My wholesale accounts are
built with trust and a sense of partnership in mind. I want them
to be as successful as they can be, and I will give them every
resource to which I have access to make that happen.

My husband has been my inspirational fire. He is the most
encouraging can-do person that I have ever met. He believes

in my hopes and dreams to make a difference in people's lives. Every business entrepreneur needs a mentor and a trusting sounding board!

Jo Khalifa

KEY SUCCESS FACTORS: Passion, Values, Can-Do Attitude, Determination, Education, Willingness to Share and Mentor, Concentrate on Following Your Dreams and Don't Chase Others, Believe in Yourself, You Have a Gift - Give Back, Join Groups and Organizations that Pertain to Your Field, Always Be the Best that You can Be

RECOMMENDED BOOKS: Any of the "Guerilla Marketing" books by Jay Conrad Levinson. My main reads are journals and magazines on the coffee and hospitality industry.

WEBSITE: www.mojoroast.com

SOCIAL MEDIA: LinkedIn—Jo Khalifa, Facebook—MoJo Roast, INC, WHOHUB—mojoroast, Twitter—MoJoRoaster

EDITOR'S NOTES: Jo Khalifa lives in North Dakota with her husband, Mo, who is a captain in the aviation field. The mother of seven children, Jo stays extremely busy with her family and business. Jo's hobbies include cooking, camping, fishing and family trips. Jo has coffee certifications in coffee grading and organics.

Courage is like a muscle. We strengthen it with use.

—*Ruth Gordon*

LOVING WHAT YOU DO

Marilyn Dawson—Love has been a big part of my life, whether it was directed toward my family or part of a tennis score (preferably my opponents'). I grew up with three brothers, two older and one younger. My father was an educator and my mom was a housewife. At the age of twelve, I picked up a tennis racket and started hitting balls with one of my older brothers. When my father was told that I had talent, he took me to a tennis pro. My father or mother (and many times both) were always at my tennis tournaments and Mom made all of my tennis clothes. My parents taught me about integrity and conduct on and off of the court. I knew never to throw a tennis racquet and to set an example for others. I enjoyed playing tennis and had the competitive spirit to want to be the "best." This and the support my parents provided boosted me to an elite level in tennis—I was ranked in the top ten of eighteen year olds and under in the nation.

After years of competitive tennis, I got married to a high-profile attorney and had four beautiful daughters. I stayed home with the girls and enjoyed being a wife and mother. I also continued to play tennis for enjoyment and exercise. Life had turned out so well that I never could have predicted what was about to happen. My husband suddenly died leaving me with daughters ranging in ages from five to fifteen. We had trust funds for the girls to go to college, but now I was faced with the question of how I was going to make money for day-to-day living.

I thought about what I could possibly do. I knew I wasn't an office type of person. I had worked in an office for two years while my husband was in college, but that was only palatable because it was temporary. As I was trying to come up with a solution, my friend Marylin said to me, "Why don't you become a tennis pro? You love tennis and could teach others what you know. I'll be your first client."

And so it began. I gave my first lesson at the Oklahoma City Country Club. After that I taught tennis lessons on a public course and my client base grew. I loved enriching people's lives by teaching a skill that could be used for a lifetime.

I had a driven desire to be the best tennis player and tennis pro possible, so I went to Victor Braden Tennis College where I studied the laws of physics. I received publicity for this with headlines like, "Marilyn Niles Combines Tennis with Science." I learned from people who were the best. I studied strategies from all angles, footage to keep the ball on the court, where to stand (especially in doubles), where to hit the ball and of course, how to put top spin on the ball.

I had great experiences in my quest to learn all I could about tennis. As I was taking lessons during John Gardner's Tennis Camp in Hollywood, the pro threw the ball down and asked me, "What in the hell are you here for?" I took that as a compliment after she asked me if I would be willing to play in an exhibition with Robert Wagner, the actor, as my partner! Janet Lee, an actress, was at this camp and asked me to come to her home in Hollywood to play tennis.

Another wonderful experience involved Bobby Riggs. Bobby was the number one tennis player in the world for three years in the 1940s. After being out of the limelight for many years, he gained fame in 1973 by playing challenge matches against Billie Jean King. I am fortunate to say that I too played in exhibitions with Bobby Riggs!

I returned to Oklahoma and a very tall man named Ted Wilcox built Hefner Courts and made them available for me to teach lessons. Later, the Quail Creek Golf and Country Club Tennis Courts were built and my client list grew even more. It was so wonderful helping people. I always taught with encouragement and optimism so that my clients left with a positive attitude toward their game.

I was blessed to have many high-profile clients who enjoyed learning tennis, a lifetime sport. One of my clients loved tennis so much that her husband built her a tennis court with a bubble top so that she could play in any type of weather. What he hadn't planned for was the Oklahoma tornado that blew it away!

Throughout the ten years of my tennis pro career, I taught the governor, his wife, doctors' wives, celebrities, politicians and many more. The relationships I established were invaluable and many are dear friends today. Through my friends, I met my second husband, Ray Dawson, to whom I had a fabulous marriage. I was also fortunate to have my mother-in-law from my first marriage help out with our daughters so that I could work.

My advice to entrepreneurs and aspiring entrepreneurs is to ask yourself if you love what you are doing. If the answer is no, you should find something to do that you love. If the answer is yes, you should share it with someone else so they have the satisfaction of enjoying what you have. And remember, do not focus on the negative. Always do things in a positive manner with LOVE!

Marilyn Dawson

KEY SUCCESS FACTORS: Passion, Integrity, Determination, Drive, Relationships

RECOMMENDED BOOKS: *The Mystic Eye* by Sadhguru Jaggi Vasudev

EDITOR'S NOTES: Marilyn Dawson changed the face of women's tennis in Oklahoma. She has three living daughters and eleven grandchildren. Marilyn recently relocated to Atlanta, Georgia, to be near her youngest daughter and family. She lives at Canterbury Court, a continuing care retirement community, and enjoys playing tennis, reading spiritual books and meeting people.

If you have ever felt such tremendous enthusiasm and desire for something that you would gladly spend all your waking hours working on it, that you would happily do without pay, then you have found your passion.

—*Sharon Cook & Graciela Sholander*

MY FAVORITE PLACE
TO "SHOW UP"

Avis Scaramucci—My favorite thing about being an entrepreneur is having the opportunity to dream the dream and make it happen. I love the possibilities, the challenges and coming up with new ideas.

Born with an entrepreneurial spirit, there were experiences throughout my life that influenced me. I began cooking at an early age taking over for my mother, a confessed "awful" cook. I loved to cook, so this made us both happy! Always looking for a way to earn some money, I sold cookies at the local grocery store.

As a teenager, I would go with my friend to her parents' clothing store and imagine what it would be like to be the owner. I loved going there! I loved the feel of it! As a young adult, I had a favorite gift store, Sand-Mark, in Norman, Oklahoma. The owners treated me so well and made me feel special regardless of how much money I had to spend. I knew someday I wanted to open my own store and provide the same excellent service to every customer as they walked through the door.

Working part time in the family owned manufacturing business gave me a solid business background and also allowed me to be with our children when they were not in school. This job was perfect because it allowed me to attend their events. When our son was a junior in high school, I started thinking about opening a retail gift business. Instead of jumping into this unprepared, I spent a year doing research, looking for property, going to market and deciding on the type of business I wanted to start. After an extensive search, I found land and a building that was easily accessible from two major interstates.

In 1991, I opened Painted Door, a gift and decorative accessories store. The people came and it was my favorite place "to show up." I looked forward to each day and worked seven days a week even though we were closed on Sunday. Always changing products around, thinking of new ideas and continually adding new merchandise enabled me to grow through the years.

In 1995, I opened Nonna's Bakery located "under the same roof" as Painted Door in a new addition to the original building. I decided to see if my customers would like some of my homemade cookies, pies and cakes. I brought my recipes from home and taught my baker how to prepare them the way I did for my family and friends. It's not easy to find freshly baked goods. I named the bakery Nonna's after my husband's Italian grandmother. Nonna was a wonderful cook.

Soon after I opened Nonna's I decided to offer a sugar cookie hoping to take orders for Valentine's. I took so many orders that my husband, baker and I had to stay up all night for two nights to make the cookies ordered. My error was in judgment; I was so excited about the sales, I didn't think about how long it would take to decorate hundreds of sugar cookies by hand. These are lessons learned through experience.

Nonna's Bakery grew into Nonna's Bakery and Café with a few offerings for lunch. The quality of food, the unique variety of gifts and accessories and the exceptional treatment we give each customer has made a difference in our success. My original store had four thousand square feet and grew to fourteen thousand square feet before moving to Bricktown in 2005.

Many people questioned why I would move when things were going so well. My customers kept talking about Bricktown, an area of Oklahoma City that had undergone a major renovation with additions of a ballpark, canals and restaurants. So I decided to see for myself. One Saturday afternoon I left work early to take a walk through Bricktown. Wow! What a change! I just knew one of the warehouses should be the future home of Painted Door and Nonna's.

I talked to my husband and convinced him to take a walk through Bricktown with me. We looked at every building in Bricktown and found a warehouse on the corner of Sheridan Avenue and Mickey Mantle Drive. This was really a huge decision to move from such an established location, but we identified potential markets that were nonexistent in our present location and purchased the building.

It took two years to remodel the existing warehouse and also add a three-story addition. Our new location is a ninety-year-old warehouse with ten thousand square feet of meeting space, a Hospitality Suite on the second and third floors, Painted Door gifts and decorative accessories, Nonna's Euro-American Ristorante including a bakery, the Purple Bar, an outside patio, and a second floor kitchen that enables us to serve "in house" banquets, as well as off-site catering.

I have been very blessed to have a great team who has bought into my dream, to have an established customer base, and to have a loving family that provided encouragement and assistance. Have there been challenges? Of course, some of the challenges I have faced along the way include:

- Profitability. It takes up to five years to be profitable in a new business.
- Establish procedures. If you expect to grow, empower employees by putting procedures in place.
- Finding the right personnel. It is important to understand and staff according to your weaknesses. Hire people who have strengths you or others in the company don't have.
- Establishing credibility and maintaining a positive attitude. You must believe in yourself or others won't.

Do I miss being at the previous location? Yes! Would I move to Bricktown if I had it to do over again? Yes! It's my new favorite place "to show up."

Avis Scaramucci

KEY SUCCESS FACTORS: Passion, Customer Service, Location, Providing an Exceptional Experience to Customers

WEBSITES: www.nonnas.com, www.painteddoor.com

EDITOR'S NOTES: Avis Scaramucci is involved in numerous entrepreneurial ventures. A life-long epicurean, Avis began cooking at an early age. This love has not only helped her form a successful restaurant and bakery, it inspired an agricultural venture—Cedar Spring Farms. Cedar Spring is a greenhouse operation owned by Avis and her husband, Phil, to supply fresh produce to Nonna's. Painted Door has two locations with the other in the Skirvin Hotel in Oklahoma City. Avis has a goal of providing an exceptional experience to every customer. It's not a surprise that she has enjoyed much deserved success!

Above all, be true to yourself, and if you cannot put your heart in it, take yourself out of it.

—Author Unknown

RISKS WORTH TAKING

Susan Neal Rhode—It was my first board meeting as the first female member of my law firm's board of directors. I had been advised to sit there quietly and listen … figure out who the players were, observe and learn. I intended to do just that. Instead, in response to a sexist statement, I found myself confronting a named partner and fellow board member with, "And just what the *&$%#@ do you mean by that?"

I come by my willfulness honestly. My mother learned to drive solely because my father let it be known that if she insisted on voting for "that Catholic" John Kennedy, he wouldn't be driving her to the polls. So she took driving lessons and got her license. When my father refused to loan her the car on election day, she managed to find another ride so she could cast her vote.

My mother was a full-time nurse at a time when most mothers did not work outside of the home. From the time I was thirteen, I was working in the hospital with her as a candy striper, a receptionist, whatever they needed. What I saw in that environment was the enormous difference my mother made in her patients' lives.

My intention was to go into mortuary sciences. While I knew I had compassion for patients and appreciated what a wonderful job my mother did, I didn't want to follow her into nursing—I didn't like the idea of the necessary pain inflicted by nurses … shots, bandage changings, etc. From my time spent working in the hospital, I saw how lost a family seemed after the death of a loved one. I hoped that by becoming a mortician, I could help them navigate through their terrible loss. My plans changed after the first week of classes, however, when the head of the program pulled me aside and let me know that no single woman should go into the field. Apparently, only women whose fathers, uncles, brothers, or husbands owned a funeral home obtained such a degree. That discussion and a particularly gruesome cadaver convinced me to transfer into the business school.

In college, I went from geek to freak in the span of months, changing out of my plaid skirt and knee high stockings to love beads and fatigues. It was the sixties and my peers and I were greatly influenced by the volatile political climate.

After graduating with my associate's degree, I worked as a secretary for two disagreeable bosses who enjoyed fighting over me. I was very unhappy in that position, but was supporting my new husband as he earned his degree. For four years I had to work in that miserable environment and bide my time. I made a promise to myself then that I would never be so unhappy in a job again.

After convincing my husband that after eight years it was time for him to graduate, I was able to leave that company and become a legal secretary. My new boss, Dick Alexander, ended up changing my life. Mr. Alexander so enjoyed the practice of trademark law, it rubbed off on me. Intellectual property work was creative and challenging. Sometimes attorneys would represent a plaintiff, sometimes a defendant, sometimes an individual, sometimes a big corporation. It had a lot of intrigue and Mr. Alexander played it as if it were a chess game.

I started as a secretary to an associate lawyer in that firm and then became Mr. Alexander's secretary. I eventually moved on to become a paralegal, but they didn't take away my secretarial work, so I was working long hours. One day Mr. Alexander told me that I should go to law school. I didn't even have a bachelor's degree at that point (nor did anyone else in my family), and I told him he was crazy. It had never occurred to me to pursue something like that. But he had planted a seed.

I decided to go back to school to get my paralegal certificate. After one semester, I thought that if I was going to put that much effort into it, I might as well get my bachelor's degree. So for the next six years I worked during the day, attended class at night and studied when I could.

I entered law school a few weeks short of my thirtieth birthday. Back then, thirty was not the new twenty ... thirty was ancient. As I finished up school, I got hired as a law clerk. The firm I joined had never had law clerks, so they didn't really know what to do with me. I didn't have a desk, merely a carrel in the library and a box containing my files and personal belongings that were routinely moved around to different locations.

My position squarely in this sort of no-man's (or no-woman's) land was most evident at the firm's yearly prom. The time came to take pictures and they lined all the attorneys up. Only one was a woman. They relegated me, the law clerk, to the picture with the spouses. After the picture was snapped, I went into the restroom in tears, unsure if I'd made the right decision to pursue law.

When I graduated from law school, I was hired as an associate. I noticed that the one female attorney in the firm had modesty panels on her desk and she had to type her own correspondence. It seemed ironic that I had just spent all these years surviving law school only to be stuck behind a typewriter again. My fears were confirmed when one of the partners came into my office and said, "Once a secretary, always a secretary."

Being one of only two female attorneys was rough going at first. I remember making some phone calls for a client to negotiate a deal, and I was asked to provide my boss's number. Since I was a female, it was assumed that I couldn't be a lawyer. Another time, I was questioning a witness on the stand and he kept calling me "sweetie." The judge finally had to instruct the witness to call me "counselor" instead.

In spite of the quickly changing world around us, it was still very much an old boy's club behind the mahogany doors of big law firms. Because I came of age during the Vietnam War and protests, I knew what it was to find your voice and actually use it. Thanks to Gloria Steinem, I also started picking up on women's rights and issues. Why the heck should I be treated differently than the male attorneys in my firm? Why the heck should I make less?

Despite these inequities, or perhaps because of them, I worked hard and became a partner. Over the years I served on the board of directors and helped build the firm's trademark practice while working hard to develop strong relationships with our clients.

I had been toying with the idea of starting a firm of my own for a few years. Initially, I spoke with three colleagues about that possibility. After preliminary discussions, however, it seemed the timing and makeup of our group wouldn't work, so we did not continue to explore it.

When my firm joined with a much larger firm of about seven hundred and fifty attorneys, I was serving in the Washington, D.C. office. Then I was selected to head up the trademark group and I moved back to Chicago. I had only been there for a few weeks when I realized it wasn't what I wanted to do. The new firm was enormous with offices all over the world. Large firms are notoriously very bureaucratic, and my new firm's sheer size made it very difficult to function. We had clients with whom we'd had relationships for years and we had been able to negotiate hourly rates, but there was little flexibility in the new firm. There was the very real possibility I would lose some of my clients even though some of them had been clients for decades. I sat at my desk in my beautifully appointed office with amazing views of downtown Chicago, and I realized that I was as unhappy as I had been long before when

I made a simple promise to myself. No job was worth such unhappiness. It was time to leave.

When my law partner, Kevin McDevitt, and I started working to form our new firm, we didn't know which of our clients would come with us. We went to visit with one of our biggest clients and kind of tip-toed around the issue because there was case law that made it unclear if we could come right out and ask a client to move with us. We were just kind of chitchatting and weren't really saying anything definitive—we were just hoping to plant seeds. The client finally interrupted me and said, "Susan, if you asked me what I think you'd like to ask me, you would be delighted with my answer." That was a sign of things to come—all of our clients agreed to move with us.

When we started our firm, a lot of our colleagues thought we were crazy to give up our high-level positions. Our beginnings were certainly humble. In order to get us started, Kevin and his wife picked up our clients' files and drove a U-Haul across the country to our new office—a two-story suburban office building located next to a dry cleaner. We had second-hand office furniture, a fax machine, a coffee maker and three employees. If the restrooms or kitchen needed cleaning, we did it ourselves. Some of our former colleagues couldn't believe we were working in such unglamorous conditions. The truth is, we were in our shorts and t-shirts and having the time of our lives.

What we did was risky, but we felt that if it didn't work out, we weren't going to suddenly lose our skills. We could always use our capabilities and talents at another firm. We knew the time was right. We knew the partnership was right. Our goal was to treat our clients fairly and to have the flexibility to do what they needed us to do. We wanted to build that practice with a group who cared about each other and was more like a family. And that's what Neal & McDevitt became.

Neither Kevin nor I had run a business before, but we felt confident that we knew what *not* to do in starting our own business. We did not have a long-term business plan, but we knew what we needed to get started: a docketing system, a billing system, computers and some filing cabinets. Our support staff came from other large firms and took a chance with us. There was a level of dedication because everyone working there had given something up to take a chance on our firm. That strengthened us all.

In 2008, Neal & McDevitt celebrated its ten-year anniversary. Additional lawyers and staff have been added through the years and all of them have truly helped make the firm a success. It wouldn't have happened without them.

I recently retired from the practice of law after nearly thirty years. As I reflect on my career, I realize that Neal & McDevitt is a lot like Dick Alexander's firm. There's a similar level of dedication and excitement, and an emphasis on client service. I take great satisfaction in realizing I created something I can be proud of and that it continues to thrive even in my absence.

For me, it's time to turn to the next chapter in my life. For those just starting out, trust me when I say: Go make it happen. It's worth the risk.

Susan Neal Rhode

KEY SUCCESS FACTORS: Taking Risks, Self Confidence, Work Ethic

RECOMMENDED BOOKS: *Good to Great* by James C. Collins and *You Can Negotiate Anything* by Herb Cohen

WEBSITE: www.nealmcdevitt.com

EDITOR'S NOTES: Susan Neal Rhode earned her AA from Southern Illinois University, and her B.A. and J.D. from DePaul University. She joined Willian, Brinks, Olds, Hofer, Gilson & Lione in 1980 as a law clerk and ultimately became a shareholder. She remained at the firm as a shareholder until

1996 when she joined McDermott, Will and Emery. As a Capital Partner, Susan headed up MWE's trademark practice. In 1998, Susan Co-founded Neal & McDevitt LLC with her partner, Kevin McDevitt.

During her career, Susan served on numerous committees, was a frequent lecturer and authored articles on trademark law. She was also an adjunct professor of advanced trademark law at DePaul University College of Law, and an instructor at Mallinckrodt College and The John Marshall Law School.

Susan has been an active supporter of charitable causes including Aid for Women and the Family Resource Center. A scholarship set up by Susan enabled five women to attend DePaul University College of Law.

Susan retired from the practice of law in 2009. She now looks forward to spending quality time with her husband, Greg, and her daughter, Cary Jo. She plans to focus on charitable work and enjoying life as a newlywed.

I make the most of all that comes and the least of all that goes.

—Sara Teasdale

AN ACCIDENTAL ENTREPRENEUR

Phyllis Larson—After working in corporate America for twenty-five years, I wasn't planning to become an entrepreneur. I simply wanted something to keep me busy two to three days a month. But someone wise told me, "There's no two to three days a month. You either do it or you don't." As my business took off, I learned the truth of that statement. If you do your job well, you can do pretty well … sometimes too well.

My corporate career began in 1978. Prior to that, as I raised my three children, I took on some special projects and public relations type work for our local library. I had also taught junior high and high school English. I was always interested in writing and teaching others to write.

When my kids started to reach school age, I applied to the largest local employer, Conoco Inc. (now known as ConocoPhillips) and took placement tests, but I assumed there was nothing there for me when I didn't hear back. After all, companies didn't hire writers, did they? Well, in this case, the graphics department at Conoco needed a proof reader. This was a new position born out of a spelling error on some stock certificates. Because they wanted to ensure not having a big reprinting job and I had gotten an excellent score on the spelling test, I was invited to come in for an interview.

I still had a young child at home and didn't want a full-time job, but I decided to interview just in case I needed a job later. Since it was a new position, they agreed to take me on part time initially. That lasted for three years until a job opened up in a new public relations office in my location.

Previously Conoco just had someone preparing news releases and an internal newsletter. But they were building up their PR department across the country and posted a job for a newsletter editor. Even though I hadn't done that sort of thing before, I applied for the position and was hired for it. Most of the people hired at that point for the PR department had backgrounds in journalism or English. People weren't necessarily specializing in PR in those days.

When I had been in that job for a few years, my first boss left the company and then my second boss retired. I was given the job of Public Relations Director for the mid-continent region, but it took a year for the actual title to catch up with the promotion.

I loved working in PR, but the benefits group kept trying to convince me to join them. They were spending $300 million a year on benefits, but weren't able to communicate that effectively to the employees. No one appreciated their benefits, largely because they weren't understood. The benefits group used so much legalese that the information became too complicated to understand.

I moved to benefits because I felt it should be a rather simple thing to directly and succinctly explain benefits. Of course at that time, I wasn't aware of the various government requirements that sometimes dictated text. Right after the move, I thought I had ruined my life. I didn't have anything to do that first month, so I read through investment fund prospectuses. I had moved from a PR job I liked into something I found quite boring. Fortunately, that first month ended up being an aberration. The pace of the job picked up and as I learned about benefits, I grew to like the work. I eventually became Director of Communications for Human Resources Leveraged Services.

When DuPont bought Conoco, we were kept busy with some huge projects early on. Most of the benefits stayed the same. When we did take on a new benefit—for instance, offering flexible benefits—we had to effectively communicate the new options or the program would not be successful. I got to hire the people I wanted on my team and develop a whole new communications program.

I focused our strategy on my belief that it isn't necessary to tell everyone everything. It's more effective to only tell them what they need to know to make a decision and then tell them where to go for more information. It was just overwhelming to employees when they received a huge packet.

So we developed a format of friendly newsletters with head-lines that clearly guided employees to the applicable informa-tion. We used humor in our communications and people loved it. During that time we also opened a call center to answer questions about the benefit changes. After that initial benefit offering period ended, we kept a line of communication open so that employees could ask questions or provide feedback.

Our communications materials and support systems changed our employees' attitudes about not just the benefits but the company. My manager of benefits at the time said it changed his whole world. He would meet once or twice a year with his counterparts from other companies. If one of our communica-tions had already been distributed, he could share it. Over time, many other companies learned through our products that communication didn't have to be so stuffy.

This work ended up being a really good fit for me. I was a stickler for accuracy, but I was able to convey information in a friendly tone. It changed the whole way Conoco presented its benefits.

When I had been with the company for twenty-five years, I decided it was time to retire. I teamed up with two former col-leagues to consider different opportunities. We didn't know what kind of work we wanted to do; we just knew we wanted some-thing to occupy our time. One of my new business partners had worked for me, been a long time journalist and had a lot of writ-ing experience. My other partner was the former manager of employee benefits at Conoco (and my former boss). He had a varied career, but was also a published author. We all had that communications background, but we didn't set out to start a communications company.

A financial company in San Francisco that we had dealings with put us in touch with one of their clients in Chicago that needed communications materials related to their 401(k) plan. We developed a communications piece for them. They liked our work and we kept picking up more jobs. Pretty soon we were working every day and retaining some very large clients. So much for the two to three days a month!

When it was clear we were focusing on communications in our new business, my partners—both of whom are men—decided that I should be the president because I had more experience running communications projects.

That first year we were really busy in the fall. When January came along, we didn't have anything to do. We wondered if we'd run our course. Then the next fall, business picked up again. We finally figured out there's kind of a season to it and there are certainly hills and valleys.

Moving from a large corporation to starting up a business took some getting used to. When something happened to my computer at Conoco, I could just call a number and an IT professional would make it all better. The first time I had a computer issue at my new business, I realized there was no one to call.

At Conoco, when we were going to put out any kind of publication, we had in-house staff to do it. If we had an impossible job, I would call the print shop and let them know when it had to get out and they would make it happen. Now, if something has to get out, we have to be the ones to do it. Fortunately, I like the challenge. If it's a huge job, I like figuring out how to make it happen.

I also had to check my ego a bit. When I was working for a huge corporation and I needed to call on someone doing business with us, I was never kept waiting. Now when I call on a prospective client, I'm at the mercy of his or her schedule. Sometimes they're on time, sometimes they're not.

Heading up my group at Conoco helped prepare me for owning and running a business. Working for a big company allowed us to learn far more than we realized at the time. We were exposed to a lot of different things, and we figured out how to do a lot of things. I don't know if that was unique to Conoco or not, but I've noticed that sometimes other people don't have that. They don't know how to do something we do almost without thinking about it.

We try to stress to our clients that they need to get value out of what they're spending. If the recipients of the benefits or programs don't understand them, our clients aren't getting their money's worth. We try to present our communications from the employees' point of view so they'll want to read them and they won't sound so corporate.

We've built our business through word of mouth. We don't advertise. Our clients have heard of us from someone we have worked for and that's how we get new business. We are finally getting ready to put up a website. We hadn't done that in seven years. It's kind of like the cobbler's children not having shoes; we were always working on our clients' communications and didn't work on ours.

We don't take on too much work at one time. If we're really busy, we're not out marketing. If we commit to a job, we focus on it one hundred percent. If it's not something we can do really, really well, we won't take it.

One of our only regrets in starting our business is that we didn't start it earlier. I believe we've had success because we focused on doing something we knew how to do and knew how to do well. We've been able to deliver the product our clients have asked for and have never skimped on quality. We also love what we're doing and the people we work with. We don't have to be doing this, so we'd better enjoy what we do.

I suppose at some point I might consider retiring again. For right now, I'm having too much fun.

Phyllis Larson

KEY SUCCESS FACTORS: Having a Full Understanding of Our Business, Taking on Only those Jobs that We Know We Can Do Well, Delivering on Promises

WEBSITE: www.writecommunications.net

EDITOR'S NOTES: Phyllis Larson lives in Ponca City, Oklahoma, with her husband, Dan, a high school orchestra director. They have three grown daughters, two sons-in-law and two grandchildren.

In addition to running her business, Write Communications, Inc., Phyllis has given back to her community by volunteering at the Opportunity Center (for developmentally disabled adults) and serving as that organization's president. She has also been on the board of the Ponca City Medical Center for eleven years. She served as the chairman of the board last year.

Love begins by taking care of the closest ones ... the ones at home.

—Mother Teresa

FROM EGGSHELLS TO ENCHANTMENT

Sarah Little—What do you do when you're stuck in a dead-end job, have a special needs child and feel like you are wasting your potential every minute of every day? If you're like me, you start a business of your own! My name is Sarah Little, and I am the owner of White Peacock Productions LLC.

Prior to starting my business, I worked as a graphic designer for another local publication. However, the publisher of that publication was in financial trouble and was not producing issues in a timely manner. It was a volatile workplace environment, full of stress and walking on eggshells. Each day, I would go home, nearly in tears, fearing I would be fired.

Our first son was born profoundly deaf. At nine months old, he was approved for cochlear implant surgery. We had his first surgery done on his first birthday and second when he was twenty-two months old. We do not live in a deaf community, and there is little to no deaf culture in our community. We made the choice for Blake to listen and talk, which meant a significant time commitment on our part (not to mention financial commitment!). Each week, we would take off four hours a day on Friday and drive sixty miles to the clinic so that Blake could receive auditory/verbal therapy. In addition, we would have other visits for audiology, equipment and surgery checkups.

With all of these factors in play, it became apparent to my husband (who comes from a long line of entrepreneurs—unlike myself) that I needed to start my own business. We started discussing it and putting together a plan. We sat down with our families and told them what we wanted to accomplish and what kind of support we would need until we got our little venture off the ground. They agreed to help us and I started my business: *Stillwater Living Magazine*, produced by White Peacock Productions.

Getting Started

I quit my job on May 14, 2004, and started talking to advertisers the following Monday. I started branching out to my contacts to cover stories, get contributing writers and find content that I thought the people of my hometown would be willing to buy. My first issue was published in July 2004. My mother and I sold subscriptions by making door hangers in the morning, and then spending the afternoons walking, baby in stroller, door to door through neighborhoods hanging door hangers on door knobs.

It wasn't long after we started publishing issues when our clients began asking us to design other items for them. As a one-woman show, this wasn't a service I marketed! I had my hands full with ad sales, covering stories, shooting photos and design. The requests started coming in more and more frequently as time went by, and I began to think that I might be able to market myself as an agency.

Giving Back

One of my greatest joys in owning my own business is the ability to give back to the community that has supported me in my endeavor. We gladly accept press releases and try to print each one that we get from non-profit agencies in need of publication. When their cause is best served by advertising, we are happy to donate ad space as well. One of my favorite causes to promote is Relay for Life. I lost both of my father's parents to cancer, and it has made an indelible mark on me.

In 2005, we featured the stories of two cancer survivors. Our cover photo was of a young boy, and a middle-aged woman, both in remission from cancer. When we staged and shot the photo, I had no idea what a mark it would make on so many people. Last year, I attended the celebration of life of the young man who was on the cover. I was proud to have played a part in a proud moment of his amazing life. To this date, we have promoted not only Relay for Life routinely, but also partnered with other businesses to help raise money for David's Army, the team in honor of our favorite little cover model.

Growing Pains

They say that imitation is the greatest form of flattery, but flattered was not my first feeling when I suddenly had head-to-head competition in my small town. Some of our biggest challenges have come from competition. In five years, another media has spawned five different forms of another local magazine. Four of the five have ceased publication to date. We have embraced the competition as a gauntlet thrown down and an opportunity to rise to the occasion. We have chosen to turn our gaze inward, and examine how we can be our community's premier magazine and advertising business. We have set an aggressive publication calendar and sales goals to match.

Looking Forward

In the next decade, print media will continue to decline. That's a fact that I have to embrace and have to plan for accordingly. At White Peacock Productions, we are trying to get ahead of the curve, for ourselves and for our clients. Consumers do not communicate the way today that they will next year, or in ten years. We want our clients to be prepared as well, so our focus is changing. We are working with our clients to develop progressive communication methods and advertising strategies to stay in touch with their current market, and grow with emerging markets as well.

In five years, we've gone from a spare bedroom and a lofty idea of working for myself, to building a company that is fun, family friendly and successful. I've followed in the footsteps of media giants that are known by first names only such as Oprah and Martha, and have loved every minute of it. It has not been without pitfalls and problems, but knowing that I'm building my own legacy makes it worth it, and it is truly enchanting!

Sarah Little

KEY SUCCESS FACTORS: Tenacity, Drive, Ability to Adapt

RECOMMENDED BOOKS: *Gone With the Wind* by Margaret Mitchell (even though it's fiction, it's a wonderful story about a strong woman who fought tooth and nail to get what she wants!), *Can We Do That?* by Peter Shankman, *The New Birth Order Book* by Kevin Leman (Key to knowing why people act why they do at a very base level, and why I always ask people about their families in interviews)

WEBSITES: www.stillwater-living.com, www.whitepeacockproductions.com

SOCIAL MEDIA: Twitter—stwmagditor, Facebook—Stillwater Living Mag

EDITOR'S NOTES: Sarah Little is Editor, Publisher and Owner of *Stillwater Living Magazine* and White Peacock Productions LLC. She is married to Ray Little, and they have two sons, Blake and Connor Little. She currently operates a full service agency, wedding and party invitation business, and monthly magazine.

Let no one come to you without leaving better and happier.

—*Mother Teresa*

MEETING WITH SELF: STAYING TRUE TO YOUR OWN COURSE

Cheryl McPhilimy—When I suddenly—and it was sudden—started my public relations agency in the 1990s, at the age of twenty-five, I had been working for three years as an account executive at a couple of successive agencies in Chicago. Economic times were tough. I'd graduated in a down cycle in the economy, and I, like the other entry-level PR people I knew, was fortunate just to have a job.

Those first jobs were a training ground. We typed press releases and worked the phones hard, pitching our clients' stories to reporters. We went to events, partly to network and partly to eat hors d'oeuvres and conserve grocery money. I learned a lot in those days about subtext and such nuances as what the client said he wanted versus what he *actually* wanted or what phrases like "this doesn't have teeth" or "where's the drama" really meant. We honed the angles and got our clients on *Oprah* and plenty of other high-profile news outlets.

It hadn't been my intent to start my own business. After a few years in the agencies, I met up with an unjust business situation. It wasn't anything so eye-popping or shocking; I've since learned there's a fair amount of fraud and dirty pool people try to pull in business. I was young, though, and it was my first encounter with such. It left me reeling and knowing I had only one option. I had to listen to my inner sense of right and wrong and move on.

I resigned quickly and found myself staring entrepreneurship in the eye. I knew I'd learned an awful lot, but not everything about the public relations business. I also knew I could bring in new business—at the last agency I'd secured our second-largest client. I considered applying for jobs at other agencies but wasn't convinced I'd find anything better than being on my own.

In hindsight, the smartest thing I did then was to give the decision of becoming an entrepreneur some space. Quitting what ostensibly looks like a perfectly good job with no offers in hand, no clients and not a whole lot of life experience leads plenty of people to share their unsolicited concerns: "What if you don't find any clients?" "Are you sure about this?" "You are looking for a new job too, though, right?" And the more worrisome, "How are you going to survive?" and, of course, "Aren't you afraid?" Questions like these were driving me right out of my mind at a time I needed to be totally focused on the task at hand: running a fledgling business.

So I did what I've since told anyone pondering entrepreneurship: I gave it some space. I set an appointment with myself for six months down the road. I'd gone out on my own in April, so I entered a meeting in my black vinyl-bound datebook for October 15th, 9 a.m., "Meeting with self. Decide whether this is working." In the meantime, I was just going to give it an honest go. If anyone questioned me about the wisdom of my choices, I demurred and didn't let my own mind obsess over whether it was a mistake to start my own firm from utter scratch. I couldn't afford to let these thoughts haunt me on a daily basis. I'd never survive.

With the appointment lodged in my book, I turned my energies to immediate concerns and there were many: find clients, set up a workspace, network with everyone I knew, introduce myself to anyone I didn't know. Those early days were an experiment. What would I be if I gave it six months and it didn't work out? Age twenty-six and unemployed? If fears edged in, I'd remind myself that on October 15th I would look them head on and deal with them fully.

It was rough. I had no idea where my first client would come from. I bought a computer and a laser printer on credit. A friendly guy at the neighborhood Mail Boxes Etc., whom I plied with homemade cookies and fudge, sent my faxes until I could afford a second phone line and a recycled fax machine. I picked up a side job to keep a little money coming in.

What happened next is that someone, the owner of an electrical products company, signed my contract and became my first client. I'd gone to her place of business twice to convince her to entrust me with her family owned company's reputation and public relations efforts. I worked hard on her account and managed to find two other clients. Through a contact, I found a small, marketing firm with a bit of office space to rent me.

October 15th arrived. The meeting with myself was brief. This was incredibly challenging, downright difficult at times, but I loved it and could say that, yes, it was working out.

Over the next decade, the firm grew. There were daily challenges and issues, but the next big test of mettle hit at year ten. In the intervening years I'd measured my growth by revenues and headcount. It was an easy yardstick. Others would ask me, "How many people are on your team now?" and I would proudly report on my growing cohort.

While I loved new-business generation and the ability to sell larger and larger projects, in accordance with the size of my firm and its capacities, I found I wasn't enjoying the agency nearly as much as I had in the early days. A few mis-hires for a senior-level associate had put me in the position of being personally stretched too thin for too long. My days were filled with the management of my team and not enough time with clients doing the work I loved. I'd outgrown my comfort zone and sweet spot.

It was then that I had my second "meeting with self." This time the decision took a bit more thinking and strategizing. I was either going to sell my firm or rein it in so I could do the work I enjoyed and at which I excelled. For a number of reasons including the economics and my interests, reining it in made more sense. Just as others had said, "Aren't you afraid?" when I had started, now they were saying, "What are you thinking!?" They couldn't understand my desire to be smaller and more, not less, involved with my clients.

Believing you don't mess with success, that you don't change something that is working, can be a scary trap. Others couldn't understand how I could possibly want to change my business model when I was successfully supporting myself and my team. Had I followed their frequent and unsolicited advice, I might be pocket rich but certainly soul poor. Your heart has to be in the business to succeed long haul.

Today my firm is a boutique, executive communications, strategy, messaging and media training company. My clients are senior executives and business leaders. I have a small cadre of talented colleagues, clients I enjoy and projects that are both challenging and rewarding. Ironically, while my revenues are lower, my profits have increased. And I'm doing the work that I love.

Cheryl McPhilimy

KEY SUCCESS FACTORS: Self Motivation, Purpose, Heart

RECOMMENDED BOOKS: *Deep Change: Discovering the Leader Within* by Robert E. Quinn

WEBSITE: www.mcphilimy.com

EDITOR'S NOTE: Cheryl McPhilimy works with executives, leaders and organizations on issues of visibility and public perception. She is the president of McPhilimy Associates, a public relations strategy and spokesperson coaching firm she founded in 1995. Individuals in the spotlight, including CEOs, spokespersons, attorneys, consultants and celebrities, turn to her to develop strategic messaging and positioning and to learn how to navigate such settings as media interviews, public speaking and high-stakes presentations. She also serves as adjunct faculty at Loyola University Chicago where she teaches public relations.

CHAPTER **6**

CONFIDENT, PROSPEROUS
AND ENTREPRENEURIAL

Put your future in good hands—your own.

—Author Unknown

Always act like you're wearing an invisible crown.

—Author Unknown

LESSONS OF
AN UNEXPECTED LIFE

Jane Jayroe—Like most students in high school, I loved to hang out with my friends or watch television. In our household, however, we went to choir practice at the church every Wednesday night.

"But Mother," I wailed, "none of my friends have to do something so stupid."

"You're going," she said with that warm smile that made it hard to be mad at her.

A loving and sweet woman, my mother enforced a few firm rules. If her daughters received a gift from God, they did their best with the gift and used it for His purpose. I stomped out to the car and slammed the car door. "You can make me go," I pouted, "but you can't make me *want* to go."

Mother put the car in gear and off we went in the cold night down Main Street. Passing the high school on the right and the football field on the left, we saw the only stoplight in town ahead, blinking red. We pulled into the church parking lot next to a few others.

I gave it one more try. "Everybody here is old. Why do I have to be the only kid who comes?"

Mother switched the car off and turned to me. "Janie, you know that argument doesn't mean a thing to me. You have received a gift and it's up to you to develop it and use it in service to others. You sing so well, there's nobody I would rather hear sing than you and your sister." I heard my mom's message but I didn't like it, except that part about being a good singer.

Inside the sanctuary, my resentment faded. The church felt warm in ways not just physical; the other folks were so kind. And singing, after all, was my joy. Even with that woman on the organ who played the keyboard with one hand and directed us with the other, singing praises to God felt somehow right. Besides, I was crazy about my mother who sang alto behind me. As a popular teenager, I knew it wasn't the cool thing to love your parents, but mine were special and I knew it. I didn't have to act like it, however.

After practice, the power struggle faded as Mother and I chatted all the way home. Mom helped me prepare for the next school day. She was like that, spoiling us rotten, except for those funny rules about being grateful and giving back. In my family, it didn't matter that you made the top grades, won the highest award, or were the star athlete; being a good steward of what you'd been given was the goal. You could and should risk yourself in life because the purpose was the living and learning, not just winning.

Those lessons of hard work, discipline and risk taking have always served me well, especially when, as a nineteen-year-old small town girl, I became Miss America. The shock of winning one of the most recognized titles in the world was overwhelming and downright scary. The night I won the crown, insecurities switched my internal channels from trusting a big God to negative voices that insisted on my smallness. They played on my fears of being alone, not being enough and having no control. They knew exactly what buttons to push. They said: you're not smart enough, not thin enough, not sophisticated enough, not pretty enough, not brave enough, or good enough to be Miss America. You are just a kid from a little town in Oklahoma. What were the judges thinking? I would be found out, I feared. I could perform the walk and wave of Miss

America, but not the real deal that would require confidence and communication skills. Heck, I had never even flown in an airplane. What if it made me sick? I didn't compare favorably to my standard of Miss America perfection. I wasn't even close, but I worked like crazy anyway—that's who I was raised to be.

What followed was a year of wide-eyed wonder. In time and with layers of experience heaped upon me in a hurry, the title eventually fit. The blessings of that experience were indeed fairy tale fabulous.

Ten years after traveling the world as Miss America, I found myself divorced with a new baby and no job or money. By the grace of God and the love of family and friends, I found my life again by taking it a step at a time. Soon, my first real career fell into my lap—anchoring the television news in Oklahoma City and then Dallas/Ft. Worth. I auditioned for the prime time anchoring position with no prior experience. The television station had never hired a woman to report the news. I prepared as well as I could, did my best and, when I was hired to do the job, I worked hard to earn my place. My first male co-anchor was so disgusted to think that a female was hired—a former beauty queen—that he quit in protest. He was already overworked by writing the whole newscast; he was determined not to do my work as well.

Nobody has *ever* done my work for me.

I grew in my position at KOCO-TV in Oklahoma City. After two years of learning about writing, editing, and speaking for television, opportunities flew in the door. I accepted an offer from the NBC affiliate in Dallas/Ft. Worth (one of the top ten television markets in America). The station wasn't too far from home and the allure of such a big market was thrilling. It was also affirming for my ability as a journalist. The station leadership was not excited about my pageant background, however, and they almost left it out of my publicity material. The move to Texas was the most rewarding professional step

I have ever taken. I worked with the best of the best—people like Scott Pelley (now of *Sixty Minutes*) and Karen Parfit Hughes (right-hand communications person for President George W. Bush).

The job was the best I could hope for, but my personal life did not work well. Every year on the anniversary of my contract signing with KXAS-TV, my friend and current General Manager of the NBC affiliate in Oklahoma City, Lee Alan Smith, called me to ask, "Are you ready to come home?" He must have known my heart. In 1984, the call struck my chord of loneliness. Raising my son in a place with little support, working long hours into the night, and never finding a church home all led to my desire to come home to Oklahoma. It was truly the place I belonged.

I continued to work in television news. First, for Lee Alan at Channel Four where I shared the news room with two of my best friends: Linda Cavanaugh and Kerry Robertson. After an ownership change at KFOR, I moved back to KOCO. In total, I worked as a broadcast journalist for seventeen years. I never tired of the work, but the long night hours wore me slick. I was missing out on my son's activities and had a pitiful social life.

Flexibility and resourcefulness were my twin helpers in working out the days of my career. I left television with an arrangement that kept me on the air weekly, but gave me a day job at the Oklahoma Health Center. Being the spokesperson for that incredible complex felt like earning another educational degree and I met some of the finest people in Oklahoma.

Years later, I received the opportunity to enter the political world when Governor Frank Keating invited me to join his cabinet as Secretary of Tourism. That position included being the director of an agency with a multi-million-dollar budget and approximately one thousand employees. I was naïve about what my reception in the legislature would be; it was a tough world. I've never worked harder.

Most of my professional life was unexpected, without traditional roads through the open gates of employment. I trusted my well rounded education, my skills, my history of endeavor, and the whisper of a loving God. Besides my mother, who would have imagined those many years ago when I was sulking in the car on the way to choir practice that I was also learning an important life lesson? It's simply this: If you receive talent, intellect, energy, health, organizational skills, writing creativity, anything of use, then you have a responsibility to God and to yourself to develop and share it for good. Living with a sense of purpose, coupled with offering what has been given to you, creates a rich life of joy and meaning. And after these many years out of my hometown, I still love to sing in my church choir.

Jane Jayroe

KEY SUCCESS FACTORS: Determination, Work Ethic, Turning Failures into Opportunities, Grace of God

RECOMMENDED BOOKS: *More Grace than Glamour: My Life as Miss America and Beyond* by Jane Jayroe with Bob Burke, *Oklahoma III* by Jane Jayroe with David Fitzgerald

WEBSITE: www.janejayroe.com

EDITOR'S NOTES: Jane Jayroe is currently pursuing a career as a writer and a speaker. She is a graduate of Oklahoma City University and holds an M.A. degree from the University of Tulsa. Jane is the author of several articles that have been included in *McCall's* magazine and books such as *Out of the Blue, Delight Comes in Your Life* and *Chicken Soup for the Mother's Soul*. Ms. Jayroe produced a set of audio-cassettes by area ministers called "Daily Devotionals," and created seminars for women titled "Living Grace-fully" and "Esther Women." Her most recent publications include *More Grace than Glamour: My Life as Miss America and Beyond* written with Bob Burke and *Oklahoma III*, a book published with David Fitzgerald for the centennial year of Oklahoma's statehood that portrays the diversity of the state. Jane was inducted into the Oklahoma Hall of Fame, one of the highest honors bestowed upon an Oklahoman. She has been the recipient of many awards and is extremely active in civic activities.

It took me a long time not to judge myself through someone else's eyes.

—*Sally Field*

FROM POTATOES TO PIES:
AN UNEXPECTED JOURNEY
INTO ENTREPRENEURISM

Paula Marshall—My intentions were never set on becoming an entrepreneur. Whose are? I didn't plan to run my family's business. I can safely say that very few of the business owners I know say they felt they were born into their roles. I became the CEO of our family's multi-national company by way of many, many pieces of a puzzle coming together from very different realms. I call it my pre-destined puzzle. All the pieces finally began to take shape when I was about thirty years old. My story begins, however, long before the pieces of my puzzle fit together.

My grandmother, Alabama Marshall, never knew about entrepreneurs. All she knew was that Winnsboro, Texas, was a tough place to be in 1927. Her seven kids were hungry, and she was done inventing new ways to cook sweet potatoes for her entire family. She was sick and tired of tilling dry soil that resisted the hoe and trying to convince her husband that there was a better way to raise their children. One hot August day, she took matters into her own hands by loading up her children and herself on a covered wagon and moving to Dallas where she became an entrepreneur by opening a soda fountain and selling delicious homemade pies.

My dad began working for his beloved mom, Alabama Marshall, when he finished eighth grade. "Didn't have no use for school," he'd say, "Cause Mama needed help with the business." Yep, my dad loved this business, mostly, I believe, because his mama started it. And he sure did love his mama.

I was born in 1953 in Tulsa, Oklahoma, the third child and the first daughter. As the story was told, it was the happiest day of my momma's life. She had two boys, and now she had a girl child. Little did my mom know what surprises I had in store for her.

Puzzle Piece #1—Love learning:

Mom was the disciplinarian in our family and believed in church on Sundays and school on Monday through Friday. She let us have a little fun on Saturdays, but that was it. My mom believed so strongly in education that if we were sick during a school day, we had to stay home that weekend. Needless to say, I probably went to school sicker than a dog some days, just so I wouldn't miss out on my weekend activities! I believe it was her focused determination to see us all educated beyond her level (Mom finished high school and Dad completed eighth grade) that gave me such a burning desire for learning.

Puzzle Piece #2—Be open to other doors that lead to unexpected places:

I'll never forget being called into my high school counselor's office in the spring of 1972. I was asked, "Where do you want to go to college, Paula?"

"Sophie Newcomb College, Sir. I want to study foreign languages and go work at the United Nations as a translator."

"Whaaaaaat?" He laughed out loud for several moments before continuing. "With these SAT scores, you'll be lucky to get into a junior college!!"

My face went red and my eyes started to burn with tears; I was humiliated.

"You did poorly on your tests, honey. You won't be going any-where. Sorry."

"What about a tennis scholarship?" I asked hopefully.

He looked at me with surprise and replied, "Tulsa Junior Col-lege has a tennis program." I think he finally felt my pain and wanted to help me.

Puzzle Piece #3—Do what you think is right:

"I just can't be pregnant; my mom is going to kill me!" I cried to my family doctor when I was in my second semester at Tulsa Junior College.

"I'm afraid you are," he said in the kindest voice I'd hear for a long time.

Puzzle Piece #4—Look upon things that happen to you as blessings rather than punishments:

In 1974 I found myself picking up little pie shells at my family's factory at six in the morning. I was a nineteen-year-old single mom living at home with my parents. Mom was angry about my circumstances, and Dad was elated to have me back at home. I was confused, and lacked the understanding of exactly what was happening. I continuously ran a video of my life through my brain while I engaged in mindless activities like feeding my baby, changing diapers, or picking up pie shells. I was determined to figure out where I messed up and how my life had turned out this way.

Was it that girl I was mean to on the cheerleading squad? Was it that guy I said I would go out with one Saturday night, and then ditched? Even at the tender age of nineteen, I believed that life had "karma," and that I must have done SOMETHING WRONG to be in this predicament. I was horribly unhappy, and was the cause of a lot of arguments between my parents. I just wanted to get out of their house!!

Puzzle Piece #5—It's okay to be afraid:

A few years later, a family crisis made us all re-evaluate my place in the company. My older brother, John, had a heart attack and was in the ICU fighting for his life. When I arrived at the hospital, I found my mom crying. It felt like another bad dream.

My mother told me, "You're gonna have to help take over some of John's duties until Roger (my second brother) gets here. Your dad and I have already talked about it. He will tell you what we need you to do."

I already knew what a big role my brother played in our business. His would be hard shoes to fill. I began to feel sweat pouring down my back.

"Mom, is he gonna be okay??"

"Pray that God will make him well again. That's all we can do."

"Okay, Mom, and don't worry. I'll do all I can to help Bama now."

"Yes, I know, you really love the business, don't you?"

"Yes, Mom, I do. I really love it."

"Your dad always says you're like his mama. He's getting you a new license plate for your car. The name he's putting on it is 'Bama II.'"

The next year my family was faced with another crisis. I was working at The Bama Companies in Tulsa when I heard the news that my father had been rushed to the hospital. I was in disbelief. John was somewhat recovered. I mean, he was back at work, but he didn't feel well a lot of the time and he had to take a lot of pills; bottles and bottles of them. It scared me because I never knew when he might have another heart attack ... he'd already had two.

Now my dad was being rushed to the emergency room. I sat in the waiting room with my mom. She was crying. I was crying. She told me, "Paula, you know your dad has been trying to sell the business?"

"Yes, Mom, I know."

"I don't want him to, and he really doesn't want to, but he thinks John's too sick to run it, and he doesn't want to put that pressure on him. He's worried about Roger not really being interested in the pie business. We've been talking about you a lot lately. Dad doesn't want to put this burden on you, but I keep telling him that you love this business and that we should keep it, and not sell it to anyone else."

"Mom, I don't know if I'm capable of doing Dad's job or not. Maybe it would be best if you did sell it."

"Are you just saying that, or do you really want to have a chance to see what you could do??"

"I think I'm saying I'm scared. What if I mess everything up?"

As I stated in the beginning, my earliest intentions were not on becoming an entrepreneur. It was pretty clear in my family, from my recollections, that girls DIDN'T RUN COMPANIES! Now, I don't want you to get the wrong idea here, but my dad was a very traditional man. He put me on a "tuffet," and treated me like a little princess. I knew from the earliest days that I had him wrapped around my little finger. He never wanted me to HAVE to go into the business world and slay dragons; as he put it. His work life was hard and tough; grueling, some would say. The thing about my dad was, he loved this business, the "P-u-i-i-i" business as he and my grandmother called it in their best east Texas drawl. Now I was being asked to do what father and grandmother had so successfully done before me and that was an intimidating prospect.

Puzzle Piece #6—Women just need a chance:

Five years later my father and I were visiting our largest customer. We were greeted with, "Paul, it's good to see you again. How are you feeling?"

"I'm doing okay, but you know, I'd like to have my daughter here take the business and run with it. That way, I would have less to worry about, and anyway, it's time for the next generation to take over."

"Well Paul, we thought you were still entertaining third parties, you know. In fact, we thought you were selling to one of our other suppliers. If you're telling us that your daughter is taking over your business, then we'll have to have an offline discussion about this matter. This is a very concerning proposition."

"Why do you say that? She's my daughter. She's been working in the business for over ten years, and she's got her college degree. What more do you need to know?"

"Well, we're just surprised, I mean, she is a woman and all."

Right then and there my daddy got up and picked up his coat. He started to walk out. He looked around at me and said "Get up, and let's go!"

I said, "But Dad, we're not....."

He said "YES WE ARE!!! I just want these xxxxxxx's to know that we were eating three squares at Bama before they came along, and I reckon' we'll be eating three squares after they are gone. NOW LET'S GO!!!"

It was a very long flight back to Tulsa. Two weeks later we hadn't heard anything since we left that awful meeting. It was like any courtroom verdict, the longer it goes, the more you think the verdict might be in your favor. I had gone from feeling sick at my stomach, to just feeling anxious and somewhat depressed. I did have my college degree, but it sure would be nice not to have to go work for anyone else, after all this time.

We all believed that we could save our family's business, and that we wouldn't have to sell it to anyone else. That is, unless our largest customer disagreed with our direction.

Fortunately, two weeks later, my father and I received the phone call we were hoping for. Our largest customer agreed to accept me as CEO.

The last fifteen years have been somewhat of a blur for me. Being part my grandmother's gene pool, making pies has come naturally for me. Being part of our company, named for my Grandmother Bama, has enriched my life more than I could have ever imagined.

Bringing all the pieces of the puzzle together!!

Today, our sales are over $300 million annually. We are growing every year exponentially. We have great customers and suppliers. We have great team members who believe they are loved and cared for. We are a family. Even though my dad has passed, and my brothers are retired from the business, my mom and I still have great pleasure from being women who "get 'er done." We expect to be "getting 'er done" for a long, long time to come.

What I have learned in my life is that all pieces of the puzzle are beneficial to our personal development. Not one piece was wasted on my journey. Each piece has benefited me in many different ways.

By holding my head up day after day, I have put one foot in front of the other. Whenever I was down, I just kept walking, one step at a time. Through the pieces of the puzzle of my life coming together one at a time, I have been able to realize a dream. I have traveled the world, been able to speak with many of our team members about their lives and done what I could to help people wherever I have gone.

My dream of going to college and working for the United States has manifested, just not in the way I thought it would. What college degree or translation job at the U.N. could have allowed me to do the things I do for our customers, our team members and our suppliers? Every time I had a pitfall, I either just fell in it and made the best of things, or I managed NOT TO FALL IN!!

The lessons I have learned are woven throughout the puzzle pieces of this story. Most of the puzzle pieces are finally in place. I believe all the lessons I have learned were, and still are today, part of a pre-determined pathway for me.

I would never go back to any point in my past because I believe the best is here now, not "yet to come." The puzzle has come together, but isn't completely finished. I look forward to seeing how future pieces fit together.

Paula Marshall

KEY SUCCESS FACTORS: Self-Confidence, Perseverance, Building a Great Team, Quality, Relationships, Focus

WEBSITE: www.paulamarshall.com, www.bama.com

SOCIAL MEDIA: Twitter—paulamarshall, Facebook—pmarshall@bama.com

EDITOR'S NOTES: Paula assumed responsibility as CEO of The Bama Companies in 1984, which now includes Bama Pie, Bama Foods, Bama Frozen Dough, Base and Beijing Bama. Under her leadership, Bama has expanded to provide a wide variety of frozen desserts and baked goods to fast food chains and casual and family dining restaurants. The Bama Companies, Inc. has been recognized with numerous awards including McDonald's® USA Highest Quality Honor and the Malcolm Baldridge National Quality Award.

Paula received her B.S. in business from Oklahoma City University (OCU) in 1982, and her Ph.D. in commercial science, also from OCU, in 1993.

The Bama mission is "People Helping People Be Successful," and Paula has created loyalty, prosperity and FUN for all of her employees and stakeholders while growing the family business.

What I am looking for is not out there; it is in me.

—Helen Keller

A SCRAPPY LITTLE NEW ENGLAND GIRL DREAMS BIG

Ann Sachs—I burst onto the scene sixty-odd years ago, a grizzly creature with frizzy hair and crossed eyes, born to question and challenge the world. I was blessed with two parents who believed that anything was possible. Sometimes I think they birthed six children to put their theory to the test: "If you do what you love and work hard at it, you'll be successful and have a happy life." The dark part of this story is that neither one of my parents really did this, which must have deepened their resolve to pass it along to us. Dad became a neurosurgeon and not the conductor he dreamed of being, and Mom became the doctor's wife and stay-at-home mom when she longed to continue as the virtuoso cellist she had been as a child.

My earliest memories of my New Hampshire girlhood were scuffling with siblings over turf and toys, and a non-stop quest to carve out a time and a place to dream. One morning when I was about six, I told my dad that I dreamed I had sprouted wings and could fly like a bird. "If you can dream it, you can do it," he told me. Dad's words became imprinted on my psyche, and I believed that I could do anything I chose if I really wanted it and if I worked extra hard. So that's what I set out to do.

When I was seven I played the witch in *Hansel and Gretel* in my second grade play. Being onstage was the most exciting experience I'd ever had: to be applauded for being mean and nasty! What could be better for one of six kids, constantly vying for attention? I was hooked. My dreams swept me away to New York City and the bright lights of Broadway, and by the time I was ten I had chosen my career: professional actress.

Drama School at Carnegie-Mellon provided a more serious approach to the work, as well as the solid training required, and in my early twenties I moved to New York. Within a few years, I…

…co-starred on Broadway opposite Frank Langella in *Dracula* and had my neck sucked 8 times a week;

…performed in world premieres of plays by Wendy Wasserstein, Jules Feiffer, and did my share of Shakespeare and Shaw on Broadway; and

…recorded dozens of radio plays—among them the National Public Radio *Star Wars* trilogy, in which I was the voice of Princess Leah. (To this day the series has a cult following—I get fan mail on Twitter!)

When I turned forty, I didn't really enjoy being "in it" anymore; I wanted to have impact on the whole thing. Also, the market for women my age in the theatre was rapidly disappearing, so I decided it was time to move on. Actually, my "pivotal moment" (an actor's term) was when I overheard Sam, my six-year-old son, talking to his best friend, Alex:

Sam: What does your mommy do?

Alex: She's a writer—she writes. What does your mommy do?

Sam: She's an actress. She auditions.

With one hundred percent of my knowledge and expertise in the theatre, I had never spent a day working in an office, didn't know how to type, had never even tried to balance my checkbook and I had no idea where to begin. So I did what actors always do before starting to act: We give real meaning to imaginary circumstances (or objects) that *impel* us into action. We say: *"What if..."* in such a way that we have no choice but to ACT. We ask a question that in its very description demands an answer: "What if my LIFE depends on using everything I know about working in the theatre? What do I know? What do I know to be true?"

There were four things I knew:

1. The theatre is a collaborative art form; it doesn't exist without collaboration. You can't do it alone in your room, like a violinist, a painter or a writer.
2. In the theatre there is no such thing as a missed deadline: "The show must go on!" is our work ethic, which we take very seriously. The work *matters.*
3. In the theatre everybody knows what everybody else does. There is a tightly organized collaborative structure—not hierarchical—that works.
4. The theatre's structure demands that everyone excels at what they do, and everyone is accountable for his or her piece. If you don't do your job in the theatre, you're fired. It's as simple as that. Finished. Kaput.

There's an old theatre saying, "It's all in the timing", and sure enough an impeccably timed gift fell into my lap.

My husband, Roger Morgan, is a Tony Award-winning lighting designer. During the years I was performing, he had begun consulting successfully with architects on designing theatre buildings. Roger is a brilliant designer, and deeply uninterested in business. He'd always envisioned a "Mom n' Pop Shop" for his studio, sort of like a Chinese laundry, with the wife and kids in the back. I joked that he'd have to do that with his *next* wife—it certainly wasn't for me. Until I asked myself, *"What if...?"*

When Roger and I teamed up at the Sachs Morgan Studio, I actually thought of it as helping him out until I determined what I was *really* going to do. I mean he had a staff to manage and clients to please and fees to calculate and, heaven-help-me, *billing* to get out the door. To my complete astonishment, I loved it. Why? I learned that the only thing I knew how to do actually worked in *business.*

That was almost twenty years ago. Together, we built the company to one of the leading firms in our industry, and had a wonderfully wild ride doing it.

Now I'm ready for the next phase! As I witnessed the impact of theatre concepts on small business owners, I decided to write a book about it: *Theatrical Intelligence.* It's in the works. The blog is launched. And Roger and I continue to collaborate in the studio every day.

Colleagues often call me to say: "Ann, will you provide—you know—some insight and inspiration?" They might be referring to a party, or a business event, or sometimes a speech for one gathering or another. I always end up talking about the theatre, of course, because it's the insight and inspiration I truly know.

It has been my blessing. And when I count my blessings? I count my parents first, and I count the theatre twice.

Ann Sachs

KEY SUCCESS FACTORS: Passion, Work Ethic, Customer Service

WEBSITE: www.sachsmorganstudio.com

EDITOR'S NOTES: Ann Sachs spent twenty-five years working as a professional actor prior to 1992, when she joined Roger Morgan in what is now Sachs Morgan Studio, Theatre Design Specialists.

She runs the business and Roger is the Director of Design. Studio projects and clients range from Broadway to Hollywood, from Disney to the Kennedy Center and just about everything in between.

A graduate of Carnegie-Mellon's Drama Department, Ann made her Broadway debut opposite Frank Langella in the Tony Award-winning *Dracula*, and played dozens of leading roles on Broadway, Off-Broadway, and in our country's finest resident theatres in premieres of plays by Wendy Wasserstein, Jules Feiffer, Horton Foote, Gunter Grass and Eugene Ionesco. She is (still!) the voice of Princess Leia on the NPR Radio Series *Star Wars,* which has had a cult following for thirty years. Ann collaborated with four other women to write *Mama Drama,* a play about motherhood published by Samuel French, performed by professional and amateur groups nationwide.

Since 1998 Ann has been a member of the Women Presidents' Organization (WPO), an international peer advisory organization for successful women business owners. She serves as Chapter Chair of two WPO Chapters in NYC. In 2006 she launched an online quarterly publication with useful information about theatre buildings: *Theatre By Design,* of which she is Editor. Her newest venture, *Theatrical Intelligence™,* www. theatricalintelligence.com, uses theatre concepts to impact business performance—it's the fun part of being smart! She is currently writing a book on the subject.

Ann was honored to receive the *2008 Lifetime Achievement Signature Award* from the National Association of Women Business Owners (NAWBO) in New York City. In May, 2010, she and Roger were honored by the Ensemble Studio Theatre, the Off-Broadway theatre that develops new American plays.

Ann and Roger have been personal and professional partners since 1970. They are the proud parents of two grown children, Abigail, a doctor of traditional Chinese medicine, and Sam, an architectural photographer.

Life is what we make it, always has been, always will be.

—Grandma Moses

SENIOR CARE WITH CLASS

Sue Loftis—Traveling the world as the child of a military dad prepared me for my life as an entrepreneur and created a philosophy I still hold today: *Wherever you are, be there.* My entrepreneurial spirit first came through when I was sixteen years old. I made Holly Hobbie key chains and placed them on consignment at a local resale shop. The owner allowed me to trade the revenue from sales of the key chains for clothes.

As a compassionate, caring individual, I pursued a career in nursing and graduated from the St. Anthony School of Nursing. After graduation, I worked in intensive care and cardiac rehabilitation for fifteen years before becoming a health administrator for a women's prison and case manager consultant for the U.S. Postal Service.

In the face of crisis there is often opportunity and this is where my story really begins. I was fifty and going through a divorce when my friends suggested I would be a perfect franchise owner of Home Instead Senior Care®, a business they were opening in Vero Beach, Florida. Home Instead Senior Care is the world's most trusted source of non-medical companionship and home care for seniors with more than eight hundred franchises in twelve countries. It seemed logical that my experience as a caregiver and R.N. would serve me well in this business. And it did, except I had never *owned or operated* a business.

I explored the Home Instead opportunity, mortgaged my house, took out an SBA loan and opened in an eleven-hundred-square-foot renovated house. Eleven hundred square feet and me! Oh, did I mention that the first bank I went to denied me, so I went to another bank and was approved? I went through training with the franchise. For me, buying into a franchise meant the difference in my success. I still had to work hard, but the franchise provided guidance and invaluable materials.

I set up the office, attended senior fairs, hired caregivers and had no clients. When I got my first client, I had no caregiver so I did a lot of shifts myself. After my first client, it was six weeks before the second one called. From that point, business improved and I now have over one hundred caregivers and ten employees in the office. I am fortunate to be able to say that all ten years in business have been profitable.

As I reflect back on the success of the business, there are several things I believe have made a difference. Although we are a franchise, clients find a locally owned and operated, growing home care business that began with the desire to serve the needs of our community's elderly adults. It's that simple. This is what we do and I make sure that the Oklahoma City Home Instead Senior Care office is passionate about exceeding the needs of the elderly in our community.

For years, I have been apologizing because people were not getting what they needed from the health care system. I took control—the opportunity to control the quality of care is intoxicating. Providing services that are needed by seniors such as non-medical care is what brought me to this career. Services may include assistance with trips to the doctor, reminders to take the right medication at the right time, meal preparation, light housekeeping, errands, shopping and even Alzheimer's care. The result is companionship allowing seniors to feel safe and independent while they age in place in the home they've lived in for years. We also provide certified home health aid for clients who need hands-on care.

Our clients have high expectations and our goal is to deliver. Before a caregiver goes out on a job, we provide training. I value our caregivers and like to empower them. They make a difference in people's lives, so I want to honor, respect and reward what they do. Recognizing and letting employees know they are valued is important. We have a "Caregiver of the Month" award and a "Caregiver of the Year" award to recognize excellence.

The corporate philosophy of Home Instead Senior Care® is to give back. They started a program five years ago for seniors called "Be a Santa to a Senior." We obtain the names, addresses and wishes of seniors in need. These are placed on trees or wreaths at companies or stores that most recently provided gifts for one thousand seniors. This, along with the other services our company provides, is rewarding and gives me a real sense of peace and satisfaction.

Among the rewards, entrepreneurs also face challenges. My greatest challenge has been finding quality caregivers. We have a great team of caregivers, but much time is taken to select those who will provide the type of care our clients deserve. I believe reputation and earned trust from clients have been critical success factors.

Focus on what you are doing, do the right thing and make your own oasis. Mine is a hot tub, cabana and music with a sign that reads, "Welcome to the Now."

Sue Loftis

KEY SUCCESS FACTORS: Integrity, Customer Service, Finding a Niche, Conscientious Delegation

RECOMMENDED BOOKS: *The Power of Now* by Eckhart Tolle, *Kitchen Table Wisdom* by Rachel Naomi Remen, M.D., *Loving What Is* by Byron Katie and Stephen Mitchell

WEBSITE: www.homeinstead.com/okc

EDITOR'S NOTES: Sue Loftis is the owner of the Oklahoma City Home Instead Senior Care franchise. She is an RN, CCM (Certified Case Manager) and CHCA (Certified Home Care

Administrator). Sue remarried three years ago and her son now works in the business, which allows her more balance in her life. One of Sue's favorite inspirational quotes is: *Everyone has the power for greatness, not for fame but for greatness, because greatness is determined by service.—Martin Luther King, Jr.* It is understandable why this quote is meaningful to Sue who has committed her life to serving others. Those who are lucky enough to know her and have been touched by her kindness are truly blessed.

*No life ever grows great until it is focused,
dedicated and disciplined.*

—Author Unknown

BRINGING A DORMANT
DREAM TO LIFE

Brooke S. Murphy—My grandfather, my uncle and my father were all attorneys, and my father became a judge. Yet when I was in college, it never occurred to me to study law. Instead, I did what was expected of a woman in that era—I became a teacher. It wasn't until years later that my family's profession became my own.

I was born and raised in Oklahoma City, Oklahoma. I earned my degree at the University of Oklahoma and got married right after graduation. I taught first and fourth grades for a year and a half—long enough to know that teaching is really the most demanding profession there is. While I loved teaching, I knew there was something else I wanted to do, though I didn't yet realize what it was.

My husband was a Naval Officer and we moved to the East and West Coasts early in our married life. When we lived in Concord, California (right across the bay from San Francisco), I got a job as an insurance claims processor. The company was located in downtown San Francisco, and I looked forward to working in a fast-paced urban environment. It was my first nine-to-five job, and it took some getting used to. While the lengthy commute wasn't an ideal situation, it did allow me to experience employment in a large corporation … something everyone should experience.

About that time, my husband's service in the military was coming to a close. As I seriously thought about returning to school to get a Ph.D. in history to become a professor, another idea crept into my consciousness. It seemed daunting, but also completely right: law school. The truth of the matter is, I think I had always wanted to go to law school, but I never let myself admit it or recognize it. Even though I was pregnant with our first child, I moved forward with the plan and applied to law school.

My husband accepted a job near Madison, Wisconsin, so I enrolled at the University of Wisconsin School of Law. My class was one of the first which included a greater number of women. Ten percent of the first year students were female. I may not have been the only woman, or the only mother in my class, but I think I was certainly the only mother with a new-born at home. To the extent possible, I scheduled all of my classes in the morning so I could go home in the afternoon and evening. After putting the baby to bed, it was time to study and then get as much sleep as I could.

After graduation, we decided to move back to Oklahoma to be near our families as we raised our children. I interviewed with a number of firms. I am still practicing law at the firm I originally joined thirty-four years ago. The firm didn't have any women lawyers when I was hired, but it was ready and willing to add a female attorney.

The partners of the firm were extremely progressive and supportive of me. In 1975, there were men's clubs where women were not usually allowed, and events women weren't invited to attend. Instead of leaving me out, the partners would indicate that they were bringing all of their attorneys to an event and one just happened to be a woman. If I wasn't allowed to come, they would cancel. In fact, there was a club downtown that had a men's only room where the firm sometimes held attorney meetings. When I was hired, the club hesitated to allow me to attend. One senior partner threatened to withdraw the firm's membership if I wasn't included. The club changed its policy.

I have since learned that there were several other instances, unbeknownst to me, where the firm took the initiative to make sure there was no discrimination. It was and is truly a unique place to practice law.

Initially some clients were a little hesitant to have a woman lawyer, especially a woman litigator. There were and still are some stereotypes in litigation that a woman won't be "tough enough." But a wise partner told me before my first jury trial to just be myself. And that's what I did. I had the support of the firm's senior partners as they assigned me to clients. When the clients got to know me, gender was no longer an issue.

Once I began to practice law, I was humbled to find out how many really smart lawyers there were. In dealing with these very talented people, both my law partners and my opponents, I came to appreciate other people's abilities and to learn from them.

As a lawyer, I'm a perfectionist and I'm competitive. If a client presents a litigation matter to me, I take complete ownership of it. I don't let any stone go unturned. I want to win … not just because I'm doing a job, but because I'm involved personally.

I'm fairly decisive. I look at the facts and the matters at hand and then I'm able to make a decision and move forward and execute it. That has served me well in my career.

In the practice of law there are ups and downs, but I've generally loved every minute of it. One reason law has continued to keep my interest is that every case presents something new. You learn about a new industry, business, group of people, or a new way of doing things. I've handled cases about water pollution and learned how water moves through the earth. I've handled cases about franchises and had to learn about the operation of fast food chains. I've had cases in the insurance industry and had to unravel different policies and sort out agents and policyholders. In the healthcare field I've handled cases involving physicians' hospital privileges, among other healthcare issues. These were all new to me, and that's one of the things that has been so great about a career in law.

In the years since I joined my firm, I have been a litigator, an owner (as a share-holder), have served several times as a member of the firm's executive and compensation committees and have served a traditional two year term as President of the firm. While all attorneys in a firm environment have to be entrepreneurial in developing client relationships and seeking out new business, as a Shareholder I became much more involved and interested in seeing the firm succeed as a whole instead of solely focusing on my clients and cases.

When I served on the firm's executive and compensation committees, I was able to learn about operations, expenses, compensation and client issues. I was also able to study the different areas of practice. It's easy to simply focus on your area of practice without being cognizant of what your peers are accomplishing.

When serving on the executive or compensation committees, and as President, I was definitely wearing a different hat than when I simply practiced law. It gave me a sense for the first time that in addition to being a professional organization, the law firm is a business that has to be run efficiently. Policies and procedures have to be instituted, accounting must be managed, attention must be paid to client development, marketing, personnel and other business matters. In a leadership role, you have to think in terms of the profitability of the firm, the future of the firm and the strategic planning of firm. Indeed, you are acting as a business owner.

When I first joined the firm, there were no women to mentor me. Fortunately, my male mentors were fantastic. Now I enjoy serving as a mentor to young attorneys, female and male.

Looking back, I don't see how I could have been in a better situation. The influence of the attorneys in my family caused me to have a respect for the law from a young age. My early working experiences as a teacher and corporate employee provided a base from which I was able to build my future career. My husband's support of my desire to go to law school and practice law was absolutely essential to my success. My firm's unique progressiveness helped me to achieve and thrive.

All these elements have come together to contribute to a very satisfying career. A personal drive for excellence and the support of others are very powerful forces.

Brooke S. Murphy

KEY SUCCESS FACTORS: Work Ethic, Drive, Supporting Others

WEBSITE: www.crowedunlevy.com

EDITOR'S NOTES: Brooke Smith Murphy, Esq. is a Shareholder and Director at Crowe & Dunlevy, one of Oklahoma's largest law firms. Ms. Murphy earned her B.S. at the University of Oklahoma and her J.D. at the University of Wisconsin (*magna cum laude*). Since joining Crowe & Dunlevy, Ms. Murphy has served in a variety of management positions including President from 2006-2008. She focuses her practice in the area of general civil litigation, including business, commercial, intellectual property, insurance defense, class actions and healthcare litigation.

Brooke has been named to "Best Lawyers in America" for Bet-the-Company Litigation, Commercial Litigation and Insurance Law; Super Lawyers Corporate Counsel (Business Litigation); and named in Super Lawyers' Top 25 Women Attorneys in Oklahoma.

She is a member of Leadership Oklahoma, Class XIX and the Oklahoma Bar Foundation, Board of Trustees. She has served as President, Oklahoma County Bar Association; President, Westminster Day School Board of Trustees; President, Phi Beta Kappa of Oklahoma City; and Master of Bench and Secretary-Treasurer, American Inns of Court. She is a past member of the Magistrate Selection Panel and the Local Civil Rules Committee for the United States District Court for the Western District of Oklahoma; Mandatory Continuing Legal

Education Commission; Legal Aid Services of Oklahoma, Inc., Board of Directors; Oklahoma City University School of Law, Executive Board; and For Youth Initiatives, Inc., Board of Directors.

Brooke has been named by *The Journal Record* as one of "Fifty Who Make a Difference" in 2004 and 2007. She has also been awarded the following: Mona Salyer Lambird 2004 Spotlight Award; *The Journal Record's* 2006 Leadership in Law Award; 2007 Lawyers for Children Service to Children Award.

Brooke is the proud grandmother of four and lives in Oklahoma City, Oklahoma, with her husband, Mike.

CHAPTER 7

COURAGEOUS, CREATIVE
AND CAPABLE

Courage can't see around corners,
but goes around them anyway.

—Mignon McLaughlin

*Courage doesn't always roar. Sometimes courage
is the little voice at the end of the day that says
I'll try again tomorrow.*

—*Mary Anne Radmacher*

BE PREPARED

Patty Roloff—The wonderful days of college life and summers at the swimming pool ended abruptly upon graduation. I was newly married and looking forward to our new adventure of moving to Augusta, Georgia, so that my husband could attend medical school. Cold reality, however, soon set in. I got a job at the mental health clinic at the Richmond County Hospital. My monthly salary of $300 as a receptionist and the G.I Bill of Rights only enabled us to rent the upstairs apartment of a house in the oldest section of downtown Augusta. Since my job didn't start for several months, I spent most of my time trying to be quiet so as not to disturb the downstairs folks and looking out the windows at strangers shopping in a small neighborhood grocery store. What a glorious relief to go to work!

In the four years we lived in Augusta, I stayed very busy. I was promoted from receptionist to social worker at the clinic and worked with Dr. Hervey Cleckley and Dr. Bill Brooks who treated the patients written about in the book and movie *The Three Faces of Eve*. After the clinic closed, I sold office supplies and worked as a filer with E.I. DuPont. And as planned, I had my first child in April before we moved back to Oklahoma City, Oklahoma, where my husband began his internship in General Practice and shortly thereafter opened his private practice.

Fifteen years and four children later, we divorced. My "settlement" was generous, but not adequate enough to continue a lifetime of private schools, camps and all we had been able to offer our children. Most importantly, my equilibrium was shattered and I needed to "find myself" and a direction for all of our lives.

I dreamed of some exotic jobs: airline stewardess, secretary for a Washington politician or a travel organizer for Hollywood stars. I wanted a job that would give me a total change and allow me to be able to show my independence. But again, reality set in and I began to get my emotions and way of thinking in check. I had a college degree and a double major in psychology and social work, but to pursue jobs in those fields I would need more degrees. I also ruled out being a librarian for the same reason. I really wanted to do something that my kids would and could enjoy being a part of, hoping I could keep them busy and divert them from the temptations of the day.

I contacted a family friend, Art Garretson, who was Manager of Local Sales with WKY TV and Radio. He set up a luncheon for us with Norman Bagwell, Station Manager. I relayed a plan I had been cooking up to buy a radio station in a small town. Norman wisely suggested that I find a job with an advertising agency and learn something about the business before I made such an investment. I took his advice and worked at an ad agency and later at a successful public relations firm.

By this time, my children were all in school and involved in many various activities. I had a wonderful lady named Dorothy at home who helped with the housekeeping, laundry and cooking, but I wanted to be available for school plays, practices, games and the necessary chauffeuring. This was my motivation for starting my own business. On a piece of paper I listed the accounts I thought I could take with me, their billing, and the expense of an office and a bookkeeper. I determined I could do it and Cox Advertising Agency was formed. The agency never became big or well known, but it adequately supported us.

Two years after establishing the agency, I obtained the account of the Triple A professional baseball team, the 89ers.

I fell in love with the business of baseball and had a chance to put all of my theories into practice in marketing, promotions and advertising. Two years after obtaining the account, the out-of-town owner, Harry Valentine, wanted to sell the team. He had an offer from the Quad Cities area to buy and move the team, but he said if I could meet the offer within a week, he would sell to me and leave the club in Oklahoma City. With the figures and business plan in hand, I had several meetings with potential investors, but to no avail. I was running out of time when the media took up my cause. They printed, televised and talked about the looming loss of Triple A baseball and what it would mean to Oklahoma City.

The public response was unbelievable and within three days of presenting the story and plan to strangers, the money was raised and we bought the club. Instead of selling professional winning baseball, we adopted the theme of "good time baseball," promising family entertainment at reasonable prices, the hottest hot dogs and the coldest beer in town. The business plan worked. I became the first and only woman owner and General Manager of a Triple A professional baseball team and all investors received their money back, plus, in a short time.

Baseball took me to Chicago when, in 1982-83, I was named an Executive Vice President of the Chicago Cubs. During this time, I returned home at least every six weeks to spend time with my club in Oklahoma City. The Tribune Company had bought the Cubs and named Dallas Green Director of Player Development. Mr. Green reorganized the "front office" of the Cubs and named me Executive Vice President of Tickets and Public Relations and my husband Executive Vice President of Marketing. We enjoyed a long and close relationship with Dallas as the Director of Player Development between the Philadelphia Phillies and the 89ers.

I remained a part owner of the 89ers for many years, but my second husband contracted Lou Gehrig's disease and I sold majority interest in 1990 for more than any other Triple A club had ever sold for at that time.

My best advice is the Boy Scout motto, "Be Prepared." You never know what God's plan might be for you, and you surely don't want to miss any opportunity that comes your way.

Patty Roloff

KEY SUCCESS FACTORS: Perseverance, Being Prepared, Work Ethic

EDITOR'S NOTES: As owner of the 89ers professional Triple A baseball team, Patty received many honors, a great deal of national publicity and was in the Baseball Hall of Fame as the winner of the Sporting News Baseball Owner of the Year 1985 award. Patty Roloff currently lives in Guthrie, Oklahoma. She is an active member of the Oklahoma International Women's Forum.

One of the things about equality is not just that you be treated equally to a man, but that you treat yourself equally to the way you treat a man.

—Marlo Thomas

DON'T CALL ME "HONEY"!

Sue A. Hale—Her name was Nancy Sparks. She was petite and perky, but tough. She was my English and journalism teacher during my junior year in high school and she introduced me to my future career. Mrs. Sparks actually had a journalism background, which was unusual for a high school teacher. It wasn't long before I knew exactly what I wanted to do in life: I was going to be a journalist. It wasn't just the creativity and energy of an inspiring teacher, it was the idea that I could make a difference for people with words and creditable information. My parents weren't thrilled with my decision, especially my mother. To appease them I initially majored in music for my first two years of college before switching to English with a minor in journalism. (I still had to keep my music as a minor too, just to keep Mom happy.)

Mrs. Sparks warned me that a journalism career wouldn't be easy. Women usually got the least exciting jobs and some men would feel threatened by a female reporter who wanted to do more than feature stories. "You'll be able to tell the ones who don't think you can do the job. They will constantly call you 'honey.' It's how they put you in your place," she said. I couldn't imagine anyone calling this little fireball of a woman "honey," but I took her at her word.

The early years of my career were a constant battle for my right to be considered a "real" journalist. I had a city editor in Topeka who was reluctant to assign me to city hall. They had never had a woman on that beat and he didn't think I could handle the "language problem." I asked him what he was talking about and he said, "They use swear words." I told him I was married to a sailor and thought I had heard or perhaps even used a few of those words. When I began to make progress in establishing relationships with the mayor and the city council members, my editor asked me if I had to "sleep with them" in order to make that happen.

I hung in there and achieved many "firsts" in my career: I was the first woman Sports Editor at the *Winfield Daily Courier* in Winfield, Kansas, first woman City Hall Reporter for the *Topeka Capitol Journal*, first woman radio broadcaster and Assistant News Director in Kansas when I worked for WREN Radio in Topeka, first woman News Editor at *The Oklahoman* in Oklahoma City, first woman Assistant Managing Editor and then, finally, the job I wanted most, Executive Editor.

My career prepared me to think like an entrepreneur, make decisions that would improve my skills and push new technology. Many times over the forty-five years I spent in journalism, I thought about what it would be like to be my own boss. The closest I came was in 1996 when I had a unique opportunity to run a subsidiary of The Oklahoman Publishing Company when I started the Internet side of our business. I was the General Manager of Connect Oklahoma (now NewsOK.com) for four years. It was a business venture and I had no real business experience, but I learned on the job.

My stint as an Executive Editor after that also was entrepreneurial in nature. I still reported to the editor and publisher, but they let me run the news operation on my own unless I asked for help, or if I needed to alert them to a controversial decision before they read it in the newspaper.

Along the way, several men tried to "put me in my place," but there were also fantastic male mentors. I was fortunate when I ended up at *The Oklahoman* that no one at the paper called me "honey," although in the mid-1970s when I was reporter and I asked for a raise to match the salaries of male reporters, I was told I was not a "bread winner."

But times were changing as more women came into the field. In fact, I was sitting in a conference one day (the only woman in management) during which the head of the sports department used some foul language and was chastised by colleagues because there was a "lady" present. I knew I had truly arrived when another guy responded, "That's no lady, that's our Editor."

During my journalism career, I learned that it was important to always have a plan in mind. While I was trying to advance, I sometimes went sideways or backwards, but I always kept my goals in sight. When I wanted the job of City Editor and didn't get it at *The Oklahoman*, I went to work for the *El Reno Tribune* as the News Editor. My boss at *The Oklahoman* told me I was ruining my career. He could not have been more wrong. As a News Editor, I became the first woman President of the Associated Press Oklahoma Managing Editors and the networking helped me get the job back at *The Oklahoman* as the first woman News Editor.

In 2000, I reacquainted myself with my more artistic side and started taking painting lessons again from a local artist. When she died and her son asked several of us if we wanted to take over the studio and gallery, we agreed. We renamed it "In Your Eye" in 2004 and it has a prominent place on Paseo Drive in the Paseo Arts District in Oklahoma City. In addition, I published a book in 2005 on nursing home care, based on a diary my mother kept while a resident at a nursing home.

As soon as I retired in 2008, I started Sue Hale, Inc., a media consulting company. My main client is a local journalism foundation and I work with them on their grants and the direction they should take in working with new media and non-profit journalism. What I'm doing now with my art gallery and my consulting businesses is the culmination of learning how women can apply their skills and create a new "place" in the world of business.

Sue A. Hale

KEY SUCCESS FACTORS: Trust Your Instincts, Don't Be Afraid to Take Risks, Passion, Continuing Education

WEBSITE: www.Suehaleart.com

EDITOR'S NOTES: Sue Hale lives in Oklahoma City, Oklahoma, with her husband, Bob. She has a stepson, David. Sue is active in First Amendment organizations, civic groups and health education.

Life is a song. Love is the music.

—Author Unknown

SISTERS AND MUSIC
AS A BUSINESS

Stephanie Farrar—From Jennifer's fourth grade award-winning performance at her regional little theater as Annie, to my trek across the United States with my previous band Agent Sparks, we sisters began our musical careers singing *Grease* tracks on the opposite ends of the same jump rope. Jennifer, the blonde East Coast thinker and I, the West Coast liberal, began our journeys from our home base in Chattanooga, Tennessee. We could never imagine, individually or as a team, where our musical passion would one day lead us.

I moved west from Tennessee to Texas, where I graduated *magna cum laude* from Southern Methodist University with a double major in film and creative writing. I fulfilled my dream of relocating to Los Angeles shortly after finishing my degrees ... precisely four days after! After appearing in several short films and television spots like *MTV Undressed*, I eventually made my way back into the music field becoming a sought-after studio singer.

Ultimately, music led me into the arms of my new husband, Sam Farrar, bassist of renowned California band Phantom Planet and producer for artists like Maroon 5 and Sara Bareilles. Not only is he the son of Grammy winning songwriter John Farrar (*You're the One That I Want* and *Hopelessly Devoted to You*), but also the son of Pat Carroll Farrar, Olivia Newton John's debut singing partner. Jennifer and I never thought our childhood heroine from *Grease* would become like family, but as luck and time would have it, that dream was fulfilled. And that was just the beginning.

In the nearly ten years I have spent on the West Coast, I have been involved in numerous musical projects. I was a backup singer for Maroon 5, sang with Weezer on *David Letterman*, *Hard Rock Live* and *Jimmy Kimmel*, and wrote, most recently a theme song for the NBC sitcom *Quarterlife*. My resume doesn't end there. My most demanding and fulfilling role as keyboardist and singer in Immortal Records' band Agent Sparks proved to be the most enlightening. Agent Sparks' debut EP, *Not So Merry*, and full-length record, *Red Rover*, were produced and recorded by Incubus guitarist Mike Einziger.

From the opposite coast, after performing on five of the seven continents with Children's International Summer Villages and Buckner Orphan Care International, Jennifer was awarded a music scholarship to Baylor University, where she studied vocal performance and English. Following graduation, Jennifer's keen awareness of the business world led her to direct a leadership team of high potential candidates for prominent Fortune 500 companies. After succeeding in the business community, Jennifer's true calling to music reemerged, leading her to perform for a wide range of artists and dignitaries featuring Kenny Loggins, John Denver, President George Herbert Walker Bush and the Pointer Sisters.

Needless to say, Jennifer and I not only have the musical "chops," but we also have the resumes to back up our diverse roles in this crowded industry. By the time 2007 rolled around, Jennifer and I began brainstorming inventive ways to position ourselves as musicians in the marketplace, as well as help other rising talent. With only music and a bloodline connecting the two "opposite" sisters, Jennifer and I discovered a shared passion for finding and developing the best of the unknown musical talent.

After years of successful career moves in the industry, Eagle Ear Entertainment was born when we decided to point the compass at upcoming unknowns and create a "new" way to discover these artists by merging best practices from traditional scouting methods and our own original online talent incubator. We put our heads and hearts together and created an online platform for emerging artists to post their online electronic press kits (including music, music videos, photos and contact info) and enter the monthly Curtain Call music video battle to win prizes.

We also eventually scouted talent for a "Cinderella Story" Rockumentary created for network television, featuring the monthly Curtain Call music video battle winner and the Eagle Ear Team. We are in the midst of securing financing from venture capital frms and investors to fulfill this dream of launching a network television series, focused on finding the best of the unknown.

Upon pitching the idea for Eagle Ear and Curtain Call, Jennifer and I immediately secured initial financing from an angel investor. After partnering with business developer, online marketer, and one of my oldest college friends, Lamonte Guillory, and the marketing genius of Jennifer's husband, Jason Young, Eagle Ear has successfully launched two websites (www. eagleear.com and www.CurtainCalltv.com), signed, developed and distributed its first recording artist Samantha Shelton, and pre-produced the Web/TV series Rockumentary *Curtain Call*.

Eagle Ear boasts a laundry list of celebrity key endorsements, industry and business executives, artists, tastemakers and consultants to help deliver a unique and progressive method to not only finding and showcasing the best emerging musical talent, but also doing so with integrity and intellect. We were able to put aside our differences and focus on our shared love of music to connect not only with each other, but with others in the music community who have struggled to find their voices. By coming together and creating a team of valuable employees and consultants, we have put music and education first ... and whatever differences we may have beyond last.

Stephanie Farrar

KEY SUCCESS FACTORS: Selflessness, Perseverance, Humility, Sacrifice

RECOMMENDED BOOKS: *Mapping Your Legacy* by Charlie Eitel, *The Business of Music* by M. William Krasilovsky, *The Magic of Conflict* by Thomas F. Crum

WEBSITES: www.eagleear.com, www.CurtainCallTV.com, www.LamonteGuillory.com

SOCIAL MEDIA: MySpace—eagleear, MySpace—samanthasheltonmusic

EDITORS NOTES: Jennifer lives in Austin, Texas, after a recent move from Atlanta, Georgia, with her husband, Jason, and two children, Jackson and Julia. She is a member of ASCAP and the Academy of Gospel Music Association. She has produced one record, *The Word Through Music* and several recordings for corporations.

Stephanie lives in Los Angeles, California, with her husband, Sam. Their first baby girl, Vesper Pearl Farrar, was born in August 2009. Stephanie is a member of AFTRA, ASCAP and SAG. She has recorded two records with Agent Sparks *Not So Merry* and *Red Rover*.

Jennifer and Stephanie have successfully recorded and released debut record label artist Samantha Shelton's EP *Good Morning Tonight* and LP *Are You Kidding Around*.

Listen or thy tongue will keep thee deaf.

—Native American Indian Proverb

THE VALUE OF LISTENING

Molly Tovar—My eleven brothers, sister and I worked alongside my father to tend to farmers' fields. At dusk when we walked home, my father would occasionally impart bits of wisdom. Although my father seldom spoke to us, when he did, his carefully chosen words carried deep meaning. We always listened closely and took his words seriously, although many times we did not recognize the value of his thoughts until later.

His face was stern when he spoke, but there was love of life in his voice and strength in his words. Once he told us, "Don't talk so much, but listen. Remember, once you speak, those words are no longer your words; they belong to the universe. They are for people to use, both good and bad, so speak wisely and carefully."

My father also told me that one day I needed to go to those buildings that the "white" people go to, to have a better life. He did not know that "those buildings" were universities or how expensive it would be to attend college. As an Indian American, he recognized the value of education and he knew it would make his children's lives better. My father's wisdom and advice will be with me all of my life.

I learned to listen very carefully, and I went to "those buildings that the white people go to" and earned my degrees. This would have been a very difficult task without the lessons I learned from my father and other individuals who became wonderful influences in my life.

One of my first experiences in listening, learning and then taking a leadership role was during my first year of college. Since I could seldom go home, I sought out other students like myself and we became a family. During our social events, we went bowling, skiing and hiking. It was clear that we all wanted more, however; we wanted a formal group with definite and stated objectives that the university would recognize as they did other established organizations and associations. I not only succeeded in finding new friends, but I was also involved with establishing the first American Indian Student Association at the university. We gained strength to believe in ourselves and to persevere against the status quo of the administration to spark positive change for underrepresented students.

It was my father who first helped me find my path in life, and guided me toward a better life. I was also influenced by two very special American Indian women, La Donna Harris (Comanche) and Wilma Mankiller (Cherokee). The traditional role of women in American Indian society has been that of Bearers of Life, to ensure that a sustainable environment exists for generations to come.

In many tribes, the American Indian woman's voice was included in the decision-making process both at home and in her tribal community. Throughout American Indian history, American Indian women have greatly influenced the women's rights movement and played a strong role in government. La Donna Harris, President of Americans for Indian Opportunity, and Wilma Mankiller, former Principal Chief of the Cherokee Nation of Oklahoma, inspired me to grow as a leader and as a strong woman.

Mankiller's great leadership style and accomplishments revitalized the Cherokee people, and inspired me to set and achieve compelling creative leadership goals. Mankiller showed American Indian women that they could do more than influence others; they could be respected and accepted as leaders. Her philosophy that "people learn to survive by helping each other" is a key element of all facets of life, including leadership in the workforce. She demonstrated how strong leaders consider the voices of all constituents and support them in numerous ways.

I remember listening to La Donna Harris discuss and reflect on traditional cultural values. She explained that four concepts are universal in Indian communities: Relationship is a kinship obligation, responsibility is *based* on community obligations, reciprocity is a cyclical obligation and redistribution is our sharing obligation.

During my first year as COO of the American Indian Graduate Center in Albuquerque, New Mexico, I was given an exciting responsibility of creating a program comparable to a student services department for the American Indian/Alaska Native Gates Scholars. The first task was to identify hundreds of American Indian/Alaska Native high school students across the country who met the criteria for this very competitive scholarship. There were only a few months to identify students to apply and meet the scholarship deadline.

Upon my arrival, I went right to work by assessing the staff resources and learned there were three full-time staff members to assist with the initiative. I visited with the staff at length and asked them questions like: "Where do you want to go with your career and why? Explain to me what you believe is your role and responsibility within this organization? If you had all the resources you needed, what programs would you design?" I reflected on how each would respond to a fast-paced, rapidly changing environment. I assessed how well they worked with each other. I learned quickly that they had untapped talent and were passionate about their jobs: the receptionist became the outreach coordinator, the director of financial aid took on additional responsibilities, and the secretary became the assistant to the financial aid director.

As I reflected on La Donna Harris's "Four R's" concept of redistribution, it was only natural that my next responsibility was to mentor each of these individuals on recruitment, retention, alumni relations and team building. It definitely was fierce and fast mentoring.

We called volunteer programs in the area. Volunteers are a cost-effective solution in providing additional skills to your organization. Individuals who want to volunteer tend to have a strong will to learn and an all around good attitude. One member, a retired engineer, provided guidance with office expansion ideas needed for future hires. Another member helped with the databases and website development. A retired teacher helped to edit reports.

We called an American Indian training and placement service program and arranged to have two of their clients handle the receptionist duties. We also called upon our colleagues and alliances to assist with the Gates initiative.

I contacted local high schools and worked out agreements on mentoring students on research techniques and other skill sets needed for the organization. It was especially rewarding to work with high school students since research has proven that those students who take part in carefully planned mentoring programs have higher grade point averages, are more likely to attend college and have improved social relationships.

The team set up appointments to meet with tribal representatives throughout the United States to discuss the Gates Millennium Scholars' (GMS) mission. The tribal educational staff worked with us to set up GMS computer labs. We worked with the high schools to gather students together with their parents, tribal education coordinators and teachers. Some of these GMS labs had up to five hundred students in attendance.

My experience shows how utilizing all of the local resources and talents can benefit an organization's mission and goals. I have learned that one of those most important skills is the ability to truly listen to others. When we listen to others, we show respect, build relationships and concepts are generated. We also learn a great deal about ourselves.

I am grateful and blessed to have listened closely to Wilma Mankiller, La Donna Harris and my father. I have benefited from their wisdom and words of encouragement that have and continue to guide me personally and professionally.

Molly Tovar

KEY SUCCESS FACTORS: Respect for Wisdom Found in the Words of Others

RECOMMENDED BOOKS: *Everyday is a Good Day* by Wilma Mankiller and *West with the Night* by Beryl Markham

EDITOR'S NOTES: Dr. Molly Tovar served as the Director of Leadership and Scholar Relations for the Bill & Melinda Gates Millennium Scholars Program. She has been nationally recognized for her expertise in strategies for ensuring the success of underrepresented students in undergraduate and graduate education. Dr. Tovar has garnered positions on state and national committees and was selected as a fellow of the prestigious International Women's Forum Leadership Program. She is currently a consultant focusing on developing leadership skills in academic and corporate communications.

When patterns are broken, new worlds emerge.

—Tuli Kupferberg

DEFINING THE ART OF JUNKIN'

*Cathy Guess—***JUNKIN'***[juhngk-in] verb; the ability to find undiscovered treasures and transform them into desirable possessions that ya just can't live without* (as defined by Girls Gone Junkin' AKA Cathy Guess and Deidra Morgan)

I guess you could say we went junkin' before junkin' was cool. I experienced my first flea market in 1969 with my boyfriend (now husband). Deidra worked alongside her grandparents at Canton Trade Days (one of the largest and most attended monthly flea markets in the South) selling homemade candy. We both loved "The Hunt" for treasures at garage and estate sales, flea markets and just about any other location, not barring junk on the side of the road awaiting trash pickup.

By coincidence, we ended up working at the same elementary school office nearly forty years later. With our shared love of The Hunt, we became close friends. Summers were a treat for us as we had many weeks off when school was not in session. In the summer of 2007, we decided to open a booth at a local antique mall. We started out with a small space and two months later moved to a larger booth. As sales climbed and our client base continued growing, another move was in the works.

Around this time, our friend, Pam Burnett, asked if we would like to bring some of our wares to sell the next month at Canton Trade Days since she had some additional room in her space. By this time we were back at the school working and still had our antique booth. We were unsure if we could add anything more to our plates. After much deliberation and assurance from family and friends, we went for it.

We loaded a trailer full of junk (treasures), packed our bags and like a band of gypsies, we were off for a unique and unforgettable experience. In our haste, we forgot one very important thing: lodging! Here we were at the beginning of a four-night stay, over one hundred miles from home, without hotel accommodations. Always resourceful, we made a pickup cab our temporary sleeping quarters. With our decorating talents, we hung our jewelry on the rearview mirror, placed our hats and hair apparel on the dash and draped our clothes over every hook.

In spite of being pounded by Texas-sized mosquitoes and having to shower in the designated vendor's bathhouse, our first Canton experience was a success. We loved it! Over the next few months we continued to work at the school and operate the booths at the antique mall and Canton Trade Days. It didn't take long to realize we were in over our heads. A decision had to be made!

After continued encouragement from family and friends, we decided to resign from our jobs at the school, close the booth at the mall and devote all our time to our new business Girls Gone Junkin'. This was the beginning of a fun-loving, eye-opening, junk-filled new chapter in our lives.

At first we primarily sold shabby chic style furnishings and décor at Canton Trade Days. As our business has grown, we've added unique handmade jewelry. Deidra creates primarily soldered jewelry, while I prefer wooden composition. Custom bedding and pillows and one-of-a-kind handmade purses are supplied by my mom, Nancy Westbrook, who is an exceptional seamstress. My husband, Steve, refinishes most of the furniture.

Deidra and I are well known to all who visit Canton regularly as the "Queens of Bling." In fact, besides having a glittered carousel horse hanging from our ceiling, we display a large pink crown on the front of the freestanding building we share with friends Pam, Jerri and Sue (entrepreneurs in their own right). We attribute our success to three important factors:

1. Keeping prices reasonable and affordable, which in today's economy is very important.

2. Staying current with the latest and hottest crazes in our décor, furnishings and jewelry designs.

3. Maintaining a courteous and friendly attitude that will have our customers coming back for more if our first two objectives are met.

Our combination of passion and talent is without a doubt our recipe for success. The journey may have been overwhelming at times, but with passion, perseverance, determination and friendship we have triumphed.

Cathy Guess

KEY SUCCESS FACTORS: Passion, Perseverance, Determination, Relationships

RECOMMENDED BOOKS: *Always Believe in Yourself and Your Dreams* by Patricia Wayant

WEBSITE: www.girlsgonejunkin.com

EDITOR'S NOTES: Cathy Guess lives in North Richland Hills, Texas, along with her husband, Steve, and their yellow lab, Dixie. They have an adult son, Dustin, who lives close by. When she's not out searching for treasures, Cathy enjoys time with her grandson, Kyan. She loves Nashville, country music and attending a good concert with hubby Steve when time allows.

Deidra Morgan resides in Hurst, Texas, with her husband, Craig, and their son, Payne. Other family members include the family dogs, Gus and Snoopy. When she's not soldering her custom jewelry charms, Deidra enjoys spending time with her three sisters and attending her son's rock band performances. She loves the beach and family trips to Florida every summer.

I've never seen a smiling face that was not beautiful.

—Author Unknown

RECLAIMING MYSELF

Karen Peterik—I have led a blessed life, to be sure. The "honeymoon baby" of a post WWII romance, I was much loved by my parents and encouraged to excel in whatever talents I was given. Mom was an RN by trade, but a natural homemaker and an incredible later-in-life fine artist. Dad, who survived his enlistment in the Army by playing trombone in the band, worked as an electronics instructor, but was self-taught in the fields he loved most—astronomy and R.C. model airplane flying. Together, they set my foundation in life and for that I will be eternally grateful.

My blessings continued when at the tender age of nineteen, I found myself marrying the man I would spend the rest of my life with. We met through our shared love of music; my appreciation and his music, as evidenced by his singing, writing and recording original songs that would soon be made famous by his groups and others. How many women get to escort an Academy Award nominee to the Oscars? (*Eye of the Tiger* was co-written by my husband and recorded for the movie *Rocky III* by Survivor in 1982. The song also won a Grammy and People's Choice Award.)

This success allowed me the luxury of pursuing my interests and talents. I graduated from interior design school and worked in a residential firm for eight years before starting my own consulting business. I was also able to delve deeper into my love for gardening, cooking and began developing my second career as a group exercise instructor. I earned my ACE certification and taught fitness classes of my own design in studios and health clubs for fifteen years.

Life was good but it was going to get even better: after eighteen years of marriage, we became the parents of our amazing son. Whatever I tell you next, please know that I would not want to change one bit of my story despite the challenges that lay ahead.

The first spot of hair loss on the back of my head was discovered by my hair stylist when I went in for a color touch-up. It usually starts out very innocently this way. Then the mere whisper of lost hair strands gradually builds up to an ear-crushing din of large clumps of hair loss eventually leaving you totally bald. I was experiencing the beginning of what I learned to be an incurable auto-immune skin disease: alopecia areata. There is no known cause, although I have come to believe that it is multi-causal with the onset frequently occurring after some kind of trigger event.

Tears silently slid down my cheeks as the dermatologist specializing in alopecia told me what I could expect. My body chose the most extreme form of the disease, alopecia universalis, or total body hair loss. Other forms of alopecia areata present in patches of scalp hair loss and alopecia totalis with total hair loss on the scalp only. After a brief attempt at re-growth, I came to the logical conclusion that silenced the cacophony of endless questions and emotions: I had to find a way to accept my baldness and get on with my life.

In our culture, hair is intimately tied to our self-image and a person's self-image forms the core which informs all emotions, thoughts and actions. How is it that what amounts to nothing more than your reflection can have this much power over us? I'm still working on that one, but I no longer dismiss this power as "superficial." After going down the requisite road of loss— anger, hurt, self-pity and depression—there is nowhere else to go but up. How was I going to find myself again, now that I had lost all of my hair?

As my ponytail got thinner and thinner, I explained to my aerobics class that I had alopecia and really didn't know how this was going to work out. I assured them that my health was not suffering—just my hair follicles. Thank God for that!

Unknowingly, I began my third career at the moment I decided to take control of my hair loss by beginning my research into all of the various hair replacement options available. I learned by starting at the bottom with a local wig shop whose employees had no idea what I was going through. They sold wigs like any other commodity and the result of that taught me that this is or rather should be a specialty business—sold by women who could relate to being bald and the difficult task of restoring a woman's self-image.

In the quest to get your old self back, you are starting from scratch. A blank canvas is much more difficult than drawing inside the lines! This analogy can be taken quite literally when one loses eyebrows and eyelashes like I did. How, where and what shape and color will look the most natural? Like poorly worn eye make-up, bad hair is embarrassing. You don't want to "own" this image, but outside of blindfolding everyone you meet or living via your computer, your appearance is the first clue people get to who "you" are. Having high blood pressure or diabetes has never been considered embarrassing; knowing that people are not looking at the real you, is!

After about seven years of wearing what I now refer to as "conventional" wigs, I attended my first National Alopecia Areata Foundation (NAAF) International Conference and made the discovery that would not only return my own self-image but provide me with a means to help others going through the same thing. I had dreamed of having a beautiful human hairpiece that looked so natural it would be undetectable, felt comfortable to wear and provided the security to pursue various activities without the fear of it coming off.

Enter the Freedom Wigs Vacuum Prosthesis. Made in New Zealand, these custom-made wigs come as close as possible to fulfilling that dream. A skin-matching silicone cap is implanted with unprocessed human hair of the length, color and curl pattern of your choosing. It suctions on your head via a laser-accurate fit and an inherent affinity to human skin. It changed my life and is changing the lives of others as I write this because put simply, it lets you forget about having hair loss. In fact, one can come to see it as a plus—never having to shave unwanted hair, never going gray and getting ready for the day much faster are just a few!

Flash forward to the thriving business I have groomed over the past ten years, New Life Hair, L.L.C.—a business I would have never gotten into had I not been affected by alopecia myself. In my position as Midwest U.S. Dealer for Freedom Wigs, I have had the satisfaction of building up to my current client base of two hundred and fifty because I did it by myself every step of the way. I have a passion for helping others "forget" about their hair loss not only through wearing and styling their vacuum hairpiece, but teaching them make-up techniques and ways to navigate social situations that are "hair sensitive." I feel I have a good balance of having empathy over what we cannot change while still encouraging each client to do the best they can with what they can change. That really opens up the discussion to go way beyond hair. That is the perspective I hope to achieve with every client.

As for the business end of my passion, I feel like I was groomed for this career through experiences from my past careers; Interior design taught me how to run a business and teaching group fitness taught me how to motivate and inspire people to find that special place within each of us that allows us to grow. The rest is a work in progress as I continue to develop my understanding of the product I wear and sell—visits to the New Zealand factory are always so enlightening, inspirational and enjoyable. I still go to the yearly NAAF conferences—but as a vendor, not an attendee. In addition to meeting new and old clients there, this is a golden opportunity to network with the other dealers; we share our experiences and learn what's on the horizon directly from the manufacturer.

Back in my home office, I divide my time between the initial client contact, whether by phone or email, face-to-face consultations involving travel to a dozen or more Midwest states, placing new orders, keeping up with accounting chores, finding ways to introduce my business to new clients, ongoing maintenance and repairs for current clients and perhaps the most dramatic time of all—attending the highly anticipated client salon styling appointment. This is where the self-transformation takes shape. A new image is born as a luxurious head of hair is sculpted (while being worn) into a shape and style that fits the uniqueness of each client. From the moment they put on their hairpiece, they take on a new image. I often feel like I am meeting the real person for the first time—it can be that dramatic. Since I know that everyone's self-image must be cultivated, what we achieve at the salon is just the beginning. But it is a crucial step in the right direction. They can move forward now and reclaim themselves … as I did.

Karen Peterik

KEY SUCCESS FACTORS: First-Hand Experience that Allows Me to Connect With Each Client, Attention to Detail, Follow Through and Personal Style.

RECOMMENDED BOOKS: *YOU: Being Beautiful* by Drs. Oz and Roizen

WEBSITE: www.newlifehair.com

SOCIAL NETWORKING: Alopecia World.com, NAAF support groups

EDITOR'S NOTES: Karen Peterik is the owner of New Life Hair, L.L.C. She is the Midwest dealer for Freedom Wigs. She is an active member of the National Alopecia Areata Foundation and lives in Burr Ridge, Illinois, with her husband, Jim. Their son, Colin, is a music student at Columbia College Chicago.

CHAPTER 8

ADAPTABLE AND TENACIOUS

*Take risks: if you win, you will be happy; if you lose,
you will be wise.*

—Author Unknown

To win you have to risk loss.

                       —Jean-Claude Killy

TAKE A DEEP BREATH AND
DO IT ANYWAY!

Marnie Walker—Uncle Charlie was the only one who knew I existed. I was the middle child and even that I shared with a brother: there were four of us.

When I was a kid, Charlie would take me out on adventures—just me. On one of these, we went swimming in Lake Simcoe. He put me on his shoulders to jump into the deep water. I was terrified. "I can't, I can't," I screamed!

"Take a deep breath," he said, "and do it anyway."

So I jumped, and the crazy thing was, I loved it.

It is passion that gives you the energy and determination to forge a new journey, to create something out of nothing, to see your business grow and flourish. But where does passion come from? When I jumped off Uncle Charlie's shoulders, it wasn't passion that made me jump. I was terrified. The passion came when I burst back out of the water like a rocket. So take a deep breath and do it anyway, the passion takes care of the rest.

In 1990 I was a cog in the wheel of a large corporation, divorced, with a big mortgage and less than $500 in the bank. I was down on my luck. Fourteen years later I was on top of the world. I was happily married, had money in the bank, no mortgage and was the owner of a multi-million dollar school bus company, Student Express, with two hundred and fifty buses and three hundred employees. I had just been awarded Canadian Woman Entrepreneur of the Year.

How did I get there? I jumped off Uncle Charlie's shoulders. It was crazy really. I didn't have enough money to buy a car, but I financed eight buses and started Student Express.

My passion was always to own my own business. I learned that school boards were looking for transportation for problem special needs children. After months in the hospital as a teenager and having to walk with canes and crutches for eight years, I knew what it was like to be a "problem" child. I also knew how to transport them.

It wasn't easy. I didn't have a place to park the buses, so the drivers took them home. The buses became billboards in the community and the drivers didn't need transportation to get to work. I didn't have a big office, so I had the supervisors ride the buses. Best thing I could have done. They solved problems in real time, so little problems didn't become big problems.

Several years ago, I got a fantastic offer from a large multi-national company to buy Student Express. Selling wasn't easy either. Student Express was my baby; I created it, nursed it and saw it flourish. I loved it. But the offer was too good to refuse, so once again I jumped off Uncle Charlie's shoulders and sold it.

After the sale, I took my personal things and fourteen years of Student Express life out my office and the depot. There were many tears—mine, customers and employees. I felt like I had fallen off a cliff. Who was I, what would I do?

After about six weeks at home, I was bored and decided a home office, housework and being what my husband called a "real wife" weren't for me. It was time for another jump off Uncle Charlie's shoulders.

It excites me to be around entrepreneurs. They are the innovators of the world, the people who make things happen. Hoping to find a new business opportunity and be involved with entrepreneurs, I joined an "angel" investment group. It was an old boys club. After several fierce encounters with angels who thought I was intruding in their space, I was asked to be on the board. It seems they needed someone to evaluate business cases and companies—someone who had actually started and built a company. That someone was me. This led to six of us founding a new angel investment group, Maple Leaf Angels, two years ago. We have about sixty members, who together have invested six million dollars to date in companies wanting to grow.

I discovered that professionals and entrepreneurs like myself needed office facilities and support services, but didn't have the time or cash flow to run an office. The result was meetings in coffee shops, lost time waiting for the courier deliveries, or worse, spending too much on an office. I searched for a solution, but came to realize that if I wanted such an office environment, I would have to create it. Time for another jump!

In the fall of 2008, I opened 401 Bay Centre, a managed office center in the heart of downtown Toronto. It has forty-five furnished executive and team offices, three meeting rooms, a business center, café, reception area, telephone service, delivery and a host of administrative services. To ensure a professional and independent image for clients, it is unbranded; the name is the address. This is an ideal setting for branch offices, professionals, organizations and companies needing short term office space.

There has been much turbulence with the financial meltdown, but the waters are calming now and 401 Bay Centre is no longer taking on water.

Will there be more jumps? Absolutely!

Marnie Walker

KEY SUCCESS FACTORS: Dream It, Research It, Do It; There is No Such Thing as Failure, Only Bumps and Turns in the Road; Do What You Love and Love What You Do; Focus and Work Hard; It's all About Your Team, You Can't do it Alone

RECOMMENDED BOOK: *Blue Ocean Strategy* by Chan Kim and Renée Maulborgne

WEBSITES: www.401bay.com, www.Marniewalker.com, www.petitude.com.au

EDITOR'S NOTES: Serial entrepreneur, Marnie Walker, is the owner of 401 Bay Centre, a managed executive office center in the heart of downtown Toronto. Marnie also is an owner of an online pet supply company, Petitude, based in Australia with distribution centers in Australia and the United Kingdom.

She is best known for her entrepreneurial achievement in building Student Express from a start-up in 1990 to a multi-million dollar school bus company with a fleet of two hundred and fifty buses. She was named Canadian Women Entrepreneur of the Year, Extraordinary Women of the Year and ranked 37th in the Profit W100 Canada's Top Women Entrepreneurs in 2004.

A key note speaker and angel investor, Marnie holds an ICD.D Board of Director's certification, teaches entrepreneurship at the Schulich School of Business, and is a founding director of Maple Leaf Angels investment group. She lives in Toronto, Canada and Gold Coast, Australia, with her husband, Bill Fahey.

Where there is no struggle, there is no strength.

—Oprah Winfrey

FROM FIRED TO FIRED UP!

Julia Erickson—I was stymied. Five months after being fired for a second time, I still had not found another non-profit Executive Director position. I believed I had ability, talent and a proven track record in my favor. Clearly, potential employers understood this because I easily got interviews. I interviewed extremely well, felt rapport with several places, and got to the finalist stage a couple of times. Alas, I got no job offers. What was going on?

For eleven years, I had led City Harvest (a New York City anti-hunger organization), taking it from near obscurity to being "one of New York City's best-loved charities," according to *The New York Times*. Then in eight months, I successfully turned New York Restoration Project from crisis to stability as its second Executive Director. Internal politics led to my being fired from both of those jobs. In the case of City Harvest, I used to joke that I built an organization worth taking over, and it was.

As I reviewed the previous few years, I realized a lot of things had come to an end. After being part of the rescue and recovery operation that followed September 11th, I moved out of New York City's Greenwich Village to New Jersey. I lost my six-year-old nephew to cancer following a two-year struggle. The icing on the cake: worsening health issues meant I could no longer consistently work full time or commute into New York City. Now, after twenty-five years in New York City's non-profit sector, I realized the universe was giving me a clear message: this path has ended! I definitely had to reinvent myself.

First, I successfully adapted to my changed circumstances—what I call "big brain, little body"—by using available technology, especially the telephone, computer and the web. With these tools, I didn't need the most able body. I got an M.B.A. online, and explored social media (especially Twitter, LinkedIn and Facebook) to connect with people outside my home. I began blogging on several topics, including my transition from influential leader to home-based solo act.

All along I asked myself one question: what is my new path? I had a few criteria. I needed to find something to do from home and using technology. I had to be able to help other people, preferably using my own experiences and successes to benefit others. Whatever I did had to be varied, intellectually stimulating, and challenging. I had to be able to interact with other people. I wanted to be in a situation where I would continue learning and growing. And I had to have enough time to write. I turned to my personal development toolbox for guidance and drew on my many life experiences. I had faith that I would find the answers as long as I kept going, kept hope alive and took the next right action.

To begin, I looked at what I loved to do, what really made me happy. I loved helping people find what they love to do, and I also loved helping staff and colleagues develop their skills and get promotions. Someone I hired at City Harvest is now its Executive Director and another of my senior staff became Executive Director of the South Jersey Food Bank. I fostered internal promotions and development opportunities. In fact, I used the "coach approach" to management.

Could I be a coach? Some years earlier I considered it, but wasn't ready to leave my job. I knew coaching worked: my coach of twelve years helped me be really effective during my years at City Harvest and New York Restoration Project. I started investigating that field on the Internet to see what kind of coaching was possible.

At the same time, I sought help from others with experience in career transitions. I joined a group in Maplewood, New

Jersey, called TransitionWorks, which helped me handle the emotional trauma of being fired and begin crafting a plan to transition from being a full-time employee to starting my own coaching practice. Eventually, I hosted "Monday Morning Get-Going Meetings" at my home and found myself guiding the conversation and coaching people informally. Through this group, I realized I wanted to help other people find their "right fit" work. Clearly, I empathized with people and could offer them support.

It all started to fall into place easily. My own track record in job searching and career development was substantial. I'd run human resources at two places, and hired and fired seemingly hundreds of people. I was well-versed in recruitment, hiring and staff development through my work building connections between job training programs and private sector employers when I was at New York City's Department of Employment.

As Executive Director, I gained a deep understanding of culture, leadership development and the critical role recruitment plays in achieving organizational goals. I endured and emerged successfully from seemingly endless job hunts, partly by using many career development tools (some more effective than others). I found my "right fit" work as a non-profit leader. I experienced the humiliation and dissonance of being fired. I knew coaching from both sides of the operation.

Soon I realized I needed both a little more training and a lot of practical experience. I began my career transformation coaching endeavor by placing one small notice on the TransitionWorks website offering free coaching to anyone willing to be my guinea pig. I offered it *pro bono* to learn "on the job." My first client was a woman in Brooklyn who received a forwarded message from someone in Maplewood. I haven't had to advertise since.

Over the past three years, I've built a part-time coaching practice based completely on referrals. I work almost exclusively by telephone and my clients live in New York, New Jersey, Chicago, California, Denver, Boston ... anywhere. Through my work with people in all kinds of fields, I've learned about manufacturing, the law, real estate, facilities operation, universities, telecom, technology and all manner of non-profits. I specialize in helping people get work in the non-profit sector. My past colleagues are excellent connections for my clients as they network. I'm blessed to be able to provide *pro bono* and very low cost coaching to people who otherwise might not be able to afford coaching.

Based on my own and my clients' experiences, I've developed a comprehensive and effective approach and tool kit for people to find and get their "right fit" work. Prior to the economic meltdown, all of my clients got work that was the "right fit." Even today, my clients are getting interviews and consulting jobs. And so far every person has found or is finding their purpose.

The coaching has led to many offshoots. I share my experience, skills and knowledge through my blog "JulieAnnErickson: YOUR ON-LINE CAREER TRANSFORMATION COACH." Through Twitter, I've become a Twitter Career Expert through Careerealism's T.A.P. (Twitter Assistance Project). This gives me a chance to help people all over the world, and to keep learning from the best career experts. I'm completing a book and workbook that captures my approach. I just finished a seven-week workshop and am planning to create a teleseminar to reach people through the web. My next steps include expanding my support team beyond my coach, chiropractor and writing group to include a virtual assistant.

Today, I can't imagine going back to traditional work. After such major upheaval, I found my next "right fit" work by following my purpose and passion, and creating my own enterprise. There are so many amazing possibilities ahead of me; the hard part is deciding what to do next!

Julia Erickson

KEY SUCCESS FACTORS: Being True to My Purpose, Practicing, Taking Action, Looking for the Positive, Providing Value, Generosity, Adaptability, Technology

RECOMMENDED BOOK(S): *Growing a Business* by Paul Hawken, *Transitions: Making Sense of Life's Changes* by William Bridges, *The Artist's Way: A Spiritual Path to Higher Creativity* by Julia Cameron, *Leading Without Power* by Max De Pree, *The 7 Habits of Highly Effective People* by Stephen R. Covey

WEBSITE: www.julieannerickson.blogspot.com

SOCIAL MEDIA: Twitter—juliaerickson, Facebook—julieerickson, LinkIn—juliaerickson, BLIP–juliericks

EDITOR'S NOTES: Julia lives in Maplewood, New Jersey, a wonderfully progressive and diverse community west of Manhattan. She lives next door to her twin sister and her family and dotes on her nieces and nephew. Julia has two cats, and enjoys writing poetry and fiction.

It is a mistake to suppose that people succeed through success; they often succeed through failures.

—*Author Unknown*

SERIAL ENTREPRENEURSHIP: DAYDREAMS TO REALITY

Jennifer Mizak—"We can't sign it. Our new parent company doesn't want to go in that direction." On hearing that, my stomach hit the floor—$42 million and an exciting future developing and marketing more effective, less toxic medical device products had just crashed out of existence. This was the "what now" moment every entrepreneur dreads.

Growing up in rural Connecticut, I sat in class daydreaming about running an international company. In my mind, there I was … chatting away in several languages, confidence coming from every pore and the feeling of success making my blood sing. Across the aisles, my peers were obsessing about the cutest boy in school. I'm not sure what happened with those girls and the cutest boy, but I got to be an entrepreneur … more than once. Chalk one up for teenage strategic planning!

I always worked—whether it was for my father as a youngster, or in retail as a teen. Both of my parents were (and are) business owners. Work ethic and strategizing how to achieve a goal were instilled in me at a young age. I don't think it's an accident that so many entrepreneurs have parents who were self-employed. I think it may be that our brains are hardwired at the dinner table when we're kids. But I also believe it's possible for anyone without this background to become a successful entrepreneur.

"Do what you love" has always been a guiding principle in my life. I don't ever remember thinking any other way as a youngster. As

I completed my undergraduate degree in fashion design, I discovered that I was much more interested in visual and written communication. Since more student loans weren't an option for me, I looked for a creative way to obtain further education in communications. I discovered that by working for a university I would be able to complete my master's degree without increasing my debt. After receiving my M.S. in communications, I began freelancing (designing and writing a direct mail newsletter for a small local company) while looking for a full-time job.

I settled at a Fortune 500 company where I worked on my business writing craft—creating sales proposals, marketing collateral materials and internal corporate communications. Eventually, I reached the point where the writing became repetitive and I wanted to learn new skill-sets. I spent another two years at the company exploring the role of management and how businesses implement change. While I had always worked with individuals at all levels of the organization, I learned more about making good business decisions and building cross-functional teams with the best people available.

When I left to join a three-year-old medical device company as Director of Marketing and Communications, my friends thought I was nuts. What about the risk, they asked. Well, what about it? I was employee number three, and quickly learned that an entrepreneur's life can feel like a roller coaster ride. But boy, the energy feels great! We developed a way to modify a certain molecule, and had created a prototype injectable wrinkle filler product. When the $42 million contract fell through the team was unable to raise the necessary bridge funding, which stopped the company in its tracks.

Just because we didn't become millionaires from that venture, I never considered it a failure. I learned a heck of a lot about starting and running a company, and that has helped me immeasurably with my latest business. Serial entrepreneurs—folks like me who just can't stay away from it—realize that you learn from *every* experience.

I thought to myself, now what? I was a new homeowner with major house repairs in a new area. Local jobs in my field didn't pay that well, but there were plenty of businesses. Besides, why should I be an underpaid employee when I could be working for myself? It would mean hard work, but I was no stranger to that. There were, however, two major challenges I needed to overcome. First, I didn't know anyone in my region and second, I was painfully shy and terrible at networking; I often became tongue-tied at the first opportunity. These issues would certainly make it difficult to get clients.

I found that our local Chamber of Commerce had about five thousand members—looking at those numbers, I thought joining would be the way to go. I also knew I needed some serious help with the challenge of being shy, and was lucky to find a free Chamber-offered mentoring program. My mentor helped me overcome my lifelong "wallflower syndrome" by working the room with me at several events. The more people I met, the more I realized that they shared the same feelings, likes and dislikes. I found it effective to ask a person what they did before they had a chance to ask me. By giving of myself—listening and learning about the other person—they give back by asking me what I do and showing genuine interest, making networking and relationship-building a great deal easier. I've found that the art of selling is about building trust and relationships. I'm no longer fearful of the sales process since I've already jumped the first hurdle by building the relationship with the potential client.

For business owners at all stages, support groups can help bring your business to new heights. Knowing that, I joined a group of business owners that help each other brainstorm ways to solve problems, look at situations differently, offer support and new ideas, make each other accountable and challenge one another to set and meet new goals. They're the advisory board that helps keep the business focused on the future.

Today, as a self-employed business writer and marketing consultant, I work with clients to craft concise, highly-targeted B2B and B2C communication materials, which allow them to meet and exceed their business goals. I often assist clients who have a marketing plan, but can't seem to execute it. I create all types of communication materials including: website content, video scripting, direct mail and online sales and marketing communications, newsletters, training materials and grant writing.

Balance is important in an entrepreneur's life. You need to work on your business and for your business. It takes both to be effective. Working *on* your business involves promoting your business, attracting clients and developing relationships. Working *for* your business means completing projects to get a paycheck. You have to work on your business *and* for your business to ensure success.

I would encourage entrepreneurs to: 1) Do the thing that is hard for you—you'll find out it may not be as difficult as you believe; 2) It's OK if you have bad days—don't beat yourself up—move forward; 3) Work on self-discipline; 4) Don't let paralysis by analysis set in; 5) Don't get stale—keep up-to-date in your field; and 6) Maintain balance in your life.

Jennifer Mizak

KEY SUCCESS FACTORS: Work Ethic, Relationships, Customer Service, Perseverance

RECOMMENDED BOOKS: *Think and Grow Rich* by Napoleon Hill

WEBSITE: www.LMwrite.com

EDITOR'S NOTES: Jennifer Mizak lives in Allentown, Pennsylvania, with her significant other. He is also an entrepreneur. She is President of LM Group LLC, a business writing and marketing consulting firm focused on providing targeted communications to businesses, local government and organizations. She works with clients from all over the United States from her home office. When not communicating the benefits of her clients, she travels as far away as she can, reads and renovates her home.

Don't be discouraged. It's often the last key in the bunch that opens the lock.

—Author Unknown

STRIP MALL SURVIVOR

Linette Shepherd—I thought I had a great retail idea that everyone would love. When I opened the doors to my shop, I thought I was offering something of value, that I had a bona fide money maker on my hands. I wondered how I'd handle the rush of customers.

I didn't need to worry. That first day, I made $20. A month later, I was only up to $50. That wasn't paying the rent, and it certainly wasn't paying me a salary. Being an entrepreneur has taught me one thing above all else: patience.

I started working when I was fifteen. In high school, I took various summer jobs, including working in my dad's accounting office. I worked with Dad long enough to learn that it was better to work for yourself than someone else. During my college years, I worked at a membership warehouse store, which was fast-paced and unrelenting. Every two minutes I was greeting a new customer. After seven stressful years of working there, it finally dawned on me that I don't like working with the general public.

After I graduated from college, I took a job with a physician contracting practice as the office manager and head of provider relations. In that job I used my organizational skills to stay on schedule and I enjoyed managing staff and negotiating contracts. Working in a professional environment was a step in the right direction, but it still had its challenges.

Then, life as I knew it came to a screeching halt when I had twins. I planned to be a stay-at-home mom to my girls, enjoying every single second of their development. What I hadn't planned on was missing work so much. I was stir-crazy and unfulfilled at home. It didn't help that where we were living at the time, Tucson, was so hot we were more often than not stuck in the house. I knew I needed to do something else, I just didn't know what. That's about the time inspiration struck.

We didn't have a lot of money back then, and I was very frustrated at how expensive children's clothing was. I couldn't believe it cost me $70 to buy two pairs of shoes for my girls. I started shopping at a children's re-sale shop where I could buy gently used shoes for $5. It occurred to me that there might be a market for this type of shop in my hometown of Reno, Nevada.

I knew we'd be moving back to Reno after my husband finished his medical residency, and I didn't recall a similar shop there. So, for the rest of time that we lived in Tucson, I paid attention to the placement of the clothes in the shop, to the pricing, to the stock. I also talked to the owner. She bought into a national franchise that required $100,000 to start and an additional $50,000 liquidity for inventory. I thought I could do a lot with that $150,000 and decided a franchise wasn't for me.

When we moved back to Reno, I started looking for a location. I knew I wanted my shop to be centrally located near a big draw. I found space in a strip mall next to a grocery store. I negotiated a three-year lease, obtained a business license, thought up a name (The Purple Pumpkin) and convinced my mom to go into business with me.

Initially I was just going to build up inventory by buying stock as it came in. My realtor had other ideas and put me in touch with a woman who had purchased fixtures and inventory to open a similar store in the area. She had just been diagnosed with cancer and was looking to sell. I was able to buy everything I needed to open my doors for $9,000.

We were off and running, but no one knew we were there. I sent out postcards announcing the store to residents in the surrounding area. I also put money into a radio commercial and newspaper ads. The best advertisement, however, was in a free pamphlet for products and services geared toward moms. It amazed me that for all the money I spent on radio and newspaper, this free pamphlet gave me the biggest return.

I planned to offer folks either cash or store credit for items they brought in for re-sale. I had assumed my customers would be parents wanting to get the best bang for their buck by opting for store credit. I was wrong. There was a surprising number of people who simply wanted cash for whatever they could sell. I knew I needed to change my policy when a young man brought in a bassinette for cash. When I looked outside, I saw a car full of young guys waiting for him. I hoped he hadn't kicked his kid out of the bassinette in order to get some cash to go out with his friends. After two months of feeling like an ATM, I decided to move to a store-credit-only policy.

I steadily built my customer base over the next three years. When my lease was up, I wanted to lower my rent and tried to negotiate with the landlord. I was a model tenant, always paid the rent on time and was beginning to see modest success. The neighborhood had really gone downhill since I opened the shop and I felt like I should have some bargaining room. The landlord wouldn't budge. I learned later that the land had been sold to a casino, so the landlord wasn't willing to put money into the development and certainly wasn't going to budge on the rent. In my experience, strip mall landlords are notorious for making tenants sign personal guarantees for the life of the lease. If a business fails, that owner will have to pay the rest of the rent out of his or her personal finances. I knew I didn't want to renew a lease with a landlord unwilling to negotiate in an uncertain neighborhood.

As I considered a move, I noticed that a lot of my customers had been talking about Trader Joe's. It clicked that there was some sort of correlation between a re-sale shop and that particular grocery store chain. So, I sought out a location as close to Trader Joe's as possible. Since the move, our profit has increased every year. We've never gone down in sales. I don't know if that's due to the shift in location, or just increased word of mouth, but the move certainly didn't hurt us.

My lease is up this year, and I've decided to move on by putting The Purple Pumpkin up for sale. The thrill of starting this business is gone. I enjoyed the challenge of getting it up and running, but now every day seems the same. I thought by the fifth year that I'd be able to fully staff my store, but I never earned enough to be able to do that. Now I'm back in a position where I'm dealing with the general public day in and day out—reminiscent of my warehouse days.

I'm also tired of being the last to be paid. The landlord, the utility companies ... everybody down the line has their hands out and if there's no money left, I don't get paid. If you have a job, you'll get paid. If you have a business that's generating a lot of money, you're probably making more than you would working for someone else. If you're running a small business, there are times you are not making money. In fact, you're probably pouring money into your business to keep it afloat.

Fortunately, being a mom has helped me weather the tough times; when you have kids, you learn some things aren't worth fretting over. When you have a business, you learn that there are way too many things to fret over to get stuck on any one thing.

During my time as a strip mall business owner, my eyes have been opened to the importance of small businesses. America is built on small businesses, but most people don't know how much work goes into running one and how little margin there is for error—whether it's a sluggish economy or a big, shiny new national chain that moves down the street. My friends don't understand that when they shop at discount chains and don't go into local stores every once in a while, they're decreasing their options. I'm more sensitive to that now. Before I would go to the big box stores and do my shopping. Now I shop at a local toy store and a little independent shoe store. I can't do all my shopping at locally owned stores, but I do try to support them when I can.

I'm hoping to now take some time off to find my next venture. Maybe I'll start another business. I suspect my personality is better suited to buying and selling businesses rather than sitting behind a counter minding the store. As a business owner, I've enjoyed having control over my ideas and the freedom to implement them and see if they work. Having a flexible schedule as a mom has also been great.

Whatever sort of business I try next, there's one big requirement … it can't be in a strip mall!

Linette Shepherd

KEY SUCCESS FACTORS: Perseverance, Patience

RECOMMENDED BOOK: *Why We Buy: The Science of Shopping* by Paco Underhill

EDITOR'S NOTES: Linette Shepherd lives in Reno, Nevada, with her husband, Scott, and her twin girls, Alyssa and Kylee. She graduated with a bachelor's degree in business marketing from the University of Nevada, Reno. A self-described adrenaline junkie, Linette took up competitive dirt bike racing a few years ago. Since "regular" exercise is too boring, she's thinking of taking up fencing. She enjoys traveling with her family and thinking up new entrepreneurial ideas.

No one can make you feel inferior without your consent.

—Eleanor Roosevelt

UNITED WE ROAR

Lillian Cauldwell—I am a peon and proud of it! We peons keep everyone else looking good.

I own a radio station that provides a conduit for voices that are otherwise not heard. The motto of the station is "Voices of the People—United We Roar." I am firmly convinced that if you get enough of us peons together, we can make a difference—just as it was with Joshua and his battle of Jericho where drums, horns and the cries of the people brought down walls.

My father was a corporate executive who had offices in four or five major cities overseas. He was decidedly not a peon. He used to tell me that without the corporate executives, we wouldn't last long. I told him he had it all backwards. If "lowly people" (I was a secretary at the time) didn't answer his phones, make his reservations, do his typing, take down his dictation, keep things organized and moving and go out and walk his dog, he would be in trouble. My father didn't argue with me after that. I knew back then that the peons kept the cogs turning.

My life changed considerably when I got remarried and was diagnosed with systemic lupus. I spent the first two years of my new marriage in and out of the hospital. I couldn't go back to my former way of life working long hours. It was clear that I had to think of something else.

My husband suggested that I write about something I knew. What I knew was how to deal with a teenager since I was in the process of raising my son. So, I wrote a book from a mother's perspective. I sent it out to several publishers and had interest from one. We ended up selling about three to four thousand copies, and *Teenagers: A Bewildered Parent's Guide* eventually was listed as one of the top ten books for that year from the publisher.

To promote the book, I spoke a lot on radio and television, learned how to field questions and think on my feet. I also learned how to be cautious when speaking to people. Adults especially can be very sensitive when speaking about their parenting. My son was fifteen and had long hair. He was also an artist, and his clothing was usually indelibly inked. I learned that it was more important to win the war versus each battle and that it's okay to lose a battle every once in a while. After all, if you get upset all the time over the small things, what are you going to do when your child comes home with news like, "How would you like to be a grandma?"

When I was doing the rounds with my book, people kept saying that my subject matter was well suited to radio. To get on radio, however, you need to know people, or have a degree. No one would hire me, let alone put me on a show, and I wasn't going to spend thousands of dollars to go to broadcasting school.

So instead, I became an entrepreneur. I self-published my historical science fiction book, *Sacred Honor*. While being an author might not seem entrepreneurial, I quickly discovered that if I wanted to have my book read around the world, then I needed to promote and market it. Since I published this book myself, I couldn't take advantage of the traditional marketing route I used for my first book. I believed the fastest and most cost effective way to spread the word about *Sacred Honor* was via the Internet.

Fortuitously, an Internet talk radio station contacted me and asked if I would be interested in becoming a guest on their program to promote my book. I would simply need to I donate a small fee; however the bigger the donation, the better chance that I would be heard. I donated fifty dollars for my book to be marketed and to be interviewed for sixty minutes.

Afterward, the host told me that I would make a good talk show host. He explained the process, and I signed on. I paid a fee for an hour's show where I interviewed other authors. I remained with this particular Internet talk radio station for one year and was told that I had thirty thousand listeners. When I switched to another Internet talk radio station, I discovered the first station owner had inflated my numbers when not a single listener followed me to my new Internet radio home.

The owner of the second station originally charged me a set amount for a month's worth of shows, but soon starting increasing his rates. I lasted six months. One day I interviewed a well-known and respected composer in the rock music business. He told me that I should run my own station because I would do a better job.

The first thing I did was homework to find out if it was possible. I went to the library, read books, studied a manual on how to run a radio station, spoke to a lot of people and poured over digital media to discover all the different types of Internet talk radio stations available to listeners. Once I collected all the information, I researched the broadcast software needed for an Internet/talk radio station. Next, I bought podcast software and contacted authors who wanted their voices to be heard.

I decided to spend a year doing talk shows to find out whether there was an audience out there for the type of programming I wanted to provide. Halfway through that test year, a talk show host convinced me to write a contract for my hosts to sign. I also put together my business plan.

I decided to call the company Passionate Internet Voices Talk Radio, Inc. (PIVTR) and based my company on three principles: 1) To market and promote published mid-list and unknown authors to the media; 2) To provide a conduit for voices not otherwise heard in this noisy sports-driven and celebrity world; and 3) To provide educational and quality content for the listeners to be used in their spiritual, personal and business lives.

Four years later, PIVTR is heard in one hundred seventy-eight countries. My largest targeted demographic audience is comprised of university and college students, followed by school districts and Fortune 500 companies. My listeners range in age from fifteen to ninety-one. PIVTR clears a thousand downloads a week. Not too shabby considering our marketing methods are by word-of-mouth, recommendation and referral.

I believe one of the biggest differences between my station and other stations is that none of PIVTR's hosts are syndicated or have doctorates after their names. They're not celebrity sports figures or former anchor folks. These are everyday people who have a story to tell. I'm saying, come to my station and tell your story and let's figure out how we make it possible for you to do your show. I learned from my work on other Internet radio stations that it was important to be honest and truthful at all times with my talk show hosts. If I'm going to get paid for offering them air time and streaming time, I have to make sure I am offering them something of value in return.

Based on my experience, I would advise an aspiring entrepreneur to not give up their day job until they have a business plan worked out. A marketing plan is also essential—you need to have a good idea of how you're going to get your product or service out to market. You've got to do your homework and then you have to really know what you want and where you want to go. You have to have vision and know that in a certain time frame you will have accomplished x, y and z. Then, focus on what you're good at and find your niche.

My focus at PIVTR is to enable our listeners to take what they need and immediately use what's applicable to them. I am thrilled that people are listening and like what they are hearing. Providing a mouthpiece for my hosts and uniting them with an audience is my way of letting the peons finally have their say. Now having found their voices, they are roaring.

Lillian Cauldwell

KEY SUCCESS FACTORS: Persistence, Passionate, Risk Taker, Flexible, Adaptable, Listener, Hard Worker

WEBSITE: www.pivtr.com

EDITOR'S NOTES: Lillian Cauldwell is CEO/President of PIVTR and Pod-cast Media Broadcast Services. She is also an award-winning author, speaker, media trainer, mentor, Long Story Short writing instructor and book reviewer.

Lillian believes a radio station should give back to the community and started radio-a-thons to raise money for charities. She has also started selling her broadcast feed and sending the proceeds to three charities on a quarterly basis. Lillian plans to expand PIVTR to offer free airtime to lesser known and unknown charities to raise money via a worldwide audience. Lillian also plans to establish an educational research and information databank where teachers, professors and instructors from all over the world will record and archive their lectures. When students want to conduct research, or they can't make it to class, they can visit PIVTR, and, for a membership fee, hear the lecture.

Pursue your dreams and outrun your fears.

—Ruth Lance Wester

OVERCOME FEARS, TAKE RISKS

Nancy Hyde—I learned about entrepreneurship from observing my father, stepfather and two grandfathers. They owned an architecture firm, a construction business and a grocery store. When I was in college, our family grocery store burned down. Even though the family business was not adequately insured, they rebuilt and kept the employees on, using up their cash reserves to do so. They survived and continued to run a successful business. Because this was still a time when few women were business owners, however, I was not given the opportunity to become an owner of the family business.

On the path to discover my own career, I started in college by using my abilities in math to study architecture. I then switched to commercial art. I finally landed on accounting when I learned it was a field where I could excel and earn a good living.

After college, I pursued a part-time job with the IRS. What an interview I endured! Four or five IRS managers all asked me difficult questions. They were important people, and I was scared of them initially. Once I was hired, the IRS provided the best training I could have ever received. My technical and communication skills developed quickly, but I greatly disliked telling taxpayers they owed more money.

I next took a job at a national accounting firm, BDO Seidman. My boss taught me what it took to have a quality accounting firm. He was a master at listening to clients, identifying their needs and solving their problems. He also believed in me, a young woman who was still very unsure of herself. At this time, there were very few women CPAs. I was working in a male-dominated profession. When I attended national training sessions, I would usually be the one woman present out of over a hundred attendees.

I left BDO Seidman to join a local CPA firm as a part owner. I was an owner of this firm in name only—the firm was controlled by one individual and never had enough money. I worked far less hours, had far less stress and made far less money.

One Friday an employee said to me, "Do you realize what the other owner is doing?" I spent the weekend looking through the records of the firm, and I saw that he had withdrawn large amounts of cash. I learned about clients he had traded out that owed the firm. This explained why so many of his clients did not pay their bills. This discovery was very shocking to me. I had not understood why working harder had made no financial difference. Now it made sense: he was draining the company of all funds he could.

I was advised the following Monday morning by my attorney to move out and take my client files with me. My husband did everything he could to support me. The whistleblower employee and two others joined me. When we moved out the following Friday night, I became the true owner of a CPA firm.

To build my business, I read, attended conferences, talked and networked with women business owners. I've now created a great firm with an even workload year round. We value time, efficiency, new technology and training. We work with clients to reach their financial goals and my clients have become my best friends. We believe in having cash reserves to withstand hard times. We are focused on becoming an employer of choice for employees. At this time, the emphasis is on developing the younger employees into successful well trained accountants. They will be the future owners of this firm.

I've also taken on leadership roles in accounting organizations. I applied for committees with the American Institute of CPAs and the Oklahoma Society of CPAs. Through the years, I served in many roles and was voted President of the OSCPAs. I was honored to serve on the Executive Committee of the AICPA for five years. My fellow CPAs chose me as the youngest woman member to be inducted into the Accounting Hall of Fame.

I recently taught thirty women entrepreneurs from Afghanistan and Rwanda to use their business plans successfully. I also hosted an Afghan accounting firm owner in my home and business.

Even though I was initially intimidated by running my own firm, one day I stopped fearing I would fail. I grew this business from four employees to nineteen in a little over seven years. I dreamed big, bought land and built a building, which we moved into in June.

I live by the mottos: "Be one who encourages, not afraid to take risks" and "to whom much is given, much is expected." I believe in giving back to others through my time, talent and finances.

Nancy Hyde

KEY SUCCESS FACTORS: Networking, Risk Taking, Work Ethic

WEBSITE: www.hccpas.net

EDITOR'S NOTES: Nancy Hyde is the President and Managing Shareholder of Hyde & Company. She earned a B.S. in accounting from the University of Central Oklahoma and passed the CPA exam at first sitting in 1975. Before starting her own business, Nancy worked for the IRS as an Auditor; then a Tax Supervisor at the International Accounting Firm of BDO Seidman CPAs; then CFO for Noble Operation, Inc.; Senior Tax Manager for the International Accounting Firm of

Grant Thornton CPAs; and the US Bankruptcy Court as a Court-Appointed Panel Trustee and Examiner.

She is actively involved with the Oklahoma Society of CPAs on the Small Firms Committee and is a Past President, Vice President, Director, Secretary and Past Chair of the Taxation Committee and the Nominations Committee. In 2003, Nancy was inducted in the OSCPA's prestigious Accounting Hall of Fame. Nancy is also a member of EWF International, an Oklahoma City-based organization offering professional and personal development for women business owners and executives. In 2007, EWF honored Nancy with the Entrepreneur of the Year award.

Nancy was recently honored as a 2010 Enterprising Woman of the Year and her firm was recognized as the 2009 and 2010 Oklahoma City Biz Readers Choice Accounting Firm. She is part of the Oklahoma City leadership team of the organization Peace Through Business

Nancy lives in Oklahoma City and serves others through encouraging her daughters, employees and other local and international small business owners by helping them define, set and reach their goals.

CHAPTER 9

INNOVATIVE AND DETERMINED

Some people dream of success ... while others wake up and work hard at it.

—Author Unknown

Every job is a self-portrait of the person who does it.
Autograph your work with excellence.

—Author Unknown

FROM NEAR DEATH TO THE BIRTH OF AN INDUSTRY

Sandy Gooch—My interest in natural foods was sparked after suffering from severe allergic reactions to antibiotics and chemical additives in food. Developing a profound allergic reaction to tetracycline frustrated me immensely and the only solution was to take action. This eventually led to my opening, what was at the time, the largest natural products market in the country.

I was raised by two idealistic parents who believed in excellence. Mother was legally blind and hearing impaired. She surmounted many obstacles with a determined "can do" attitude. My father was a research biologist and chemist and owned his own wholesale pharmaceutical company, E.L. Buckner Medical Supply Company, in Altadena, California. He sold a variety of medicines and was very familiar with the quality, function and viability of his entire inventory. He even had his own formulations of supplements and healing products manufactured by drug companies. Though young, I can remember the general theme of phone conversations he had with the doctors, dentists and veterinarians he served.

I loved visiting him in his office and warehouse. He was very proud of his selection process and his own line of private label formulations. I saw him send questionable merchandise back to the large drug manufacturers and suppliers. Dad's company was small, but he only wanted the highest quality products, including his own private label. Professionals respected him.

He was trusted. Those are the business standards by which I was raised and I never forgot them. I thought his degree of business and scientific integrity was incorporated in all businesses. Little did I know!

Decades later, I was gravely ill and trying to heal myself with the help of my father and his dedicated research. We both came to the conclusion that the food supply was compromised. For the most part, available foods in supermarkets were devoid of a full spectrum of nutrients and laced with chemicals in one form or another. The population was getting sick—and so was I. I threw everything out of my refrigerator and kitchen cupboards that had ingredients with -ic, -ite, or -ate at the end of it.

Out went anything with artificial flavor, artificial color, additives, preservatives or hydrogenated vegetable oils. Instead, I purchased foods that were designed for wellness: whole grains, meats, fish, chicken without hormones and real foods, organic to the degree that they were available in those days. I turned my life around and felt so healthy and enthusiastic.

As I experienced and read about what was happening to our food, I turned my anger into productivity by giving lectures about diseases that were fostered by a lack of nutrient density and an overabundance of preservatives. Folks would say, "Why don't you open a market that would sell the kinds of products you have been showing us? We can't find all the items you are educating us about in a single market or health food store." They were frustrated. So was I.

I quit my teaching job and joined forces with Dan Volland, who was the manager of a health food store, to open the first Mrs. Gooch's Natural Foods Market in West Los Angeles, California, in January 1977. At the time, it was the largest natural products market in the country. I developed criteria for product selection with the wise aid of my scientific father. After all, this criteria was helping to keep me alive. If it worked for me, why wouldn't it benefit others?

I can remember choosing a natural food distributor to be my major supplier. The owner scowled and shared that he felt I was a nice lady, but that if I didn't broaden my standards I would fail. Eighteen months later he took me out to lunch and said he was never so glad to have been wrong. For me, it was a validation to stay the course and hold on to my convictions.

I did listen to criticism when it involved things such as store design, employee dress, accounting procedures, better striping for the parking lot and a myriad of other observations people had. Over time, numerous positive, updated changes were made regarding the infrastructure. But the product standards were like a beacon to the community. That platform remained.

Over the next decade, new markets were launched in California in Hermosa Beach, Northridge, Sherman Oaks, Glendale, Beverly Hills and Thousand Oaks. At the store in Hermosa Beach—the second store we opened—customers were getting into fights in order to shop inside during busy times because it was so small, only five thousand square feet.

Thus, we closed it and opened a Mrs. Gooch's in Redondo Beach that was four times larger. The company was known as the torch bearer for the highest quality standards in the industry. In a time when quality issues plagued the supplements end of the industry, examining the culture that created those high standards was essential.

I gleaned information and was influenced by health book authors, health care professionals, industry organizations, customers, research scientists, other health food store owners, suppliers, educators, governmental leaders, chefs, environmentalists, color specialists, handwriting analysts, artists, technology and systems consultants, museum directors, designers, musicians, etc. My "holistic" knowledge base was continually being expanded and enriched. I did not want to be limited regarding the thinking and development of this new concept market. Mrs. Gooch's evolved, in part, because of the energetic input by a full spectrum of professionals from many fields.

The initial quality standards were in place from day one. As time went by, and new manufacturing processes and ingredients were incorporated in products, we would have discussions with staff in every department. We conducted inventory audits led by an attorney who specialized in FDA matters. Loren Israelsen was ever diligent as he reviewed product labeling, safety, ingredients used and manufacturing processes as it related to government regulations. When questionable products were observed, they were categorized. Loren's categories ranged from "definitely get rid of this" to "talk to the manufacturer to see if a specific desired change could be made." Sometimes manufacturers were very cooperative, sometimes they weren't. We didn't waiver once the products were discovered to have a problem, either with government-approved labeling or ingredients.

Additionally, staff conducted research to back up their recommendations about adding new standards or criteria for product or category selections. An example of this would be irradiation of food, which when we started the business, was nonexistent. Over time, the process was incorporated by some manufacturers. After conducting research, we decided to screen against irradiated products. The new food standard was added to our printed form for suppliers and informational handouts to the consumer. This review process happened quite a few times as new food technology and growing procedures came to the forefront. Eventually, our standards and product audits became known as "Goochable." Companies, nationwide, knew we had done our homework.

I was never in business to just "make money." That is very lineal. Money was the energy by-product of Mrs. Gooch's doing a great job. This did not preclude using prudence and fiscal responsibility in the business strategy. Too often, managers change direction only because they can have greater profit by incorporating the new idea. "What are the hottest selling products that we don't carry? Let's add them now." This is short-term thinking, not long-term strategy.

Reflecting back, what would I have done differently? I was a very trusting person. Today I would scrutinize key people in an organization and check out the validity of their statements and personal integrity more extensively. This is key whether you are hiring employees or investigating a manufacturer, supplier, broker, consultant or farmer. Business benefits by having a strong foundation of systems, products, service and marketing to name but a few. One of the strongest components of the foundation is reciprocal trust.

The Whole Foods Market acquired the Mrs. Gooch's chain in 1993. It was like losing my family. We had eight hundred and thirty employees I loved and adored. However, what is uplifting is that there are now a variety of natural foods markets throughout North America that have adhered to certain standards and are offering organic products.

Today my company, Sandy Gooch Enterprises, is involved in a variety of activities and has created a number of vehicles, from investment opportunities and property management to consulting within the natural products industry.

Sandy Gooch

KEY SUCCESS FACTORS: Standards, Research, Passion, Integrity, Reciprocal Trust

RECOMMENDED BOOKS: *The Power of Kabbalah* by Yehuda Berg, *Six Thinking Hats* by Edward de Bono, *The Power of Nice* by Linda Kaplan Thaler and Robin Koval, *Blue Ocean Strategy* by W. Chan Kim and Renée Mauborgne

EDITOR'S NOTES: Sandy Gooch is the President of Sandy Gooch Enterprises and a pioneer in the natural food store industry. Sandy was honored as 1992 Entrepreneur of the Year from *Inc.* magazine and Ernst & Young; Retailer of the Year 1990-92 from the *L.A. Business Journal*; and 1991 Woman of the Year from the National Organization for Women. She was the only woman chosen among "50 Visionary Leaders Who Transformed Food Retailing" in 2003 by *Supermarket News*.

The mayor of Beverly Hills designated a "Sandy Gooch Day."
In 2001 she was selected as one of The Leading Women
Entrepreneurs of the World by the nonprofit of the same name.
Her true legacy, however, is much more than the deserved
awards and recognitions she has received. Sandy Gooch sin-
gle-handedly created a culture and established what quality
means based on survival, dedication and standards.

In 1993, Mrs. Gooch's was the largest-grossing natural products market in the world. Sandy had seven stores, eight hundred and thirty employees and annual sales of $90 million.
In September, the company was acquired by Whole Foods
Market. The stock was eventually valued at $63 million.

Sandy lives in Marina del Rey, California, and donates her
time to many national and international women's issues organizations.

Note: This story was written based on interviews by Suzanne
Shelton, president of The Shelton Group, a boutique PR firm in
Chicago; and Shara Rutberg, a freelance writer from Denver.

All the so-called "secrets of success" will not work
unless you do.

—Author Unknown

SEVEN LANGUAGES TO ENTREPRENEURSHIP

L. Lloys Frates—My love of travel and pursuit of an academic career allowed me to attend language training and study abroad in a number of countries including Portugal, Brazil, South Africa, Austria and England. Before I really knew I wanted to be an entrepreneur, I had studied seven languages and experienced many different cultures.

My father is an attorney and my mother directed the launch of the Oklahoma Arts Institute, so I grew up with great role models with strong work ethics. I received my Ph.D. in history from UCLA and discovered that the career path for this degree was not a good fit for me. I felt the research burden would keep me from what I really aspired to do.

An opportunity to work in a business my brother and some of his friends had founded appealed to me, so I took a job at Renewable Resources Group (RRG) in Los Angeles, California. RRG is a firm that develops and invests in projects and technologies in the renewable energy, alternative fuels and sustainable water sectors. The timing was perfect because they were expanding their business and needed someone to lead an alternative fuels project.

This was never a path I envisioned for myself, but with the offer of becoming a principal of the company, I quickly learned a whole new business. It was exciting and terrifying. I took action doing what I needed to do to prepare myself, including enrolling in classes in accounting and finance. What I realized is that I had a skill set; I just needed to apply it to this situation. It turned out my research background was the key to my success.

The first three to four years were tough, and we had to take on consulting jobs to bring in money. The relationships we formed through the consulting jobs proved invaluable. We now have a group of fifteen people, seven of whom are principals. Timing is critical in any company, and we may have been somewhat ahead of our time in 2003. Now that new companies are entering this arena, we have the advantage of experience and education.

We also have investors who invest in specific projects. Recently, we purchased a sixty-eight-thousand-acre ranch with wind, water and solar potential. An organization approached us and wanted the wind property, so we sold thirty thousand acres. The other thirty-eight thousand acres are now under development for solar and water. Projects can run hundreds of millions of dollars, and the environmental hurdles take a tremendous amount of time and energy. We invest in renewable energy and sustainable projects all over the U.S., with the bulk of our projects in California, Nevada and Colorado.

Every entrepreneur encounters challenges, and one of the greatest challenges for me is letting go when a deal falls apart. I find myself emotionally invested after pouring my heart and soul into a deal. I am also not totally comfortable with the art of negotiation when I perceive conflict. Fortunately, these are strengths of some of the other principals.

We have a company culture of giving back, so we serve on boards and volunteer in various capacities. I am on the Board of the Los Angeles League of Conservation Voters. This is a group that backs the election of those who strongly support the environment. I am also a co-founder and Executive Board member of EndOil, an organization with members who are advocates to reduce our dependency on foreign oil.

Entrepreneurship has allowed me to control my own destiny, to have more flexibility and to create a world of my choosing.

The downside is that it can be really frightening, and I have never worked so hard in my life. If you like what you are doing, however, the hard work is worth it.

L. Lloys Frates

KEY SUCCESS FACTORS: Taking Action, Work Ethic, Education

WEBSITE: www.renewablegroup.com

EDITOR'S NOTES: L. Lloys Frates lives in Los Angeles, California. Lloys is a published author, has a Ph.D. from UCLA, has been a guest on various television and radio shows, and is the recipient of research grants, fellowships, and academic honors. Her academic service and training abroad have allowed her to study seven languages and experience the culture of Europe, Africa and South America.

Vision without action is a daydream.
Action without vision is a nightmare.

—Japanese Proverb

THE SPARK EFFECT

Linda Feinholz—"Jack, is there any reason we have the machines set up where they are? If we relocate them in a different order, I can get the work done in less time." I had waited days before bringing up my idea. I was eighteen and working for a friend of the family. Jack and his partners had left their employer and set up a competing records reproduction business that rapidly grew to $5 million in sales. My idea sparked changes in that business that reduced operating expenses and sped up client delivery by twenty percent, overnight. I began to understand that what I considered to be the obvious solution just wasn't so obvious to other folks.

My second suggestion to Jack resulted in a new line of revenue for his business. Clients were constantly asking for new copies of the documents but couldn't find their microfiche, so I proposed we offer to store the fiche. By adding simple storage drawers at our office, the company saved the time of sending our crew out to copy the originals again. We charged for the storage. Clients loved it and so did Jack's CFO.

As I planned my start in university, my father's cousin, told me not to rush to specialize—that the greatest value of a college education would be the access to all the ideas and subjects various professors had to offer. I confess I loved being told that by a man who had revolutionized the investment world by inventing the mutual fund and making himself and many other people multi-millionaires. I held that recommendation in the back of my mind because I had no idea what I was interested in. And I'll admit I felt overwhelming jealousy when others around me specialized, and I still couldn't figure out my own focus.

Nearing the end of my college course work, I was interviewing a forensic pathology professor—a member of the board
of advisors of the school's chamber music committee—for a
campus article. When I shared my admiration for the single-
mindedness of professional musicians, he countered, "Ah,
but I think you have the richer life ahead of you! You'll likely
change your focus every three to five years and look back on
a very interesting life with an amazing variety of experiences
professionally and personally." What amazing permission he
granted me with those words!

These three men weren't aware of it, but they were three of
the four mentors that triggered my entire professional journey.

My path has been composed of three elements over and over
again: a hunger for variety, a thirst for learning and an ability
to spot a new opportunity and take practical steps to bring it
to life. For some folks, these three characteristics feel like a
lack of focus. For me, they are the structure of my work and
my life. I've found that all I need to absolutely love the life I've
created are companions who share these values.

My entrepreneurial bent meant I wasn't a long-term fit for
working in a typical nine-to-five job. As a manager at a pre-
eminent medical center clinic, I discovered that I could turn
stalled operations around and have the entire staff loving it—
trim that budget, reorganize those procedures, hire and train
and manage staff, engage them in designing and implement-
ing continuous improvements that had them working together
ever more effectively and the physicians singing our praises.
I found myself sitting at my desk sort of hoping a little fire
would spark up that needed fixing. But no organization wants
an internal fire starter! I was getting a clear sign that I needed
to find a new way of leveraging what I was good at in a way
that didn't cycle back into boredom.

In the wonderful synchronicity of most of our life journeys, no
sooner does the obstacle arise, than so does the solution. At
lunch with several colleagues, I mentioned I was signing up for
extension courses in accounting and computer programming

to see what else I could do. A consultant working with our division looked me dead in the eye and said, "Don't. Don't do it. That's not who you are. You're a project-oriented problem solver. Go get an M.B.A. and start consulting." My fourth mentor had shown up with the final part of the formula.

Four years earlier I had been overjoyed to graduate, start working and stay far away from classrooms. And now I was being told to get back behind a desk and a pile of books. It was the last thing I wanted to do, and yet my colleague's argument was compelling, so I took his advice. I discovered that there was a wealth more to learn—new ideas on assessing what was awry; practical tools and measurable solutions to business issues; and philosophies, theories and techniques that cut through chaos and confusion like magic.

I began to recognize that I'm an alchemist.

Each course I took, each business magazine article I read, every conversation—all provided fodder for mixing—designing specific solutions that would be the perfect fit for the people I work with. Taking that new information and leveraging my own experiences in management, I began to develop a reputation for straightening out a business' culture and leadership priorities, its team's challenges and their personal distractions and obstacles.

As I completed my M.B.A. and headed into full-time consulting, I hit my stride with Fortune 100 companies. I loved every moment of the work but discovered that I couldn't stand big corporations' tolerance for living with obstacles and breakdowns. My latent entrepreneur got more and more impatient until the day I told a good friend, "I want to work with people who care passionately about their business and want to have it work better on Tuesday morning."

Have you noticed, there's nothing quite like making declarations? No sooner did I say that than the phone started ringing with referrals to small and mid-sized businesses whose owners and management teams were sick and tired of feeling stalled and wanted help now. I knew that if I accepted the gauntlet thrown down I'd be stepping into a heck of a challenge—my need for variety meant I wasn't prepared to name a niche, or declare a narrow solution or even an industry as my specialty. And that meant complicating my marketing and my role, never knowing where the next client would come from, never having a sense in advance of what the precise challenge would be that needed solving, nor how long any client engagement might last. My very real personal worries were whether I could tolerate having no predictable future income, and whether I could be more than a problem solver—I needed to become a marketer, too. I had to learn how to deliberately build relationships for the sake of business, not just pleasure.

All I was certain of was that I had to take the entrepreneurial path, step into the uncertainty, follow through with practical actions one at a time and find companions to support me just as I do for my clients. The spark effect kept igniting new opportunities. The referrals to clients showed up. The fear became faith. And I discovered my tolerance for the roller coaster of independent consulting.

My successes meant I had the luxury of complete control of my time, and I doubled my income while actually working one quarter as much time. I have had the time to learn new ideas and technologies, to join the boards of non-profit organizations and to make a difference in the community. I also took on mentoring younger consultants and start-up entrepreneurs, and have added coaching executives and solo professionals seeking new paths as well.

Entrepreneurship created an unanticipated additional advantage. In a single year, three of my family members were diagnosed with cancer. No organization would have been comfortable with the time demands I had to juggle. My independence meant that I had control of when I was with clients and when I was supporting my relatives through their challenges. The struggles actually lasted twenty-two months. Who could have imagined that?

The difference today? Modern technology has provided astounding new elements to mix together offering fresh ways of working with clients, by phone, by Internet, in groups and one-on-one. And an unexpected niche has shown up that I love. I've begun to redesign my business model so that I can work with many more people around the world who want to add six figures to their businesses. Whether they are running a business, or are solo entrepreneurs or professionals, I now show them how to repurpose their expertise by turning it into programs and informational products to use as marketing and products and services that create new, low-cost highly profitable streams of income.

Variety. Learning. Opportunity. Add the entrepreneurial spark to your vision and commit to practical high payoff actions that are aligned with that vision, and everything is possible.

Linda Feinholz

KEY SUCCESS FACTORS: Vision, Passion, Focus, Action, Perseverance.

RECOMMENDED BOOKS: *The Power of Full Engagement* by Jim Loehr and Tony Schwartz, *Transitions: Making Sense of Life's Changes* by William Bridges, *Mastery: The Keys to Long-Term Success and Fulfillment* by George Leonard, *Think and Grow Rich* by Napoleon Hill, *The Goal* by Eliyahu M. Goldratt, *The Tipping Point* by Malcolm Gladwell, *Blue Ocean Strategy* by W. Chan Kim and Renée Mauborgne, *SPIN Selling* by Neil Rackham

WEBSITE: www.LindaFeinholz.com

EDITOR'S NOTES: Linda Feinholz calls Los Angeles, California, her home. She is the founder of Feinholz, Inc., and is an accomplished consultant, coach, author and radio show host. When not designing solutions for leaders, business owners and entrepreneurs you can find her at the pond hand feeding her koi while her cat watches, or she's on an airplane exploring new places and visiting friends around the world.

*We plant seeds that will flower as results in our lives,
so best to remove the weeds of anger, avarice,
envy and doubt.*

—*Dorothy Day*

FUNK-DEFIED

Jessica White Pohlkamp—Six or so years ago I was sitting in the car with a girlfriend. Picture being stuck in traffic on a hot, sticky Midwestern afternoon. We had the air-conditioning blasting and the radio too. We were all gussied up en route to downtown Cincinnati for some summer food and fun. I pulled my cell phone out of my purse, and it was covered in make-up, dirt and grime. I began the pointless ritual of rubbing my cell on my shoulder, sleeve, pant leg and the standard thumb across the screen. This only smeared the grime across the phone and screen. I simply thought, "There has to be a better way." And "Wouldn't it be fun if I could wipe my phone off with something that smelled great too, like tropical piña colada or fresh berries?" My girlfriend and I giggled as I brainstormed flavors like bubblegum and cucumber melon. A light bulb went on over my head—click!

Later that week, I sat down at my dirty and dusty computer and recalled the cell phone dirt and grime debacle. I decided to do some research to find some scented cell phone wipes for my phone, laptop, camera or whatever else needed to be cleaned in my home office. To my sheer amazement, Google came up with empty cyber hands. The search engine brought me lots of bulky tubs of screen wipes, bottles of spray and microfiber cloths, wet/dry multi-step wipes and puffy pads that could be dangled from cell phones. None of these items fit my idea. I wanted a one step, portable wipe that was LCD safe. The kicker was that I also wanted a refreshing fragrance. I clearly recall the light bulb growing brighter over my head.

As a physical therapist, I began noticing that my co-workers would treat patients and then answer a text or call without washing their hands. I looked around the therapy room and found a huge tub of wipes for institutional use. They smelled awful, were really oversaturated, and I had no idea if they were LCD safe. The light bulb grew brighter and even began to glow! I wondered if I really was on to something. Could it be possible to invent something so simple like fragranced cell phone wipes? I wondered if I was missing something.

Back to the computer I went and search after search left me empty handed. I was so excited at the prospect of creating a fun, fresh cell phone wipe for me, my friends and my co-workers. But I didn't know where to start. I thought I had to find a cleaning solution and add fragrance to it, but how? I have a minor in chemistry from college, but I didn't know the first thing about mixing chemicals. My light bulb faded as the clouds of fear and lack of faith rolled in. The light bulb grew dim but never burned out.

A few years later, my in-laws, my husband and I were at our favorite Indian restaurant. My brother-in-law, Mark, set something on the table. It was a simple black cardboard box with a logo on it. He grinned from ear to ear like the Cheshire cat. I asked him what was in the box and he proudly exclaimed it was HIS new retail product: underglow lighting for furniture called "LIT." I opened the box slowly as if I was expecting a jack-in-the-box to pop out. I examined the contents, the box, the instructions, the neatness of it all. I can officially say the light bulb over my head turned into a meteor! I was furious with myself, but extremely proud of Mark. "That should be ME!" I exclaimed to my poor husband all the way home from the restaurant as I beat my fists on my knees.

The moment we arrived at home, I got on the computer and started feverishly searching for contract manufacturers that make wipes. Mark had asked me at the previous Thanksgiving why I didn't just call a manufacturer to see if they had fragrances in house and if it was possible to blend the solution for me. I was so scared someone would steal my idea that I remained paralyzed. With my new infusion of meteoric power, I finally stumbled onto a few leads. I contacted companies in California and China. Neither took me seriously, and it was a good thing they didn't. I had no business poking around in China. It would have been impossible to protect my intellectual property overseas as a newbie entrepreneur. And the company in California was too far away for me as well. I finally found a small company in the Midwest that actually called me back. I was driving to Put-in-Bay to watch Mark's band The Menus for the weekend when I received "the call." I gave my pitch like a teenager divulging five years worth of baggage and at the end of the query, I heard, "I think we can do that."

The process had officially begun! I chose berry, melon and piña colada fragrances for my wipes because they were commonly accepted candle and air freshener scents. I wanted a peel-and-seal multi-pack pouch because that was what was most commonly accepted by consumers. We tweaked and geeked and communicated for six months, submitting the wipes for LCD safety testing and making sure the wipes had adequate "scent transfer" onto the phone without being overwhelming. When we were finalizing the packaging concept the bomb dropped. My manufacturer said the fragrance in the wipes was "aggressive" and broke down the adhesive on the peel-and-seal, which would eventually render the seals useless and leave retailers with a short shelf life product and lots of product returns.

After I stopped belly laughing at the expression "aggressive fragrance," my belly started hurting because of the roadblock. What was I going to do? Zip it up! I decided to go with a front facing zipper lock and ended up creating the first wet wipes on the market with this packaging. It was risky, but consumers seemed to appreciate the freshness seal a zipper lock provided and we were back in business.

I got my first run of Berry Celly Smellys® in June of 2008; and after attending a tradeshow with fantastic feedback, we tweaked some design elements and rolled out all three fragrances by January of 2009, including Berry, Melon and Piña Colada. I decided to use a name like Celly Smellys® because I didn't want to be generic wipe number 584. I wanted to be unique and different.

I hired a representative and found a local distributor to warehouse and fulfill my product. I was able to nail down an electronics distributor to get my product into retail outlets and college bookstores. I also went to an expensive buyers' show, which allowed one-on-one meetings with retail buyers. I got a lot of great advice from the buyers' show, but virtually no sales.

At this point, Celly Smellys® are available on ToysRUs.com and Walmart.com, and are in over six hundred and fifty f.y.e. stores nationally and over one hundred college bookstores. My eventual goal is to expand Celly Smellys® to all major retail outlets.

Through my experience of bringing a product to market, I have learned not only what to do, but what *not* to do. For instance, targeting electronics buyers has been a tough road to travel. It seemed a natural progression to present my product to electronics buyers. I have always known my target market is teens, tweens and moms or more generally, anyone with a cell phone (four billion people globally). But approaching electronics buyers was not effective because the price point was not a match and neither was the merchandising. Electronics are expensive and most buyers did not want to deal with a lower price point item like Celly Smellys® even though it seemed like a relevant accessory. I learned how important it is for entrepreneurs to identify their niche and target market immediately. My advice is to identify a market and go after a distributor that offers both price point similarity and market relevance. Or more simply, don't try to shove a round peg into a square hole just because it looks good on paper. It has to make sense in the real world.

I also made the mistake of letting my rep advise me to buy an incredible amount of inventory to cover sales when she had not nailed down a purchase order. "I have a client that almost had Target but they didn't have the inventory so they lost the deal," she said to convince me. Well, in retrospect, I realize her client may not have been ready to deal with Target then. I also know a small business that actually requested to start small with Walgreens so they could prove they could do a good job. Walgreens eventually placed the product in all of the stores based on the focus of quality over quantity. In simple terms, many buyers and reps have subsequently advised me that all big box retailers know that purchases are made months ahead of time and sixty to ninety days for production time is standard. There is absolutely no need to buy an exorbitant amount of inventory without purchase orders to substantiate it. And if you don't have the resources, back-end office set up, or distribution to fulfill, then it is absolutely acceptable to grow at your own pace. As the cliché goes, Rome was not built in a day.

This leads me to my biggest nugget of advice. If I had gotten all of the big accounts that I thought I "needed" in the beginning, I would not have been mature or well-equipped enough to handle it. You have to know your product and business inside and out and if you don't, you'll be as transparent as rice paper. I use what my father calls the "tummy test." If it feels good in your gut, it's probably a good deal. If it doesn't, then it's not. This has saved me from many a sore mistake. Alternatively, the complete disregard for the tummy test has gotten me into plenty of trouble to the tune of over $100,000 in inventory that I couldn't sell initially just because I didn't listen to my gut. I bit off more than I could chew knowing fully it was not what was appropriate for my business.

Most importantly, I learned I don't have a wipes company that markets. I have a marketing company that sells wipes. Marketing is key!

Jessica White Pohlkamp

KEY SUCCESS FACTORS: Passion, Perseverance, Taking Action, Marketing

RECOMMENDED BOOKS: *Mommy Millionaire* by Kim Lavine

WEBSITE: www.cellysmellys.com, www.chickpreneur.blogspot. com

SOCIAL MEDIA: Twitter—cellysmellys, Facebook—celly-smellys

EDITOR'S NOTES: Jessica White Pohlkamp is a thinker and visionary. She is inspired by her husband because he is her "rock" and her family because they are an endless fountain of support. Jessica has a master's degree in physical therapy from the University of Cincinnati in Ohio. Her husband is a professional BMX racer and she uses his profession as an opportunity to market her product Celly Smellys®. Jessica has two cats, Houdie and Hammy. She works part time at a nursing home as she grows her start-up business.

Energy rightly applied can accomplish anything.

—Nellie Bly

THE ART OF E-COMMERCE

Jory Burson—Have you ever thought you would like to start a business if only you had enough money? I did it for less than $50. I repurpose broken computer keyboards into art, accessories and office supplies. I then sell the items I make on my virtual store, Jorydotcom's Epic Key Emporium at jorydotcom.etsy.com, for between $4 and $70 plus the cost of shipping. My expenses are almost negligible, which makes it so much easier to relax and enjoy what I do. And my website? The one I use is so easy, it could turn any hobbyist into an entrepreneur.

Although I've always enjoyed making just about anything with my hands, it has only been recently that I've discovered there is a market for the things I create. I didn't want to grow up to be a starving artist, so by the time I was in junior high I had given up on the idea of ever making art for a living.

In 2007, I graduated with a degree in broadcast journalism from Oklahoma State University. The job market in the broadcast industry was already slowing down, and my husband and I didn't want to move, so I made the decision to go to graduate school. For those of you who've gone to graduate school, you no doubt remember how hard it is to concentrate on graduate work and have time for much of anything else. It wasn't long before the research papers wore me down—I couldn't remember what it was like to do something fun for myself.

One day, I found an online thread of digitally altered pictures of items made from unconventional materials. One of the pictures really stood out to me: a purse made out of computer keyboard keys. I wondered why such an item couldn't be made in "real life." I decided right then to make one. My husband's former boss and friend happened to have about thirty keyboards that were just going to be thrown away, so he agreed to give them to me. I cleaned them, bought some black fabric, and about thirty hours later I had a purse made from computer keyboard keys.

Of course, I didn't finish it in one sitting. I had to work on the purse when I had spare time during the weekends. But as I worked on my project, I thought about how much I looked forward to seeing it completed and how happy and content it made me feel just to sit and make something by hand. I thought about all the electronic waste our culture creates and how hard it is to recycle those electronic components. The more I thought about it, the more need I saw for repurposing old electronic materials in new ways. By the time I completed the purse, I had thought of several other items to make from my leftover computer keyboards, and I haven't stopped since.

Shortly after I created my purse, my friend Clint told me about Etsy.com, an e-commerce site where people can buy and sell handmade items—like a virtual farmers' market exclusively for artists and craftsmen. Etsy.com handles all of the e-commerce data for a small listing fee of twenty cents per item. All I had to do was create my own shop on the website and fill it with pictures and information about each of my items. That's it.

I've been an Etsy.com shopkeeper since September 1, 2008, and it didn't take long before I got my first sale—a lady in upstate New York bought a refrigerator magnet set. Then a man in Houston bought a painting with an eight-bit style character from Super Mario Brothers. Another piece of art went to a man in Canada. Push pins to Chicago. Picture frames to Boston. And so it goes.

It continually amazes me how I can target people all across the country with so few resources. It wasn't long ago that craftspeople who wanted to sell to customers outside of their region had to travel all over the country and hope that their prospective buyers had money to spend when they got there. To be an artist was to sentence oneself to a life of poverty, or barely scraping by. When America went online in the 1990s, it became easier for artists to showcase their work to a wider audience. Rather than rely solely on their gallery fronts or touring craft shows, artists could identify potential buyers through forums and user groups without leaving home and without much expense. But despite the widened exposure the Internet provided, it still wasn't easy to make a sale. It was (and still is) expensive to process online payments. Without the technical know-how, it's difficult to do it yourself and easy to be taken advantage of by scamming opportunists. This, combined with the skeptical attitude most people had about online purchases, made it hard to make money online. Until now, anyway.

Etsy.com is one of several places an aspiring artist can go to start selling his or her work, without any significant computer know-how. Can you type? Take and upload a picture? Click a few buttons? Then you can sell your services and items online. These days, it takes more effort to update and maintain a Facebook or MySpace page than it does to make a sale online. Social networking is a great way to share what you do with people—for free. And if you're already hooked up on social networking sites, then you're halfway to having a business. Many sites have virtual marketplaces that reach millions of people, one or two of whom are bound to like your work. Never before has it been easier to turn your hobbies and talents into something profitable.

I knew the items I made would be very appealing to the young, computer-programmer set, but there aren't that many people who fit that description where I live. But thanks to Etsy.com, it doesn't matter. I'm only limited by time and my creativity. In the interest of full disclosure and honesty, this is not something I currently do full time to pay the bills. In fact, in less than a year of business, I've only made a few hundred dollars— not enough to pay my mortgage. But for something I do as a hobby, it has been an excellent way to supplement my income while finishing grad school.

In addition to teaching me some basic business skills, Jorydotcom's Epic Key Emporium has kept me thinking passionately and creatively about business, and life in general. I make money with a few broken keyboards and some spare time, just for fun. What can you do?

Jory Burson

KEY SUCCESS FACTORS: Creativity, Passion

RECOMMENDED BOOKS: *The Tipping Point: How Little Things Can Make a Big Difference* by Malcolm Gladwell

WEBSITES: www.jorydotcom.etsy.com and www.thestoryofjory.com

EDITOR'S NOTES: Jory is a freelance photographer and videographer. She lives with her husband, Tanner, and dog, Ein, in Stillwater, Oklahoma.

CHAPTER **10**

ADVENTUROUS, DARING AND HIGH ON LIFE

Adventure is worthwhile.

—Amelia Earhart

*The key to realizing a dream is to focus not on
success but on significance—and then even
the small steps and little victories along your path
will take on greater meaning.*

—Oprah Winfrey

BUILDING PEACE THROUGH BUSINESS IN DEVELOPING COUNTRIES

Terry Neese—As I stood in the midst of barren mountains and a land stripped of plush greenery, weighted down by my fifty-pound flak jacket, I found myself filled with humility and fear. I understood in that very moment what it meant to be thankful. A glance to the left—a figure draped from head to toe—what I could only assume is a woman. A glance to my right—a snapshot from a children's Bible—buildings with archways constructed of mud brick and stone the color of creamy sand. Reality hits: I am in Afghanistan. I am on a mission to help women entrepreneurs in this country.

I closed my eyes for a moment, and I flashed back to my twenty-something self making my way into the working world. It was the 1970s in Oklahoma City, Oklahoma, and I was working at a personnel agency, feeling underappreciated and overworked. The business was broke, and I was the only one left on staff; I was practically running the place, but I had no control and no reward. Like a light bulb switching on, I realized what I needed to do: open my own business and run it ... *the right way.* I had no money and no clue how to find money, but that didn't stop me. I was determined because I loved the staffing industry—I loved helping people. This was my passion.

Passion wasn't going to cut it though. I knew I couldn't do this without focus and hard work, which also meant I had to be resourceful and practical. A year after renting an office space, I worked the deal of a lifetime. In 1976, I bought my own building, financing the purchase through the building's owners—a dream come true. But six months later, that dream turned into a nightmare.

Strike One

I remember it as though it were yesterday. I was sitting at my desk, and I swiveled my chair to look out the window, only to find the pointy teeth of a backhoe chomping down on the pavement, gobbling up the road to my building's front doors. I soon discovered the city was turning the road in front of my office into an interstate.

Thoughts starting racing in my head as the fury was swelling: How did I not know about this? Why did no one bother to tell me—no, better yet why didn't they *ask* me?! How would my clients get to my office? As it turns out, the answer to that question was that women had to walk four blocks in their high heels … in black, sticky tar. Not exactly a red carpet entrance. After two and half years with no direct access into my building, and having not read even as much as a headline in the newspaper, I soon coined my motto. "If you run a business and aren't involved in politics, then politics will run your business."

Strike Two

Finally, there was direct access to my front door, even though it was from a one-way frontage road. I couldn't believe I had made it—I had even managed to keep all my staff. I had also begun to network with fellow businesswomen in my community and joined associations, such as the National Association of Women Business Owners (NAWBO). I was building my client base and generating more business. The road ahead (one-way and all) was looking bright.

Two months later, our office building burned down—a disaster invoked by kids with too much time on their hands. This was still in the pre-computer days, so all of our files were lost: client histories, employee information, account-receivables and so much more. There was no way to know who owed me money, and I quickly learned that people don't send you a friendly IOU reminder.

I was devastated. How in the world were we going to recover? But my passion, hard work and focus all began to work together, and within twenty-four hours, I had the phones up and running. I asked a business owner two doors down if he would let us set up temporary shop. We hauled the burned furniture to the donated space. A combination of cinder blocks and charred wood transformed into our make-shift desks. This was no time for vanity or pride.

Three Strikes ... And I Still Wasn't Out

After the fire, the spirit of Oklahoma truly rose to the occasion; business miraculously quadrupled within six months. Business was booming bigger than ever ... that is until the oil and gas bust of the 1980s. Not surprisingly, Oklahoma firms were hit hard; suddenly there were no jobs to offer. Employers who had been looking for employees were now the ones looking for jobs. But I just had to keep pressing on: I put my blinders on and continued forth, and quality somehow outpaced quantity.

As I joined more associations and got more in tune with what was happening in my community and my government, I attended the White House conference on small business in 1986 as an elected delegate from Oklahoma. I was the voice for Oklahoma small business owners in our nation's capital. A whole new world was opened to me—a world of power and a way to make a difference. And that's when my passion started to evolve from helping people through the personnel agency to helping people on a much larger scale—through public policy.

As my daughter stepped up to the plate to run the business, I pursued my new passion. In 2001, I decided it was critical that an organization be formed to be the voice for women business owners in our nation's capital, so I co-founded the largest women's advocacy group, Women Impacting Public Policy (WIPP), to do just that.

After learning that most businesswomen didn't have the first clue about public policy, I founded the Institute for Economic Empowerment of Women—a 501(c)3—whose mission is to economically, socially and politically empower women through education.

Soon, that mission statement grew to empowering and educating women on a worldwide scale. In 2006, I was approached by the White House and the U.S. State Department to create a meaningful business education and mentorship program for women in Afghanistan. At first, I couldn't believe what I was hearing … why would I help women all the way in Afghanistan when women here on the home front were struggling?

Still not one hundred percent sure why I had agreed to create this program, I traveled to Afghanistan with the State Department as a member of the U.S.-Afghan Women's Council. And it all became so clear. Standing on the ground in Afghanistan, as I reflected on my journey as a woman entrepreneur and what I thought to be insurmountable obstacles, I got a big reality check. Yes, I faced challenges as a business woman: I had no money to start up a business, I had no place to locate my office, I had no entrance into my business for two years, I had everything destroyed. But I had my freedom. As a citizen, and as a woman, I had my independence.

I didn't hear bombs exploding in the streets. I didn't worry about whether I would make it home alive or not. Not only did these Afghan women share the same business obstacles I had, but they were also living in a war zone, under the constant threat and fear of militants and radicals. Talk about passion, hard work, focus and sheer guts.

And so the Peace Through Business program was born. The program provides long-term business training to women entrepreneurs from Afghanistan and Rwanda. Since 2007, we have directly educated more than one hundred women in both countries. Our students attend an intensive eight-week business class in Afghanistan and Rwanda, and then thirty women are selected to travel to the United States for further training and leadership development. We also match each student with an American woman business owner with whom she lives and works for a full week.

Our philosophy is two-fold: if you educate a woman, you educate a nation. And secondly, a country that is economically sound has a greater capacity for peace. As these women grow their businesses, they are helping put their countries on the road to economic freedom and peace.

There's nothing more important to me, as an entrepreneur, than to pay forward my blessings, which is what Peace Through Business is all about. While we reach a handful of students through our program, our students reach masses by paying forward their education.

It's hard to say what the future holds, because I never thought I'd be where I am today. Plans to expand Peace Through Business into more countries and to develop a domestic business training program are already in the works. But no matter what I do, I do know this: in order to remain successful as an entrepreneur, I have to keep my family first, my passion alive, deliver on my word, stand by my ethics and abide by the Golden Rule. The rest will all fall into place.

Terry Neese

KEY SUCCESS FACTORS: Passion, Hard Work, Focus

RECOMMENDED BOOK: *How We Lead Matters: Reflections on a Life of Leadership* by Marilyn Carlson Nelson

WEBSITE: www.ieew.org

EDITOR'S NOTE: Besides being an entrepreneur, Terry is also a pilot and a member of the Ninety-Nines, an international organization of women pilots. Terry is married to Earl N. Neese. Their daughter, Kim Neese, is CEO of Terry Neese Personnel Services and is the proud mom of Emily and Erin. They all reside in Oklahoma City, Oklahoma.

Anything not attempted remains impossible.

—Unknown Author

MOVING UP

Patricia A. Henriques—I never wanted to be an entrepreneur. And the last thing I thought I would ever do was be responsible for figuring out how to move the Pittsburgh International Airport *overnight*. But I did just that. I found a unique niche in the marketplace and became the best in the country.

I was always rather ambitious, and I think that was what ultimately drove me to start my own business. As the administrator for a large law firm in Washington D.C., I got to a point where I couldn't go any further and wanted more responsibility. I was pleased when the firm considered making me the managing partner. Unfortunately, some of the junior partners opposed it because I was not a lawyer and in the early 1980s, a non-lawyer rarely made managing partner. It became clear that the only way to enhance my income and career was to start my own business.

By that point, I had worked at the law firm for three years and had another ten years of experience with a bank, advertising firm and trade association. The diversity of my positions and industries gave me broad experience; I understood operations, logistics and finance. At the law firm, I had just finished moving one hundred lawyers into new offices without losing any business or billable hours–quite a feat by any measure. I did it by moving a section of the practice every six weeks for eighteen months.

The interior designer and general contractor for the project told me they had never seen such a seamless move and suggested I offer that service to companies. My experience taught me that moving a business was a very complex undertaking. I was convinced that we could provide clients value in two ways–by saving them money on the move itself and by maintaining firm operations throughout the process with no loss of revenue.

I did market research and wrote a business plan. Some family savings served as collateral to help me get a line of credit from the bank. I identified law firms as a target market and fortuitously, a group of lawyers decided to leave the same firm where I was employed. They became my first client and we co-located. I provided a part-time administrator for them and started Management Alternatives at the same time. I was off!

At first I spent a lot of time educating the marketplace on the value of our service and relied heavily on connections and relationships in launching and growing the business. Early on, a moving company I had used at the law firm referred me to one of their clients who needed eighty thousand square feet of furniture reallocated throughout their new space. The client happened to be General Electric (GE). I won that business—our first major move project—and wrote software to solve their problem.

The move was very successful, but not very profitable. Our client knew we had gone above and beyond and gave us a bonus to cover our direct costs, so it ended up working out. Even though the pricing was wrong, our valuable service to GE led them to refer business to us for the next six years. It also gave me the opportunity to reevaluate how we priced our services. I originally thought we could offer fixed pricing for our services, but found that didn't work. Each project was unique, which made pricing much more complex. Variables such as square footage, operational complexities and schedule all impacted price. I ultimately learned to provide pricing that allowed for shared responsibility–for us and our clients–in determining our fees.

One of the reasons we were so successful was that we kept our clients in business in spite of the disruption around them.

Our pitch: We provide the highest quality service during the project and leave at its successful conclusion without loss of income or revenues to our clients. Interestingly enough, administrators or office managers who are in charge of moving their firms often lose their jobs at the end of the project because the move proves so disruptive to the organization. It's very difficult to keep a firm operational during a move project, but that's what we did and that's why our clients liked us and were willing to pay for our service.

One of our internal challenges was finding qualified people to work for the firm. This was a new service, so no one was really qualified. It was not a family-friendly business either because it required work on weekends, so it was a challenge to find and train the best people.

The external struggle of convincing the marketplace and educating companies on our value creation was equally daunting. It was a new business and a new service. We looked at our client base and realized that real estate brokers, architects, designers and moving companies could help us secure business. The realtors were among the best referrals for us. They recognized our value to their clients—everyone has a move horror story—and eliminating that problem would translate into future business. So, they pitched their clients on our behalf and "warmed up" an otherwise cold sales call for us. Other related industries also realized this and we relied on this network as sales distribution channels for the company. These referrals continued to grow because we always delivered.

I had been growing the company since its inception in 1983 and sailing along when the bottom of the economy dropped out in the early 1990s. At the time, the downturn seemed to last an eternity—I almost went out of business—but it probably wasn't more than a year long. Luckily, in the middle of it all, we won the contract to manage the move to the new Pittsburgh International Airport in 1992.

When we finished that job, the economy was turning around in Washington, D.C., and with the great press we got from moving the Pittsburgh airport, the business took off. We won the job to move one million square feet of the Pentagon in 1996 during its renovation. Being a woman-owned business was advantageous in the public sector; lots of federal projects followed.

A few years later, we landed the Sprint World Headquarters campus move, which was the largest commercial construction project in the country. Sprint moved fifteen thousand employees from fifty-eight leased buildings throughout the Kansas City area to a new two-hundred-acre campus. It was three million two hundred thousand square feet of office space in twenty-two buildings. In the last phase of the project, Sprint needed to consolidate once again, and we moved an additional one thousand people per week for sixteen weeks in a row. It was a monumental job and effort for us, but a resounding success.

I sold the business in 2002. I had identified a number of targets for an acquisition and rejected the low ball offers that came from some of them. Finally, the network served me well again: I was introduced to a major construction company that wanted to expand and diversify. It was a great fit and in six months we closed and I sold the company I had started twenty years earlier.

Now I am able to do more for my community. I have worked with my favorite organization, the Girl Scouts, for more than twenty years. I especially enjoy helping young women see that they have so many options in life. I regularly serve on community and corporate boards; I usually lead the strategic planning process for them or head up the finance committee. My passion is business, and I love to help organizations and entrepreneurs be better at business. The way that I decide to get involved in something is if I think I would enjoy the people– it's always about the people for me. I also mentor other entrepreneurs and look at businesses for investment.

The most important advice I would give to other entrepreneurs is that you need to understand your strengths and weaknesses, find others with the right skill sets to fill the gaps and build a high performance team. As entrepreneurs, we need to have courage. We can't be afraid to ask for advice or make hard decisions, such as firing people. An outside board of advisors or directors is essential. Finally, the most critical skill to acquire is understanding finance–*your* business model and *your* key financial performance indicators. For me, understanding finance and money has made all the difference in my success.

I worked very hard at building a successful business, but I was very fortunate to have been able to reap the benefit. I may not have planned on becoming an entrepreneur, but I have certainly enjoyed the journey!

Patricia A. Henriques
Contributed by Nola Miyasaki

KEY SUCCESS FACTORS: Networking, Relationships, Work Ethic, Background in Finance, Focus

RECOMMENDED BOOKS: *Atlas Shrugged* by Ayn Rand, *John Adams* by David McCullough, *Truman* by David McCullough

WEBSITE: www.mgmt-alt.com

EDITOR'S NOTES: Pat Henriques is an extremely talented entrepreneur who was able to identify an opportunity and do what she needed to do to grow her business. When one meets her, it is apparent immediately that she is a no-nonsense, relationship-driven person who is smart, adventurous and open to whatever life presents. Besides working with community organizations and advising entrepreneurs, Pat and her husband Vico are avid world travelers. Pat has been a contributing guest speaker and a mentor for women entrepreneurs for the Falcone Center for Entrepreneurship at Syracuse University. She served as a Visiting Entrepreneur in Residence for the Riata Center for Entrepreneurship at Oklahoma State University for the 2009-2010 academic year. She is also a Visiting Professor of Entrepreneurship at the School of Management at Simmons College in Boston.

The closer one gets to the top, the more one finds there is no top.

—Nancy Barcus

FLYING HIGH

Lindy Ritz—My aviation themed kindergarten graduation was complete with an airplane mock-up and airline captain as the keynote speaker. I didn't realize how that event would herald my future career—the highpoint of which was being selected as the first female Director of the Federal Aviation Administration's Mike Monroney Aeronautical Center. On any given day, over six thousand five hundred Department of Transportation employees, contractors and students work at the Aeronautical Center with an operational budget of over $1 billion annually. The center is situated on eleven hundred acres with one hundred twenty-five buildings and over three million square feet of work space.

My dad was a pilot, and I flew many times with him. I never envisioned I would follow his love of aviation into my chosen career. Being one of two daughters, I tried to be the son my dad never had, attempting to do most things boys do with their fathers, including participating in a father/son bowling league.

At the age of thirteen, this all changed when I became more interested in boys, fashion and other things that fascinate teenage girls. Ironically, my undergraduate degree was in fashion merchandising and marketing, but the runways I would ultimately be concerned with were not for fashion models.

Upon graduation from college, my husband John and I married in my hometown of Santa Fe, New Mexico, and headed for new horizons. John began his first position as a petroleum engineer in the oil fields of Louisiana. I also wanted to be gainfully employed, and as I was feverishly seeking a meaningful position, I ran headlong into many unexpected challenges. Employers anticipated that I would get pregnant or move away to follow my husband's career, which made me a less-than-desirable candidate in their minds. My first position was with the U.S. Forest Service in New Orleans. While it was at least a job (a temporary one at that), I definitely was not perfectly matched to the voucher examining vocation.

Three years later we found ourselves on our way to Corpus Christi, Texas, and for me an interim stop in the Navy's travel processing organization. I subsequently was selected for a Navy management intern position, a coveted developmental program in human resource management. It was an important turning point in my career. I began to be asked for my opinion. I felt valued and realized I could make a difference. To my surprise, one success seemed to build on another. I was exposed to every aspect of human resource management and was rewarded with four promotions in five years.

We moved from Corpus Christi to Oklahoma City, and my job search began all over again. Although under a hiring freeze at the time, the FAA interviewed me. To my delight, a waiver was obtained and I was offered a mid-level position commensurate with my former responsibilities with the Navy. I had no idea that the FAA's Aeronautical Center would prove to be my launching pad and present me with the opportunities of a lifetime.

The climb to higher altitudes included positions as a First Line Supervisor, Compensation and Classification; Manager of Training, Development and Compensation; and Manager of the Human Resource Management Division. When the FAA established a national Candidate Development Program, I applied along with over four hundred and fifty candidates. The group was narrowed down to under thirty, and I was fortunate to be grouped into the pool from which future senior executives were selected. This was a tremendous milestone in my career and a major boost to my confidence level.

I have been blessed to have had many mentors throughout my career, and my predecessor, the former Director of the Aeronautical Center, had a profound effect on me. His coaching enabled me to meet challenges head on, knock down roadblocks, and appreciate the God-given talents I possessed. Through the Candidate Development Program, I was afforded many opportunities to increase my knowledge of the agency's programs and expand my perspectives. My first opportunity was a move from Human Resources to the FAA Logistics Center as the Deputy Director and then on to Aviation Systems Standards as the Deputy Director.

The opportunities seemed to be coming at jet speed, and I was fascinated with each position that I held. After serving in the Aviation Systems Standards position, I was selected as the Deputy Director of the Aeronautical Center. Remaining in Oklahoma City was a major coup and not the norm for FAA careers. I moved organizationally rather than geographically.

Were there positions I wanted and didn't get along the way? Absolutely. They all stand out clearly in my mind. Each time I went through the normal mourning/agonizing process, picked myself up, and let each setback serve as a motivator. Obstacles and disappointments always seem to occur for a reason, and upon reflection I found that I truly benefited from each of them.

In 1997, I became the Director of the Mike Monroney Aeronautical Center, which is, in my opinion, one of the most exciting positions in the FAA. Many people think that working for the government must be bureaucratic and very restrictive. I would offer that it is all about your attitude and how you approach things. As an experienced administrator with an entrepreneurial mindset, I offer the following:

- Challenges can be opportunities.
- There are always risks in taking certain actions, but frequently they are the stepping stones to true success.

- The biggest setbacks you experience often end up being the best things that happen to you.
- As an administrator, I frequently try to put myself in the position of my subordinates.
- Be like a sponge—have a real curiosity about how things work.
- Networking and relationships are absolutely crucial.
- Being able to work as a team is essential. Collaboration and synthesizing ideas are fundamental.
- Constantly give back to those around you, your organization and your community.

In support of my last point, our entire organization works together every year to raise money as part of the Combined Federal Campaign. We set goals and this year raised over $660,000. It's a testament to our employees who have a deep compassion for others and the desire to give back. As the Director, I feel like I am flying high and humbled that I represent an outstanding group of talented and energetic professionals.

Lindy Ritz

KEY SUCCESS FACTORS: Passion for What You Do, Integrity, Strong Work Ethic, Networking and Continuously Giving Back

RECOMMENDED BOOKS: *The Road Less Traveled* by M. Scott Peck, M.D., *Good to Great* by Jim Collins, *The 7 Habits of Highly Successful People* by Stephen R. Covey

WEBSITE: www.faa.gov

EDITOR'S NOTES: Lindy Ritz received her bachelor's degree from the University of Oklahoma and her master's degree in aviation and space science from Oklahoma State University, where she was selected into Phi Kappa Phi honorary scholastic fraternity. She completed graduate programs at the University of Michigan and the Kellogg School of Management.

Lindy is a member of the International Women's Forum-Oklahoma Chapter and serves on the following boards: Oklahoma City Chamber of Commerce; Arvest Bank; the State Fair of Oklahoma; and the Aviation Advisory Boards at the University of Oklahoma and Oklahoma State University. She was in the inaugural class of Leadership Oklahoma, serving on its Board of Directors and Executive Committee, and was selected for the Distinguished Graduate Award.

Lindy has received numerous other awards including the George W. Kriske Memorial Award from the Air Traffic Control Association for an outstanding career, which added to the quality, safety or efficiency of air traffic control; the FAA's first Golden Compass Award for Exemplary Leadership; the 2007 Administrator of the Year for Public Administration; the Byliners Award for Women in Communications; the Red Lands Council Woman of Distinction by the Girl Scouts; and the President's Award from the National Black Coalition of Federal Aviation Employees (NBCFAE). *The Journal Record* inducted Lindy into the Circle of Excellence for Women Making a Difference in Oklahoma. Lindy was honored by the University of Oklahoma with the Regents Award; the Distinguished Alumni Award from the College of Arts and Sciences; and by the College of Business Beta Gamma Sigma Fraternity as the Chapter Honoree. The Delta Gamma Fraternity recognized Lindy with their highest national award, the Delta Gamma Rose, for those who have distinguished themselves on a national or international level in their chosen fields.

Lindy resides with her husband, John, in Norman, Oklahoma.

Doubt whom you will, but never yourself.

—*Christine Bovee*

LEARNING TO PLAY
THE GAME OF LIFE

Jenny Leather—The journey to find the entrepreneur within required me to tap into my deepest creative energy, a part of me that is beyond words and beyond my thinking mind. Sometimes we create unconsciously, without being aware of how we are creating. I have spent the last fifteen years understanding and mastering this process, which I am now able to share with you from a place of ease and grace.

I come from Melbourne, Australia. Married since twenty-four, I have three beautiful sons. As a young woman, I saw myself as "not smart" because my grades were average. Historically, we know many entrepreneurs were challenged in school because they found it challenging to be told what to do.

When I was younger, it did not occur to me that I was an aspiring entrepreneur—I just knew I was different. What set me apart was my bloody mindedness and determination not to allow my academic challenges to prevent me from following my dream of becoming a nurse one day. Yes there were those who urged me to reconsider and find something safe and predictable, except to me it was not an option; my dream of becoming a nurse was so dear to my heart. I had an unshakeable belief in my ability to do this and such a determination to stay committed and do whatever it took to achieve that dream—all early signs of an entrepreneur in the making. Somehow even in my youth I had this inner knowing that I could take a dream and make it into a reality no matter what challenges I faced. Little did I realize it was the core component needed for the magic of creation.

I was accepted into nursing, much to the amazement of my family and friends, and enjoyed the profession for over twenty-five years. Over the years, I found the work extremely rewarding and eventually worked as an intensive care nurse in organ transplant for small and sick babies. As satisfying as the work was, in time I burned out and once again came that deep yearning to create a new dream.

As often happens when a life change is unfolding, my husband also felt the pull to make a life change. At the same time my son was facing challenges of his own at school. Like his mother, he found it challenging to fit into the school mold. When faced with challenges what does an entrepreneurial-minded mum do? She goes in search of answers outside the box.

I contemplated starting my own business. However, paramount in my mind was the question of what made one person successful and yet another unable to take the first step? In my quest I came across the so-called "success gurus" with questionable answers. Not to be deterred, I found amazing and wonderful teachers who taught me so much, but just below the surface was a fear around venturing out on my own.

What I did was invest in positive cash flow properties. Over the following eighteen months my husband and I bought thirty properties. Our goal was to have more time to enjoy the pleasures in life. Instead, the more properties we bought, the more our time was taken up with the management of those properties. Undaunted, we thought we were invincible. We pushed ourselves to learn more, studying both business and personal development with some of the best teachers in the world. Finally we decided to raise the bar and move into property development and investing with like-minded partners.

In the beginning of our joint ventures, I thought it was about creating many millions of dollars. What I did not understand were the complexities that accompany making money of that magnitude and that there was no guarantee that monetary success would bring joy, peace and contentment. In truth, despite my financial success, happiness was elusive. What I did not expect was for my old demons to show up— "Who do you think you are? ... Remember you are really not smart enough to achieve your dreams."

I questioned whether this mental mind chatter was real—or was it just another way to hold me back from creating sustainable financial freedom and the lifestyle of my dreams. I came to understand that I co-create my life—the good, bad and the ugly. I could create magic or challenges, it was all up to me and how I played the game of life.

As we moved into larger projects, along came greater financial opportunities as well as bigger challenges. The highs and lows we experienced with our smaller properties simply increased in scale. This was when my intensive personal development training really gave me the edge. I found I was able to handle the greater financial responsibilities and the challenges with ease. On the other side, I also found that the level of doubt increased, but I still felt this unshakable belief in my ability to succeed.

We were not long into this project when our youngest son was diagnosed with Burkett's lymphoma. We were in shock, unable to comprehend. I bargained with God to save Daniel's life, and in return I would do anything including giving up my wealth. Throughout this ordeal my core inner strength came to the forefront with the same "bloody mindedness" that had helped me earlier in my life. I knew I would do anything for my son. His return to health was my main focus for many long months.

Then came the news we had prayed and hoped for—he was to be one of the few survivors of this horrific disease. I knew deep within that it was my faith in God and the universal energy together with a dedicated commitment and deep love for my son that kept my absolute focus on a positive outcome. I simply knew I was not alone, that there was an unseen force always by my side keeping me strong.

Four years later our son is healthy and clear of this disease. On the other side of the coin, our finances took a dive. Our focus and commitment was to our son and his recovery and it took its toll. We made a series of decisions affecting our finances during this tumultuous time that had a domino effect. What could have been a devastating blow has in fact been the catalyst for amazing personal growth.

I feel closer to the universal energy than ever before. I see everything as being inter-connected and therefore nothing happens by chance. We are co-creating whatever happens in our life including our financial wellbeing. I can draw on that inner core strength that was so evident during our son's illness to re-create a sustainable flow of money. It is how I approach it this time— that is the key. I have learned that my self-talk was my undoing. Although I had the entrepreneurial spirit I had some pretty strong self-talk that was contradicting all the positive moves I made. This awareness has given me enormous freedom that now I know I need to ask better questions such as:

- How can I enrich my personal journey?
- What experiences will bring me joy?
- What do I truly value on a day-to-day basis?
- How can I use my experiences and insights into this journey called life to benefit like-minded individuals?"

Looking back, I can see I have been successful all along and have achieved some amazing outcomes. What I may not have acknowledged was my own value. This amazing journey has provided me with the wisdom to accept that I do have value and once I acknowledged that I am worthy of good things happening, then it simply began to unfold magically with ease.

Everyone has a different definition of success, and I certainly spent a number of years getting in my own way until I understood that we create our own reality. It is when we are willing to examine how we are getting in the way of our own success that we start to play a larger game in life. In truth, every challenge we face is in fact a gift. It is an opportunity to learn something new. My aim now is to play the game called life flat out, moving toward a richer, heart-centered life, and to share what I have learned with others so that their journey will be smoother.

Jenny Leather

SUCCESS FACTORS: A Belief in Oneself, Persistence, Patience

RECOMMENDED BOOKS: *One Minute Millionaire* by Mark Victor Hanson and Robert G. Allen, *You Can Heal Your Life* by Louise L. Hay, *Rev. Ike's Secrets for Health, Joy and Prosperity—for You* by Frederick Eikerenkoetter

WEBSITES: www.jennyleather.com, www.freedomtobe.com.au

SOCIAL MEDIA: Twitter—jennyleather, Facebook—jennyleather

EDITOR'S NOTES: Jenny Leather lives in Melbourne, Australia, with her husband, Gary. Jenny is a speaker and coach, focusing on a well-rounded version of wealth success that includes transformational healing. She is passionate about assisting individuals and groups to "reclaim their power" so they are in the drivers' seats of their lives. Jenny believes we create our outcomes in life—however at times we need support and assistance to understand the complexities of the Game of Life.

In September 2009, Jenny entered an agreement with the creator of the FREEDOM to BE Program, a powerful transformational program that releases emotional stress in minutes and if used regularly, clears deep core patterns with ease and grace. She now uses this program in her coaching practice, achieving outstanding results.

Women, like men, should try to do the impossible.
And when they fail, their failure should be
a challenge to others.

—Amelia Earhart

ROCKET GIRL AND
HER MENTORS

Debra Facktor Lepore—When I introduce myself as a rocket scientist, people often pause a moment until they realize I'm serious. I always wanted to do things that have never been done. Growing up outside of Detroit, the auto industry influenced me, but I found cars too mundane and instead chose a different mode of transportation— launch vehicles—as my career focus. The Space Shuttle launched on its maiden flight in 1981, during my freshman year of high school. By junior year of high school, my career plan was to become an aerospace engineer, get an M.B.A., do strategic planning, and then be head of NASA.

The time was the Cold War, in the mid to late 1980s. The United States and the former Soviet Union were adversaries. Most space activities in the U.S. were funded by the government, and the idea of creating a privately funded launch company was inconceivable. At that time in my career, I only knew that I wanted to work on new space launch systems and find clever, creative and cost-effective ways of getting to space.

I started on my education plan and had summer internships at General Motors, McDonnell Aircraft Company (now Boeing), and ANSER (Analytic Services). After completing my bachelor's in aerospace engineering, I enrolled in a joint M.B.A./ engineering master's program. After three weeks, I realized that business skills came easy to me, and technical credentials were far more important for a woman in a male-dominated industry.

So instead, I earned my master's in aerospace engineering; spent a summer at the International Space University in Strasbourg, France, learning about international cooperation and space policy and law; and then headed to Washington, D.C., to work on what was the nation's first new heavy lift launch vehicle since the days of the Apollo program and landing on the moon.

At ANSER, I worked alongside several retired military officers (all men) and had my first exposure to the value of a mentor. I learned that I didn't have to figure out everything on my own. I learned that mentors could see my passion, point me in the right direction, play to my strengths and improve my weaknesses, and open doors that I didn't even know existed. Each mentor has left an impression on me and influenced my journey in some way. I could share a dozen of my favorite pieces of advice, but these three points have shaped me as an entrepreneur:

1. Be an expert where there is none.
2. You can't buy experience.
3. Pass it on.

Be an Expert Where There is None

In 1995, I was selected to be a Leadership Foundation Fellow, a new program established by the International Women's Forum and Harvard University's Kennedy School of Government through a grant with the U.S. Department of Labor. The program aimed to promote the advancement of women through mentoring by matching top women in their fields with up-and-coming young women.

I was matched with the late Bettie Steiger, then an executive with the Xerox Palo Alto Research Center (PARC), a prestigious center of innovation perhaps most known for developing the computer mouse. Bettie was the first formal mentor I'd ever had, and my first female mentor. While Bettie put a name to her advice—*Be an expert where there is none*—I realized that an earlier mentor had already started me down this path.

It started with the fall of the Berlin Wall. My mentor, then CEO of ANSER and a former astronaut, had a vision of opening an office in Moscow, Russia, to facilitate joint projects with the former Soviet Union. He wanted ANSER to establish eminence in this field since we had the technical expertise, the connections, and, perhaps most importantly, the blessing of the board to take a risk.

In July 1992, ANSER became the first U.S. aerospace consulting company to open an office in Moscow. I helped create the strategy for the office, lined up customers, and learned to speak Russian. In May 1994, I became Chief of Moscow Operations for ANSER's Center for International Aerospace Cooperation (CIAC)—officially my first "intra-preneurial" venture. I facilitated joint aerospace projects throughout Russia and Ukraine, creating partnerships with former adversaries. My analyses contributed to the U.S. inviting Russia to become a partner in the International Space Station (ISS) program. My expertise in Russian rocket engines ultimately led me to work on commercial start-up launch projects. That story comes later.

Bettie's view of becoming an expert was all about becoming an entrepreneur. It's about intentionally surveying the market, analyzing market needs, assessing existing capabilities, identifying technologies that can fill the needs, gaining the skills necessary to fill in your own shortfalls and ultimately entering the market. Bettie and I created a mentoring plan to develop my business skills and expand my exposure to other markets. We used the assets of the Fellows program, the other Fellows, IWF members, and my mentor's personal and professional network. I explored advertising, marketing, sales, finance, business planning and strategy.

One year after the Fellows program, I was offered a job at an entrepreneurial start-up aerospace company at Kistler Aerospace Corporation and relocated across the country from Washington, D.C., to Washington State. I immediately recognized that joining Kistler was equivalent to earning a "walking M.B.A." and that I could complement my technical skills in an environment that no business school could teach me. The opportunity came about because of mentors and connections at ANSER who knew I had become expert in Russian rocket engines. Kistler was interested in using Russian engines on its K-1 reusable aerospace vehicle, the first ever fully reusable rocket system, designed to take cargo and passengers to and from space.

Kistler's approach represented a huge shift in conducting business in space and the K-1 vehicle could transform both the launch and satellite market. The space transportation market was dominated by expensive, expendable launch vehicles that were funded by the government. A new commercial market was emerging, led by the demand of telecommunication satellite operators for affordable, frequent, reliable access to low earth orbit (LEO). The time seemed right for a privately funded, commercial venture to completely transform the space launch market. For a while, this was true. I played a key leadership role in the business development and strategy of the company and helped raise over $600 million in private capital—a first in the space transportation market, and a feat that has yet to be matched.

Then the LEO telecommunication satellite market fell apart. The bond market crashed. Investors got "Asian Flu." Then came the "dot com" boom ... and bomb. Kistler needed a new strategy to stay alive because our customers and our funders disappeared.

So, I became an expert in applying commercial business practices to government contracting, so that Kistler could offer K-1 launch services to the government instead of commercial customers. I led Kistler's unsolicited proposal to NASA in April 1999 for International Space Station (ISS) resupply services, which cracked open the doors for small entrepreneurial firms to work with NASA on such flights.

My proudest moment was negotiating an innovative commercial contract with NASA, valued at up to $135 million, under the Space Launch Initiative (SLI) Program in 2001. The terms and conditions served as a template for new space companies to contract with the government. These two activities ultimately begat, nearly ten years later, what are now NASA's Commercial Orbital Transportation Services (COTS) and Commercial Resupply Services (CRS) programs.

You Can't Buy Experience

Early in my career, I was anxious to succeed, be recognized for my great work, be promoted quickly and be the boss—yesterday. One of my mentors advised, "You can't buy experience." You just have to live it. So true!

As a young engineer, I thought I knew it all, and I didn't need any help. I feared that if I asked for help, I would be perceived as weak. I worked long hours, making sure everything was perfect. I really did have to work hard, and harder than all the guys, so that people would take me and my work seriously. I faced many biases: my gender, my youth and the fact that I was not a pilot or a military officer. The only thing I had on my side was time. In time, I would gain experiences that would be relevant and useful to me.

I changed my focus from worrying about every little detail to taking deliberate steps to be exposed to as many new experiences as I could, in as many areas as possible, and to soak in the advice of mentors. I originally became interested in space to work on things that have never been done before. Every time a new project came up, I evaluated it from this perspective: What is already known? What makes it new? What could I contribute? What could I learn? How could I shape the opportunity to be more than it could be? I also played these questions over whenever I faced an obstacle.

When Kistler's funding ultimately ran dry (despite a successful restructuring through Chapter 11), I joined AirLaunch LLC as President and an owner, an opportunity that was the perfect culmination of all my experiences to date. The founder, Gary Hudson, recognized my unique combination of technical, business, international and policy skills and valued my practical, hands-on experience as an executive of a small business. We saw that our skills were complementary and that together, along with the skills of our three other partners, we could make the business a success. Finally, I understood what my mentor meant by earning experiences and putting them to good use.

AirLaunch won about $38 million in funding from the Defense Advanced Research Projects Agency (DARPA) and the U.S. Air Force to develop a small launch vehicle to affordably and responsively deploy small satellites to space from a C-17 cargo airplane. The team set records for the longest (sixty-six feet) and heaviest (seventy-two thousand pounds) objects ever dropped from a C-17 aircraft. We received two patents for innovative airdrop techniques. The DARPA/Air Force program and company operations concluded in late 2008 when the funding ended.

I now run my own business, DFL Space LLC, a small business based in the Seattle area, focused on engineering innovative business strategies. I bring my clients my expertise (a unique blend of entrepreneurial, technical, business and international skills) and my experiences (from Russia, start-ups, fundraising, working with the government). I'm best at developing big picture strategies and balancing them with tactical implementation. In turn, I'm learning new skills and technologies from them, all of which go into my toolbox of life.

Pass it On

The most important advice is to "Pass it On." I am where I am in my career because of my mentors. It only makes sense, then, to be a mentor to others. Research shows that men and women benefit equally from mentoring, and it doesn't matter who does the mentoring (e.g., mixed or same gender, younger or older, same or different field). It's a matter of access, and creating a mentor culture in which mentoring becomes natural for everyone, including women and minorities.

Both ANSER and Kistler had corporate cultures based on mentoring. ANSER was full of retired military officers and experts with Ph.D.s, balanced by a team of young people eager to learn. Kistler's technical leaders consisted of a "who's who" of the Apollo space program that put the first man on the moon, and they passed on their experiences to younger engineers. With a few exceptions, the demographics of the industry meant that mentoring relationships were largely comprised of men mentoring men.

Because of the Leadership Foundation Fellows program, I am a huge advocate for women mentoring women. In addition to Bettie, I met so many other women, from all fields, disciplines, backgrounds and cultures. I credit Mrs. Lou Kerr, President of The Kerr Foundation and one of the founders of the Fellows program, with instilling in me the importance of helping other women. I had invited Lou to join the ANSER CIAC board, and she and I became fast friends and clever collaborators. Lou is the master facilitator of mentors and partners. She freely lends a hand, gives advice, makes connections and brings people together. Seeing Lou in action and how she has helped me inspires me to help others. I personally take time to identify promising, up and coming young women and to mentor them and provide pathways and openings for them and other young professionals.

I've even found a way to make mentoring entrepreneurial. I joined the board of Women in Aerospace (WIA) in 2008 and kicked off WIA's "Reach for the Stars" Mentoring Program, by sharing my tips and tricks of how to be a mentor and how to be a protégé. Under my leadership as WIA's board chair in 2009, we expanded the organization's reach to Europe by forming WIA Europe. This connection was made possible by relationships I developed early in my career. We also formed a separate non-profit 501c(3) organization, The Women in Aerospace Foundation, Inc., to award scholarships to college sophomore and junior women pursuing careers in aerospace. This year, I'm serving as the first President of the WIA Foundation and we will award our first scholarship in the fall. I'm thrilled to lay the groundwork for encouraging more young girls to become interested in science, technology, engineering and math (STEM).

As I mentor others, I always give them one condition: to pass on the advice and skills that they learn (from me and others) and be a mentor themselves.

Debra Facktor Lepore

KEY SUCCESS FACTORS: Be Clever, Believe, Persevere, Create and Nurture Relationships, Mentor Others, Pass it on

RECOMMENDED BOOKS: *When Smart People Fail* by Carole Hyatt and Linda Gottlieb, *America's Competitive Secret: Women Managers* by Judy B. Rosener

WEBSITES: www.DFLspace.com, www.AirLaunchLLC.com

EDITOR'S NOTES: Debra Facktor Lepore is President of the Washington State Women's Forum (WSWF) and a former International Women's Forum Leadership Foundation Fellow (1995-96). She is 2010 President of the Women in Aerospace (WIA) Foundation, Inc.; 2009 WIA board chair; a member of the Women Presidents' Organization (WPO); an Executive Liaison and Industry Professor at Stevens Institute of Technology School of Systems and Enterprises; and an Executive in Residence at the Babson College Center for Women's Leadership.

Among other distinctions, she is one of the "100 Top Women in Seattle Tech" on techflash.com; one of *Puget Sound Business Journal's* 2008 Women of Influence and 2006 "40 Under 40" Awardees; and recipient of WIA's 2007 International Achievement Award. She served as the final Vice Chair of the Board of Washington Works, a former Seattle non-profit dedicated to welfare to work programs. Debra served a one-year term on the Aerospace Industries Association (AIA) Board of Governors and is former Chairman of AIA's Space Council. She is an Associate Fellow of the American Institute of Aeronautics and Astronautics (AIAA); an Academician of the International Academy of Astronautics (IAA) and former Secretary of the IAA Commission on Space Policy, Law and Economics; and an alumna of the International Space University (ISU) 1989 summer session program in Strasbourg, France. She also serves on the U.S. Department of Transportation's Commercial Transportation Advisory Committee (COMSTAC).

Debra earned a bachelor of science degree (*magna cum laude*) in 1988 and a master of science degree in 1989, both in aerospace engineering from the University of Michigan in Ann Arbor, Michigan. Debra and her husband, Dominic Lepore (an entrepreneur in his own right, as founder and owner of Terrapin Consulting LLC), reside in Bellevue, Washington.

KEY SUCCESS FACTORS

Key success factors listed after each story were compiled to determine those the featured entrepreneurs deemed most important. The following are the top ten according to the number of times each was listed:

1. Passion
2. Perseverance
3. Work Ethic
4. Relationships/Networking
5. Integrity
6. Determination
7. Focus
8. Customer Service
9. Self Confidence/Belief in Oneself
10. Taking Action

The following *key success factors* were listed by more than one entrepreneur, but did not make the top ten list:

1. Taking Risks
2. Ability to Adapt
3. Drive

4. Education

5. Resourcefulness

6. Background in Finance

7. Fearlessness

8. Giving Back

9. Inspiration

10. Intelligence

11. Listening Skills

12. Patience

13. Tenacity

14. Persistence

15. Vision

RECOMMENDED BOOKS

There were a variety of different books recommended by the featured entrepreneurs, yet only seven made the list by two or more contributors. The seven books that received a recommendation by multiple entrepreneurs are the following:

- *Good to Great* by Jim Collins
- *The 7 Habits of Highly Successful People* by Stephen R. Covey
- *The Tipping Point* by Malcolm Gladwell
- *The One Minute Millionaire* by Mark Victor Hanson and Robert G. Allen
- *Think and Grow Rich* by Napolean Hill
- *Blue Ocean Strategy* by W. Chang Kim and Renee Mauborgne
- *Atlas Shrugged* by Ayn Rand

WATCH FOR THE MOMTREPRENEURS' EDITION AND NATIVE ENTREPRENEURS' EDITION OF A CUP OF CAPPUCCINO FOR THE ENTREPRENEUR'S SPIRIT

Are you an entrepreneur with a story to share? Join us in our quest to encourage others by describing your unique journey to becoming an entrepreneur! The series of books, *A Cup of Cappuccino for the Entrepreneur's Spirit*, captures entrepreneurs' true stories which are written to inspire, energize, and teach the reader. The stories include adversities, challenges, triumphs, and successes experienced by the entrepreneur to help readers discover passion and basic principles they can use to live the entrepreneurial dream.

The Cappuccino series of books includes Volumes I, II and the Women Entrepreneurs' Edition I of *A Cup of Cappuccino for the Entrepreneur's Spirit*. Future editions will include Momtrepreneurs, Native Entrepreneurs, Extraordinary Entrepreneurs, Women Entrepreneurs II, Young Entrepreneurs, Ecopreneurs, Internet Entrepreneurs, Global Entrepreneurs, Social Entrepreneurs, Disabled Entrepreneurs, African American Entrepreneurs, Australian Entrepreneurs, New Zealand Entrepreneurs and others.

If you are interested in sharing your story to inspire others, the format and guidelines are located on the website at www.acupofcappuccino.com. Just click on Submit Story.

Please send your reactions to the stories in this book. Which stories were your favorites, and what kind of impact did they have on you?

LaVergne, TN USA
30 April 2010
181130LV00003B/2/P